Saint-Saëns and the Organ

Plate 1. Saint-Saëns at the organ of Salle Gaveau, 6 November 1913

Saint-Saëns and the Organ

ROLLIN SMITH

PENDRAGON PRESS
STUYVESANT, NY

Library of Congress Cataloging-in-Publication Data

Smith, Rollin.
  Saint-Saëns and the organ / by Rollin Smith.
     p. cm.
  Includes bibliographical references and index.
  ISBN 0-945193-14-9
  1. Saint-Saëns, Camille, 1835–1921. 2. Composers—France—Biography.
3. Organists—France—Biography. 4. Saint-Saëns, Camille, 1835–1921. Organ music.
5. Organ music—France—History and criticism. 6. Organs—France. I. Title.
ML410.S15S4 1991
786.5′ 092—dc20
[B]
                                                          91-11626
                                                                 CIP
                                                                 MN

For Anthony Baglivi

Contents

ACKNOWLEDGMENTS

List of Illustrations

Sources for Illustrations

The American Organist, 1, 21, 25, 42, 46; Berger, 45; William Bunch, 39, 53; Norbert Dufourcq, 6, 7, 8, 10, 11, 20, 44; Elliott & Fry, 34; Jim Lewis, 18, 22, 49, 52; Kurt Lueders, 9, 19, 48; Christopher Ross, 40, 41; Reginald Whitworth, 51.

Acknowledgments

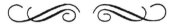

A debt of gratitude is acknowledged to those who assisted me during the research and writing of this book:

Anthony Baglivi, who encouraged and guided this study of Saint-Saëns and the organ since its inception;

Kurt Lueders, who suggested many avenues for research relative to the organs Saint-Saëns played and his connection with the harmonium;

Austin Niland, who lent invaluable assistance in researching the organs of St. James's Hall;

Michael Sayer, Honorary Archivist of the English Organ Archive, who provided the specification of the Gray & Davison organ in St. James's Hall;

The Rev. Bernard B. Edmonds of Suffolk, who provided the specification of the Bryceson Brothers & Ellis organ in St. James's Hall;

Henry Karl Baker, who provided me with the original contracts for the organ of Aeolian Hall, London;

William Bunch, who provided the photograph of the interior of Aeolian Hall, London;

L. Maxwell Taylor, curator of the San Francisco Archives of the San Francisco Public Library, for his assistance in researching Saint-Saëns in San Francisco;

Yves Gérard, for his help in gaining access to the Saint-Saëns archives in Dieppe;

Pierre Bazin, director of the Chateau-Musée de Dieppe;

Yves-Alex Agostinis, for his help in deciphering and translating many of Saint-Saëns's letters;

Richard Warren, Jr., Curator of the Historical Sound Recordings Collection of Yale University, who helped in my studies of Saint-Saëns's recordings;

Jesse Macartney, who advised me on many technical points as I transcribed into musical notation the perforations of the player organ roll of Saint-Saëns's *Fantaisie pour Orgue Aeolian*;

Howard Ross, for his help in translating into English some of Saint-Saëns's writings;

Robert Price, who assisted in researching Saint-Saëns's activities in San Francisco and who proofread the final draft of this book; and

Charles N. Henderson, who edited and corrected the final draft of the manuscript.

Legend

The designation of pitches throughout this book follows the "Plaine and Easie Code." Commas or apostrophes preceding the pitch name identify the octave placement of that pitch.

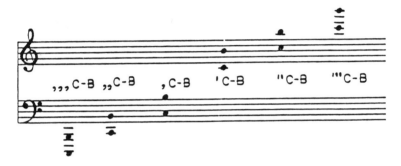

From Barry S. Brook, "The simplified plaine and easie code system for notating music, a proposal for international adoption," *Fontes Artis Musicae*, XII/2–3 (May–Sept. 1965) 156–60.

Foreword

Few lines, if any, in musicians' biographies describe their activities as organists, although many began their careers as organists or held organ posts to supplement their incomes. The lives of Mozart, Schubert, Brahms, Liszt, Bruckner, Mendelssohn, Saint-Saëns, Elgar, Gounod, and Puccini scarcely mention their association with the organ.

César Franck and Camille Saint-Saëns were the two most important French organists of the nineteenth century. Yet, Vincent d'Indy's biography devoted barely five pages to Franck, the organist—Franck, whose entire professional career was bound to the organ as a player, composer, and teacher, and who's image was immortalized in the famous painting of him seated at the organ!

Franck's contemporary and colleague, Camille Saint-Saëns, more popular and prolific as a composer, has received even less attention as an organist. Jean Bonnerot, his secretary and biographer, devoted two sentences to the five years Saint-Saëns spent as organist of the Church of Saint-Merry and less than four pages to his twenty-year career at The Madeleine.

Such biographical neglect of Saint-Saëns as organist is, in part, attributable to his extremely diverse musical talent. Biographers have viewed him from various perspectives: the composer of operas and vocal music, the symphonist, the incomparable creator of instrumental works, and as a great piano virtuoso. Even Bonnerot, writing the first full-scale biography, on intimate terms with his subject and possessing a zealot's enthusiasm, had no interest in the organ and little empathy with Saint-Saëns's passion for it.

In spite of a long and important career, Saint-Saëns's music today is often associated with lighter genres and awaits the critical reevaluation accorded to, for example, Franz Liszt. Saint-Saëns's works are numerous and, if not always inspired, are well crafted, deftly polished, and supported by a perfectly balanced, classical symmetry.

The task of researching Camille Saint-Saëns's life is made easy by his fondness for the pen: he was an avid letter-writer and an eager author of articles and essays. So tireless a correspondent was he that other biographers frequently quote him—Jean-Michel Nectoux's recent critical study of Gabriel Fauré (Flammarion) immediately comes to mind.

The present volume is intended to supplement and amend the existing biographical material and to bring together, for the first time and in English, information on Saint-Saëns's career as a church musician, organ virtuoso, and organ composer, and to chronicle the associations with his organist colleagues. In attempting to create Saint-Saëns's day-to-day life as an organist, the book is divided into sections using his church positions as landmarks.

Documentation of Saint-Saëns's organ career is plentiful but not readily accessible. At the Bibliothèque Nationale in Paris, it was necessary to go through every Parisian musical journal published during Saint-Saëns's lifetime—a time-consuming task because they are not indexed. Most of his manuscripts are in that repository and were consulted, particularly for the thematic catalog. The Chateau-Musée at Dieppe has a collection of correspondence written to Saint-Saëns and virtually every letter he received is to be found there. The San Francisco (California) Public Library has a special local history division which possesses all of the records of the 1915 Panama-Pacific Exposition; that archive, coupled with local newspapers, proved a gold mine of information about Saint-Saëns's stay in that city.

It is hoped that the compilation of this material will lead other musicians to perform the neglected organ and choral music of Camille Saint-Saëns and authors to investigate further his complex career in music.

CHAPTER I

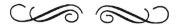

Early Influences

Camille Saint-Saëns was born in Paris on Friday, 9 October 1835. His father[1] died of consumption two months later and the child was reared by his widowed mother and great-aunt. It was from the latter, Charlotte Masson, that he received his early musical training. As a prodigy, he was equaled only by Mozart. Saint-Saëns was playing the piano at two and a half, reading and writing music at three, and composing at five years of age. At seven, in March 1843, he began piano lessons with Camille Stamaty and in October, harmony and composition studies with Pierre Maleden. His progress was so phenomenal that in three years he made his formal public debut. On 6 May 1846, the ten-year-old pianist astonished his audience in Salle Pleyel with this program:[2]

---

[1]Jean Bonnerot, *Camille Saint-Saëns* (Paris: Durand, 1923) 7–8. Victor Saint-Saëns, an audit clerk with the Ministry of the Interior, had come to Paris from Rouxmesnil, a small village some three miles from Dieppe. The name "Saint-Saëns" is not uncommon in the area; indeed, there is a town of that name of several thousand inhabitants twenty-one miles south of Dieppe. The word is a corruption of Sanctus Sidonius, a seventh-century Irish monk who established a monastery in the part of Normandy now known as Seine-Inférieure.

[2]Bonnerot, 21.

Concerto No. 4 in B-flat	Mozart
Air with variations	Handel
Fugue	Handel
Toccata	Kalkbrenner
Sonata	Hummel
Prelude and Fugue	Bach
Concerto No. 3 in C Minor, Op. 37	Beethoven

So impressive a program, which included two concerti with orchestra, played from memory, caused someone to comment to Madame Saint-Saëns, "What kind of music will he be playing when he's twenty?" To which the proud mother replied, "He will be playing his own!"[3]

Alexandre-Pierre Boëly

The following winter Stamaty went to Italy to improve his health and advised Madame Saint-Saëns that, while waiting to enroll in the organ class at the Paris Conservatoire, her son should begin study with Alexandre-Pierre Boëly. It was a fortuitous circumstance that Saint-Saëns's introduction to the organ was through this particular musician, for it was Boëly's adherence to severe classical traditions that not only helped mold Saint-Saëns's taste but served as an inspiration to him throughout his very long life.

Boëly had been organist of Saint-Germain-l'Auxerrois, the church opposite the eastern entrance to the Louvre, since 1840. There he played a four-manual, thiry-six-stop Clicquot organ of 1771, which, when supervising its rebuild in 1838,[4] he had fitted with a new "German" pedalboard—that is, one with a greater compass and longer keys than was common in French organs of the time—on which Bach's music (Boëly's specialty) could be played. Indeed, according to Joseph d'-Ortigue in 1849, he was one of the two or three French organists who

---

[3] Camille Saint-Saëns, École Buissonnière—Notes et Souvenirs (Paris: Lafitte, 1913) 11.
[4] During the time that Saint-Saëns was studying with Boëly, the organ was being restored by Ducroquet. Between 1847 and 1850 the number of manuals was reduced to three and a new expressive Récit was installed. Boëly inaugurated this organ, 27 November 1850.

2

"were capable of playing a fugue correctly,"[5] performing his own "with an ease of fingering, a purity of style and a severity of harmony worthy of Bach."[6] He is remembered as "The French Bach."

Boëly had attended Saint-Saëns's debut and encouraged him by dedicating to him his *Fantaisie*, Op. 21, for piano.[7] It was through Boëly that Saint-Saëns first heard and became acquainted with great organ music; his tribute to his mentor appears in the preface to a collection of Boëly's *Noëls* republished in 1902.[8] Yet something more than an affectionate admiration later endeared the pupil to the master: their mutual tribulations. The same antagonism encountered by Boëly as he tried to maintain high musical standards in his church was experienced by Saint-Saëns during his tenure at the Madeleine. Saint-Saëns resigned; Boëly was dismissed (for economic reasons).[9] The sixty-seven-year-old artist smiled and said, "My taste no longer keeps up with the times and I am too old to change."[10] A few years later a priest recounted the sad details:

> It was said that a priest in Paris, whose name deserves to be handed down to posterity—M. Legrand, pastor of Saint-Germain-l'Auxerrois—was not afraid to discourage, disgust and dismiss the greatest and practically the only French organist of the time, M. Boëly, whose music he found too solemn, too religious, and not entertaining enough.[11]

Benoist's Organ Class

Saint-Saëns studied under Boëly for about two years and then, in October 1848, he entered the organ class at the Paris Conservatoire. His

---

[5]Alexandre Cellier; Henri Bachlin, *L'Orgue* (Paris: Delagrave, 1933) 184.

[6]Pierre-Henri Lamazou, "Les Organistes Français,: *Revue et Gazette musicale* (4 May 1856) 140.

[7]Published by Richault in 1858. That same year he died and Saint-Saëns played his funeral, 29 December 1858, at Saint-Philippe-de-Roule. The music performed at the funeral of the French Bach—Niedermeyer's *Pie Jesu* and *Agnus Dei*, sung by the Bollaert brothers from the École Niedermeyer (*La Maîtrise*, January 1859, 156–58).

[8]Reprinted in Appendix A.

[9]The church register, 28 July 1851, reads: "Due to economic circumstances, the following measures will be taken: M. Boëly will be relieved of his duties the first of October; no organist will be appointed to replace him. M. Vast will continue in his duties as assistant." Boëly's eighteen-year-old assistant and former student, Eugène Vast, at the time a classmate of Saint-Saëns at the Paris Conservatoire, remained as "assistant" until 1909!

[10]Cellier, *L'Orgue*, 180.

[11]Théodore Nisard in *Revue de musique sacrée ancienne et moderne* (1854) 232.

teacher was François Benoist, himself a former student of the Conservatoire who, having attained first prizes in piano and harmony, won the Prix de Rome in 1815. His return to Paris four years later coincided with the death of Nicolas Séjan, and Benoist succeeded him as organist of the Chapelle du Roi and as professor of organ at the Conservatoire—the latter post he held for fifty-three years; so long that it was jokingly said that three republics and two empires had lived and died under him!

Benoist was a marvelous improviser, excelling in extempore fugues on given subjects and, according to Fétis, "was the only organist in France able to hold his own with the Germans."[12] Benoist and Boëly were considered the most serious organists in Paris: "two artists who respect their art and do not prostitute our organs with barcarolles, contredanses, galops, waltzes and polkas."[13]

Saint-Saëns described the organ class:

> I was fourteen when my piano teacher, Stamaty, introduced me to Benoist, the organ teacher—an excellent and charming man familiarly known as Father Benoist. I was put in front of the organ and was so frightened, and what I played was so extraordinary that the whole class burst into laughter. I was accepted as an auditor and given the privilege of listening to the others.
>
> I was assiduous and did not miss a note or one of our teacher's words. At home I worked, studied and toiled at Sebastian Bach's *Art of Fugue*. The other students were not as industrious as I and one day, when not many were present and Benoist had nothing more to do, he put me at the organ. This time no one laughed. At once I became a pupil and won the second prize at the end of the year. I would have been awarded the first prize had it not been for my youth and the disadvantages of having me leave a class in which I needed to remain longer.
>
> Benoist was a very mediocre organist but an admirable teacher, and a veritable galaxy of talent left his class.[14] He spoke little, but as his taste was refined and his judgment sure, everything he said was

---

[12]Cellier, *L'Orgue*, 179.

[13]Félix Danjou, "Chronique départementale," Toulouse: L'Inauguration de l'orgue de Saint-Sernin, *Revue et Gazette musicale* (13 July 1845) 232.

[14]These included such important composers as Adolphe Adam, Georges Bizet, Léo Delibes, Félicien David and César Franck; prominent organists: Lefébure-Wély, Édouard Batiste (Delibes's uncle), Alexis Chauvet, Renaud de Vilbac, Théodore Dubois, Théodore Salomé; and pianists: Charles-Valentin Alkan, Henri Duvernoy and Raoul Pugno.

valuable and important. He collaborated on several ballets for the Opéra.[15] That gave him a lot of work and, as hard as it is to believe, he brought "his work" to class and scribbled orchestrations while the students played the organ. This did not prevent him from hearing them and supervising them, leaving his work to make the necessary observations.[16]

The organ upon which "lessons" were taught was of unknown origin, with four stops on the Grand-Orgue, five free-reed stops on the Récit, two flue and some free-reed stops on the Pédale.[17] The one-and-one-half octave pedalboard precluded the study and satisfactory performance of organ literature, but this was of little consequence because, as is obvious from the curriculum, all of the work in the organ class, with the exception of the study of one composed piece, was in improvisation.

The four areas covered were accompaniment of plainchant,[18] improvisation of a fugue on a given subject, improvisation of a piece in sonata form on a free theme and performance from memory of an organ piece with pedal. Under Widor, Guilmant and Gigout, this same course of study subsequently developed the "modern" French organ school. The *emphasis*, however, was different. While Widor and his successors were concerned primarily with organ technique and literature (though in no way excluding the study of improvisation), the students in Benoist's class were little acquainted with organ repertoire. It was then, as it was to continue under César Franck, a class in keyboard improvisation—which happened to be taught at the organ. In fact, "organ" was still grouped with composition and harmony under Section VII of the General Regulations when the Conservatoire was reorganized in 1848 because "the study of this instrument, which exists principally for improvisation, is

---

[15]He had succeeded Ludovic Halévy as chorus master at the Opéra in 1840.

[16]Saint-Saëns, *École Buissonnière, 39–41.*

[17]Norbert Dufourcq, "L'Enseignement de l'orgue au Conservatoire National avant la nomination de César Franck (1872)," *L'Orgue*, No. 122 (October–December 1972) 123.

[18]Louis Vierne wrote that "it consisted of a note-for-note accompaniment of a liturgical chant in the upper part; then the chant became the bass in whole notes, not transposed, accompanied by three upper parts in a sort of florid classical counterpoint. The whole notes then passed to the upper voice, transposed a fourth higher, and received, in turn, a florid classical accompaniment. . . One did not hesitate to accompany each note with a chord—an effect about as artistic as if it were applied to *bel canto* vocal runs." (Louis Vierne, *Mes Souvenirs*, published serially in *L'Orgue* from September 1934 to September 1937. Citations refer to the collected edition, Paris: Les Amis de l'Orgue, 1970, 23.)

inextricably bound to the study of harmony and composition, both indispensable to the organist."[19]

It was a practical class. On the one hand, it stimulated the composer's creativity and, as Saint-Saëns wrote, "developed faculties of invention which otherwise would have remained latent."[20] Most of Saint-Saëns's classmates later composed for the theater and competed for the Prix de Rome; few of them ever became church organists. On the other hand, it developed a facility which would enable its practitioner to hold an organ post "to augment his resources"[21] if not for any artistic gratification. In view of the requirements of the liturgy, the ability to improvise was an absolute necessity for an organist in a Catholic church.[22]

Historically, the only music prescribed for the Mass was that to which the words of the liturgy were set—Gregorian chant or polyphony. Except for brief periods of silence at the Offertory and Communion, when the priest's movements took more time than the singing of the designated text, there was no place for the playing of solo organ music. The organ, therefore, had to usurp sections which were ordinarily sung by the choir.[23]

---

[19]Constant Pierre, *Le Conservatoire National de Musique et de Déclamation* (Paris: Imprimerie Nationale, 1900) 358.

[20]Camille Saint-Saëns, "Music in the Church," *The Musical Quarterly* (January 1916) 8.

[21]In this way many celebrated names in French music were connected with the organ: Léo Delibes, the ballet composer; Raoul Pugno, the pianist; and Charles Gounod, the composer of *Faust*. Widor and Fauré, who spent their lives teaching and writing for the theater, held two of the most prestigious organ posts in Paris. So, too, it was with Saint-Saëns, for, though he held two successive organ positions, he remained very much a musician of the world—the concert hall and the theater.

[22]The distribution of musical forces is charmingly explained by S. Sophia Beale in *The Churches of Paris* (London: Allen, 1893) 324–25.

> The organ. . . in all the Paris churches is at the west end of the nave and is only used for voluntaries and solo performances, never to accompany voices, for which purpose a small instrument is always placed close to the choir, either at the side or behind the altar. This is a much better arrangement than our modern one of having a huge organ in the chancel thundering away and drowning the voices. Of course, it necessitates two organists, but the gain in refinement is worth the outlay; and there is no reason why the choirmaster, who would accompany the singers, should necessarily be a first-rate player.

[23]The organist's position was well defined in a directive from Rome:

> Composers of church music must always bear in mind that instrumental music in church is merely tolerated; it must serve primarily to sustain and enrich the

6

The practice of plainchant improvisation goes back to at least the fourteenth century, when, to relieve the singers from the strain of continuous chanting, [24] the organ alternated with the choir. Although this ritual use of the organ declined during the seventeenth and eighteenth centuries everywhere but in France, such alternative performance continued to flourish well into the twentieth century, and only with the directives of the Second Vatican Council has its practice been curtailed.

Aside from these short improvised interludes, called "versets," each lasting forty to fifty seconds, the organist played during moments in the service when the priest's actions were not accompanied by singing. These were opportunities for improvisation also because the length of time needed to be filled was so unpredictable—some priests read more quickly than others, there might or might not be incensation, and the length of processions and the number of people receiving communion varied.

The Students

During the two-and-one-half years Saint-Saëns spent in the organ class, seven of his classmates competed for the first prize[25] in organ; three never attained it. Édouard Silas, a Dutch organist, won first prize in 1849. He later settled in London, where for sixty years he was active as a pianist, teacher, and organist (for a time at the Catholic Church at Kingston-on-Thames). In 1871 Saint-Saëns dedicated his *Gavotte in C Minor*, Op. 23, for piano, to Silas. Léonce Cohen won the first accessit in 1849, later played the violin in the Orchestre de Vaudeville and at the Théâtre-Italién and composed two one-act operas. Céleste Morel competed only one year and won the accessit in 1850. Joseph Franck, César's younger brother, won the second prize in 1850 and the first in 1852. Eugène Vast, Boëly's assistant at Saint-Germain-l'Auxerrois, and like

---

chant, never to dominate it, still less to overpower it and reduce it to a mere accessory. (Cardinal Patri, Vicar of Rome, *General Directions and Instructions for Directors of Music* [20 November 1856]).

[24]Benjamin Van Wye, "Ritual Use of the Organ in France," *Journal of the American Musicological Society* (Summer 1980) 291.

[25]Official graduation depended upon winning a first prize at the competition (concours) held in July, at the end of each school year. A jury awarded four prizes: first and second prize, and first and second accessit, or honorable mention.

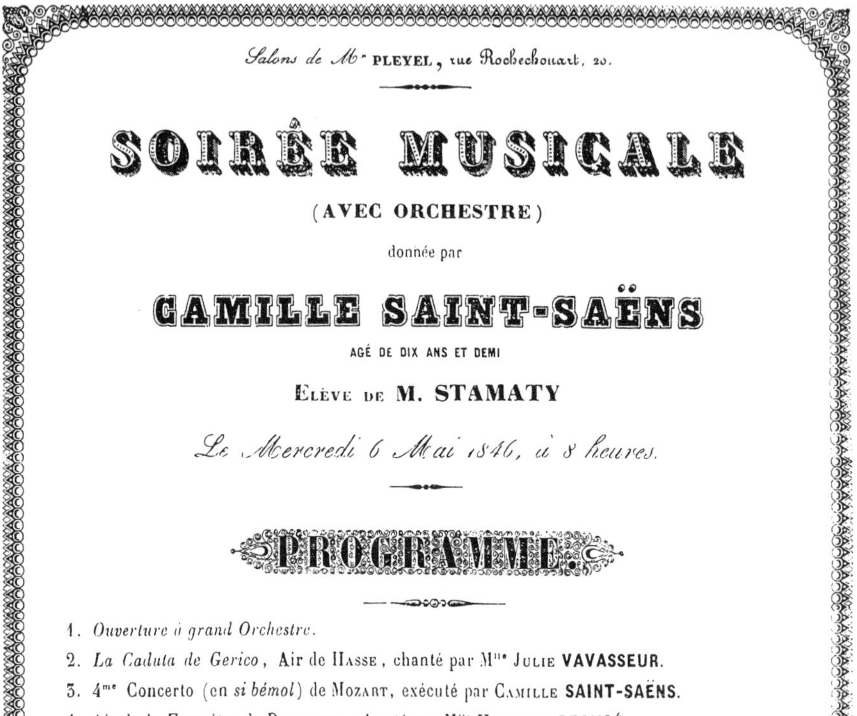

Salons de Mr PLEYEL, *rue Rochechouart, 20.*

SOIRÉE MUSICALE

(AVEC ORCHESTRE)

donnée par

CAMILLE SAINT-SAËNS

AGÉ DE DIX ANS ET DEMI

ÉLÈVE DE **M. STAMATY**

Le Mercredi 6 Mai 1846, à 8 heures.

PROGRAMME.

1. *Ouverture à grand Orchestre.*
2. *La Caduta de Gerico*, Air de HASSE, chanté par Mlle JULIE **VAVASSEUR**.
3. 4me Concerto (en *si bémol*) de MOZART, exécuté par CAMILLE **SAINT-SAËNS**.
4. Air de *la Favorite*, de DONIZETTI, chanté par Mlle HERMINIE **BEAUCÉ**.
5. Thême varié (en *mi majeur*) et grande Fugue (en *mi mineur*) de HÄNDEL, exécutés par CAMILLE **SAINT-SAËNS**.
6. Scène d'*Ariodant*, de MÉHUL, chantée par Mlle JULIE **VAVASSEUR**.
7. Toccata de *Kalkbrenner*, Prélude et Fugue de J.-S. BACH, exécutés par CAMILLE **SAINT-SAËNS**.
8. Récitatif et Romance de *Guillaume-Tell*, de ROSSINI, chantés par Mlle HERMINIE **BEAUCÉ**.
9. 3me Concerto (en *ut mineur*), de BEETHOWEN, exécuté par CAMILLE **SAINT-SAËNS**.
10. *Final.*

L'Orchestre sera dirigé par Mr Tilmant aîné.

Le Piano sera tenu par Mr A. DE GARAUDÉ.

Imp. Pollet et Cie, rue St-Denis, 380 (Carré).

Plate 2. Program of the ten-year-old Saint-Saëns's recital at Salle Pleyel, 6 May 1846

Saint-Saëns, had been one of his former organ students. The year Saint-Saëns won first prize (1851), Vast succeeded Boëly as organist; he won first prize in 1853. Jules Cohen became a friend of Saint-Saëns and later assisted him occasionally at Saint-Merry. He won first prize in 1852, taught ensemble singing at the Conservatoire and succeeded Benoist as chorus master at the Opéra in 1877. Charles Lecoq, who won only first accessit in 1852, later enjoyed great success and popularity with his forty operettas and comic operas. Saint-Saëns, himself, won first prize in organ on 28 July 1851.

Saint-Saëns at Sixteen

The following October, Saint-Saëns enrolled in Ludovic Halévy's composition class to prepare himself to compete for the Prix de Rome.[26] He entered the competition the next summer but was unsuccessful. Léonce Cohen, one of his fellow students from the organ class, was the winner. Saint-Saëns's disappointment was brief, however, for in October he entered a competition sponsored by the Société Sainte-Cécile. His *Ode à Sainte-Cécile* won the prize and was performed the day after Christmas.

Appointment to Saint-Merry

The following year, 1853, the seventeen-year-old musician succeeded the seventy-eight-year-old Vincent-Edmond Govin[27] as organist of the Church of Saint-Merry, an appointment due less to Saint-Saëns's credentials and talent than to his mother's friendship with the pastor,

---

[26]The Prix de Rome was France's highest academic prize for composition. The winner of the First Grand Prize received a gold medal, four years in Rome at the Villa Medici and a monthly stipend. Works composed while in Rome were given public performances in Paris. The Second First Grand Prize was a silver medal, a smaller stipend and a shorter period of residence at the Villa Medici. The Second Grand Prize was only a bronze medal and a cash prize of 1,800 francs.

[27]Govin (1775–1853) had studied with Gervais-François Couperin and had been organist of the Cathedral of Blois (1805–1809), Saint-Paul-d'Orléans (1809–1811), Saint-Eustache in Paris (1820–1830) and of Saint-Merry from about 1841 until his death in 1853. (Félix Raugel, *Les Grandes Orgues des Églises de Paris*, Paris: Librairie Fischbacher, 1927, 33 and 195.) Two of Saint-Saëns's illustrious predecessors were Nicolas LeBègue, organist of Saint-Merry from about 1660 until his death in 1702, and Jean-François Dandrieu, who held the post from 1704.

Jean-Louis Gabriel.[28] The church, situated on the rue Saint-Martin, one block north of the rue de Rivoli, is roughly seven blocks east of Saint-Eustache, whose organist, Édouard Batiste, ranked as the second most popular organist in Paris (Lefébure-Wély held the place of honor), and seven blocks west of Saint-Jean-Saint-François, where the thirty-year-old César Franck was organist—his severe style was matched only by that of Saint-Saëns. The parish of Saint-Merry was very large; a census taken in 1863 numbered 26,000 Catholics and mentioned that 232 weddings had been performed during that year. The stipends from those weddings, additional fees from funerals, and a modest salary provided Saint-Saëns with enough income and leisure to pursue his musical career as a pianist and composer.

The Parisian Organ World

The organ world in which Saint-Saëns had grown up, and of which he now found himself a part was much different from what it was to be by the end of the nineteenth century. The music in the churches of Paris was a scandal to all of northern Europe, as it had been since the middle of the eighteenth century, when "French music gradually became less a handmaid of religion than a lady-in-waiting to the court. The old organist-composer gradually forsook the organ for the more popular and lucrative clavecin."[29] Fétis attributed the inferiority of French organ playing to the organist's

> . . . obsession with what they call improvisation . . . Not one of them has what may be called an organist's training. Not one of them could master the great compositions of Bach. All their attention is turned towards special effects, tonal contrasts . . . and ways to arouse and gratify sensual instincts. This situation is far from new, for men like Marchand, Calvière, Daquin, Balbâtre, and Charpentier were headed in this direction. There have been no distinguished organists in France since the seventeenth century: Couperin was the last . . . Storms have been the standard ever since.

---

[28]Abbé Gabriel, a native of Cantal, had been a canon of Notre-Dame Cathedral before his appointment as pastor of Saint Merry, 23 December 1851. (Norbert Dufourcq , *Les Grandes Orgues de Saint-Merry de Paris à travers l'histoire*, Paris: l'Association des Amis de l'Orgue, 1983, 48.) When Saint-Saëns went to Saint-Merry, one Canon Delacroix was maître-de-chapelle, but in a short time, Paul Wachs, the father of César Franck's student (and later organist of Saint-Merry, 1874–96), took over the choir.
[29]An address given by Harvey Grace on 14 May 1918, entitled "Modern French Organ Music."

> When I was young, a certain M. Miroir enjoyed a great reputation for that kind of wizardry ... The audience was terrified, but M. Miroir had enough good taste to calm their excitement with little solos on the Musette, Petite flûte, Voix humaine with tremulant, or Cromorne en taille.[30]

Of the last organists of the "old school"—all of whom had died by the year of Saint-Saëns's birth—Guillaume Lasceux, Nicolas Séan, Éloi-Nicolas Miroir, François Blin, and Jean-Nicolas Marrigues, Félix Raugel wrote:

> The distinctive characteristic of their talent was a spontaneity, a faculty for improvisation and a knowledge of organ effects, but, except for Séjan (whom Cherubini liked to go to hear at Saint-Sulpice), the others left no works worthy of their reputations. Their style was generally cold and incorrect and none of them had seriously studied the art of composition. As Benoist said later, "They spoke the language very well but did not know the grammar."[31]

Montalembert wrote in 1839 that in playing tunes from the latest operas, waltzes and contredanses "there was nothing more grotesque or irreligious at the time than the practices of the Parisian organists."[32] The previous year the organist of Saint-Étienne-du-Mont, Gabriel Gauthier, had played a well-known drinking song on Easter Sunday. Waltzes reminiscent of the Opéra or Salle Musard could have been heard at Notre-Dame-de-Lorette and, in other churches, at the offertory, a waltz followed a galop and, on major feast days, the Overture to *William Tell*, the March from *Le Prophète*. For the offertory on Easter, a priest had ordered his organist to play the waltz from *Rosita* "and, above all, up to tempo!" Romanzas from *Loïsa Puget* and polkas blared forth at the Magnificat.[33] Musettes were heard at one of the most solemn moments of the Mass; when the priest takes communion. Hunting songs alternated with the *Dies irae*.[34]

---

[30]François-Joseph Fétis, "L'Orgue mondaine et la musique érotique à l'église," *Revue et Gazette musicale* (6 April 1856) 1.

[31]Félix Raugel, *Les Organistes* (Paris: Henri-Laurens, 1923) 109–10.

[32]Montalembert, *Du vandalisme et du catholicisme dans l'art* (Paris, 1839). Quoted in Cellier, *L'Orgue*, 84.

[33]Cellier, *L'Orgue*, 176.

[34]Ibid., 177. How similar to Mercier's observation in 1781: "During the elevation of the host and chalice they play ariettas and sarabandes; and at the Te Deum and at vespers, hunting songs, minuets, ballads and rigaudons." (Louis-Sébastien Mercier, "On Organs," *Tableau de Paris*, Vol. II, Chapter 131, p. 78.)

Adolphe Hesse, on a trip in 1844, observed that the organ playing

. . . in France was generally irreverent, although once in a while a significant talent came to my attention within this irreverence. Not rarely is a gay pastorale heard during a church service which turns into a thunderstorm before closing with a sort of operatic grand finale in free style. Given that this is untenable from the German religious point of view, it must be admitted that such things are often done quite talentedly. A requiem mass for Lafitte in the church of Saint-Roch gave me the opportunity to hear one M. Lefébure-Wély play in a solemn, appropriate manner, whereas he worked up a tremendously gay mood during the mass on Sunday. In response to my astonishment over this I was told that the clergy as well as the congregation expect lighthearted music.[35]

Such was the state of the art as Camille Saint-Saëns entered the organ profession and began his lengthy career as organist and organ composer. It was to be a career as seemingly impervious to the decadent influences about it in church music as it would be later to the modern harmonies of Wagner and Strauss. Boëly's student would bring the pure classic tradition into the twentieth century and he would die eulogized by Reynaldo Hahn as "Musical art's last great classicist."

[35]Adolph Friedrich Hesse, "On organs, their appointment and treatment in Austria, Italy, France and England," *Neue Zeitschrift für Music* (1853) 53.

CHAPTER II

Saint-Saëns and the Church of Saint-Merry (1853–1858)

Although construction began in 1520, the Church of Saint-Merry[1] was built in the Flamboyant Gothic style of the preceding century. It was not finished until 1612 but, because the succession of architects adhered to the original plan, there were no stylistic changes—a rare instance in a church so long under construction.[2] All of the statues on the richly ornamented west front date from 1842, replacing those destroyed during the Revolution. The bell in the north tower (above the left door), cast in 1331, is the oldest in Paris, escaping destruction during the Revolution only because it was impossible to get it down without destroying the tower itself. In Saint-Saëns's day, houses rose in tiers above the left side of the church and what is now the hotel at the corner of the rue Saint-Martin and the rue de la Verrerie was the rectory.

---

[1]The name Saint-Merry is an abbreviation for Saint-Médéric who died 29 August 700 and is buried beneath the site of the present church.

[2]Detailed descriptions of the church are to be found in: S. Sophia Beale, *The Churches of Paris* (London: Allen, 1893); Walter F. Lonergan, *Historic Churches of Paris* (London: Downey, 1896); and Martin Garay, *L'Église Saint-Merry de Paris* (Paris: Association pour la Culture par les Loisirs et le Tourisme, c. 1982).

Plate 3. Church of Saint-Merry in 1856

The Organ

The original seventeenth-century organ of Saint-Merry, considered by contemporaries to be one of the best in Paris,[3] was restored by François-Henri Clicquot some years before the Revolution, repaired in 1800 and rebuilt by Dallery in 1816–18. Further repairs were made in 1828 and 1841. Already "one of Clicquot's oldest instruments"[4] at the time of Saint-Saëns's appointment, it was in deplorable condition and all but unplayable.[5] The thirty-seven stops were disposed over four manuals and a primitive pedalboard. Two of the manuals, the Récit and Écho, had a compass of only twenty-seven notes; the Pédale's twenty-one-note range was from ,,,A to ,F—a compass making the performance of Bach's music impossible.

As titular of an organ that was barely playable for two years (and which was out of commission most of the next two years while it was being rebuilt, Saint-Saëns exercised his talents not only in composition and piano playing but also in playing and demonstrating and, in one instance, composing for three new musical instruments: the harmonium, the harmonicorde and the pédalier.

The Harmonium

The harmonium as we know it dates from 1841. While Alexandre Debain did not *invent* it, he did synthesize all of his predecessors' work with free reeds, controlled the pitches from a keyboard and developed four contrasting colors of reed tone which could be selected and combined by using stops, as on the organ. Those who came after Debain either added to or perfected his work. Because he had to patent the name "harmonium" to protect his legal rights, his competitors, Alexandre and Mustel, adopted the term "organ" for their instruments: orgue expressif in France, and in English-speaking countries the familiar reed organ, parlor or cabinet organ, American organ, pump organ and

---

[3]Félix Raugel, *Les Grandes Orgues des Églises de Paris* (Paris: Librairie Fischbacher, 1927) 31.

[4]Georges Schmitt, *L'Organiste* (Paris: Encyclopédie Roret, 1855) 85.

[5]Norbert Dufourcq, *Le Grand Orgue et les organistes de Saint-Merry de Paris* (Paris: Librairie Floury, 1947) 26.

15

even Liszt organ.[6] So named, it is little wonder that the public has come to think of the harmonium as a substitute for the pipe organ instead of the expressive free-reed instrument it was conceived to be.

Debain devised a system of numbering the stops[7] and of printing harmonium registration. A number or letter in a circle written above the staff indicated which stops were to be drawn; a line drawn diagonally through the circle indicated that the stop was to be shut off. Debain centered the stops in a row above the keyboard with the Grand jeu, or Full Organ stop, in the middle:

0 4 3 2 1 G 1 2 3 4 0

The four sets of reeds consisted of two ranks at 8' pitch, Nos. 1 and 4; one of 16' pitch, No. 2. and one of 4', No. 3. The keyboard was divided at middle E so that an entirely different registration could be drawn for the left hand, playing below middle E, than for the right hand, playing middle F and above.

The popularity of the harmonium paralleled Saint-Saëns's organ career. Of the celebrated composers who wrote for the harmonium he was one of the first. The following is a chronological list of early works for solo harmonium by important nineteenth-century French composers.

1845	Hector Berlioz	*Trois Pièces*
1847	Charles-Valentin Alkan	*25 Préludes*, Op. 31
1852	Camille Saint-Saëns	*Trois Morceaux*, Op. 1
1856	Camille Saint-Saëns	*Élévation ou Communion*, Op. 13
1858	Georges Bizet	*Trois Esquisses Musicales*
	César Franck	*Cinq Pièces*
	Camille Saint-Saëns	*Six Duos* pour harmonium et piano, Op. 8[8]
1862	César Franck	*Quasi Marcia*, Op. 22

[6]In 1876 The Mason & Hamlin Organ Co. of Boston brought out the Liszt Cabinet Organ, a fifteen-stop reed organ with seven sets of reeds (and one octave of 16' Sub-Base [sic] reeds). Having been sent one of these instruments, Franz Liszt replied, "What a magnificent organ I have to thank you for; even players of moderate ability will be able to create great admiration in its use." (Letter from Franz Liszt to Mason & Hamlin, Weimar, 12 June 1883.)

[7]Patent dated 3 March 1843. Michael Dieterlen, *L'Harmonium une aventure musicale et industrielle* doctoral thesis, Université de Reims, 1982.

[8]Bizet also published *Trois Duos pour Orgue et Piano* in 1858. They were arranged after the *Trois Esquisses Musicales*. However all registration in the two-stave Régnier-Canaux "organ" part is for the harmonium. These are not original pieces but rather potpourris of Mozart's *Don Juan*, Grétry's *Richard Coeur de Lion*, and Rossini's *Le Barbier de Séville*.

It has been estimated that some 2,260 pages[9] of original music were composed for the harmonium in the 100 years between 1849 and 1949. Between 1850 and 1859, 24.69% (1,570 pages of both original music and transcriptions) was published, and between 1860 and 1869, 2,236 pages of music (28.68%) were published.[10]

The *Trois Morceaux*[11] were actually written the year before Saint-Saëns went to Saint-Merry but were not published until late fall 1858. Three pieces comprise the set: *Méditation*, *Barcarolle* and *Prière*. The *Méditation* is of little interest, but the *Barcarolle* is directly inspired by Mendelssohn's "Venetienisches Gondellied," Op. 62, No. 29, of his *Lieder ohne Worte*, composed about ten years before Saint-Saëns's work. The barcarolle was a genre to which Saint-Saëns returned several times and, curiously, seemed to associate with the harmonium. (A five-and-one-half-page manuscript dating from April 1897 of an unpublished *Barcarolle* scored for violin, cello, organ and piano is in the Bibliothèque Nationale.) On 7 March 1898 Saint-Saëns composed the *Barcarolle*, Op. 108, for violin, cello, harmonium and piano.

The prière, although not a "form," was a genre which few nineteenth-century organ and piano composers ignored. César Franck's *Prière* in C-sharp Minor, the fifth of his *Six Pièces*, is the greatest, but the example by the seventeen-year-old Saint-Saëns is noteworthy for its curious 11/4 meter.[12]

Saint-Saëns's three pieces for harmonium do not use the Debain numbers to indicate registration. Instead, he calls for "Cor anglais,"

---

[9]Dieterlen, *L'Harmonium*, 255.

[10]Ibid., 251.

[11]Six other harmonium pieces are to be found in the Bibliothèque Nationale under Ms 914 a–e; No. d, *Morceaux pour harmonium inédit* includes:
1. Moderato in C Major (59 measures)
2. Moderato in D Major (54 measures)
3. Andantino in E Major, headed *Communion ou O Salutaris*
4. Moderato in F Major, Ave verum (40 measures)
5. Allegretto non troppo in G Major (73 measures)
6. Andante in A Major (22 measures)

[12]Other examples of his use of unusual meters are in the restatement of the theme—in 5/8—of the *Étude de Rythme*, Op. 52, No. 4 (1877), for piano; *Carillon*, Op. 72, No. 2 (1884), for piano, is in 7/4; the Allegretto of the *Trio in E Minor*, Op. 92 (1891–92), is in 5/8 and 5/4; and the first movement of the *Triptyque*, Op. 136, for violin and piano (1912) is in 5/4.

17

Plate 4. Advertisement for Estey's two-manual and pedal reed organ with
Saint-Saëns's testimonial, 1908

18

"Bourdon," etc. They were probably written for the Alexandre orgue expressif. Had he written them with the Mustel instrument in mind (as did Bizet), he surely would have called for either "Double expression" or "Harpe éolienne," the new stop Mustel developed in 1855.

At the 1867 Paris Exposition Saint-Saëns acquainted himself with American reed organs and signed testimonials for Estey of Brattleboro, Vermont, and Mason & Hamlin of Boston. Of the former he wrote:

> I have played the Estey organs and have been charmed by their tonal quality which so closely resembles that of the pipe organ, and by the resources which they offer the performer.[13]

With Édouard Batiste, Auguste Durand and Edmond Hocmelle, Saint-Saëns recommended the Mason & Hamlin Cabinet Organs "for the rendering of all sacred music, and also as an indispensable auxilliary of the pianoforte in the drawing room."[14]

Years later when Saint-Saëns visited the French exhibit of musical instruments at the Brussels Exposition in 1897, he stopped at the exhibit of Mustel "organs," talked about them at length and played both the harmoniums and the célesta "which, under the famous artist's fingers, produced marvelous effects."[15]

In 1903 Saint-Saëns wrote a testimonial for the Orgue-Mustel:

> It is with the greatest pleasure that I take the opportunity to say how much I think of the Orgue-Mustel, the only one of its kind in the world . . . I have played this marvelous instrument many times and it cannot help but be admired.[16]

Noted performers did not disdain playing the harmonium. At a concert given by Jacques-Nicolas Lemmens and his wife at Cavaillé-Coll's atelier, the Belgian organist alternated solos between the organ and the orgue expressif—the first time he had played the latter before the Parisian public.[17] But, in spite of its popularity and the seriousness with which it was regarded in the music world, the harmonium never

---

[13]*Illustrated Catalog of Cottage Organs Manufactured by J. Estey & Co., Brattleboro, Vermont* (New York: Biglow & Co., 1876) 22. This same endorsement was run in *Musica* from June 1908 to August 1909.

[14]*Mason & Hamlin Cabinet Organs*, Illustrated Catalog (March 1880) 27.

[15]*Le Monde musicale* (30 October 1897) 223.

[16]*Le Monde musicale* (15 January 1904) 24.

[17]On 14 August 1864. A review by Louis Roger of this concert appears in "Chronique," *Revue de musique sacrée* (15 August 1864) 315.

achieved academic recognition. Nothing ever came of the proposal made in 1846 by the harmonium manufacturer, Jacob Alexandre, to the director of the Paris Conservatoire, Daniel-François Auber, of creating a harmonium class with himself (Alexandre) and Lefébure-Wély in charge of it.[18] But, shortly after Charles-Marie Widor's appointment in 1890 as professor of organ at the Conservatoire, the director, Ambroise Thomas, announced his intention of creating a harmonium class which could be considered a stepping stone towards the study of the organ. When asked his opinion, Widor replied, "My dear director, that's an excellent idea. Only for it to be complete it will be necessary to go further by planning a logical gradation in the teaching of our blowing machines: accordion, harmonium, and organ!"[19]

The Harmonicorde

Another new instrument of the period, and surely the most unusual, was the harmonicorde. A combination harmonium and piano, it was patented by Alexandre Debain in 1851. Fétis[20] mentioned that it would have been better to choose a name other than "harmonicorde," which was already used for an entirely different instrument, invented in 1809 by the famous acoustician Gottfried Kaufmann and his son Friedrich in Dresden. Debain's instrument combined his harmonium with a set of wire strings arranged as in an upright piano but with only one string to each note. The hammer struck the string at the same time that the reed was set in vibration; the attack was precise and firm. The strings could be played with or without the reeds and vice versa; coupling the two was accomplished with knee-levers. The effect was that of a harp accompanying a wind instrument.[21]

The year 1856 saw the harmonicorde at the height of its popularity. "It was positively all the rage!"[22] and fifteen special concerts were

---

[18]Michel Dieterlen, "L'Orgue Expressif de la Maison d'Education de la Légion d'Honneur de Saint-Denis," *La Flûte Harmonique*, No. 17 (1er trimestre 1981) 13.

[19]Charles Tournemire, *Petite Méthode d'Orgue* (Paris: Max Eschig, 1949) 67.

[20]Adrien de la Fage, *Quinze visites musicales à l'exposition universelle de 1855* (Paris: Chez Tardif, 1856) 62.

[21]Ibid., 63.

[22]Ad. de Pontecoulant, *La Musique à l'Exposition de 1867* (Paris: Bureau de l'art musical) LXV.

devoted to it alone. Queen Victoria and Prince Albert ordered two Debain harmonicordes.[23] Rossini had it played at his soirées and even wrote to Debain that he had heard it "with genuine pleasure . . . It is a very beautiful invention which cannot help being well received in the musical world."[24] Lefébure-Wély did not ignore the new medium and in 1857 published his three movement *Caprice Originale*, Op. 120, for two harmonicordes.[25]

Saint-Saëns, Lefébure-Wély, Freslon, Miolan, Henri and Alfred Lebeau and Paul Jujat demonstrated a harmonicorde at Salle de Herz in the latter part of November 1854.[26] On 9 March 1855 at Lebouc and Paulin's fourth and last soirée, Pauline Viardot sang arias by Handel and Schubert, Mme. Mattmann played Beethoven's *Trio in B-flat* with MM. Maurin and Lebouc, and M. Paulin sang pieces by Sacchini and Gluck. Saint-Saëns played the Andante of Beethoven's *Fifth Symphony* on the harmonicorde[27] and Henri Blanchard wrote that:

> The detached tones of the piano keyboard coupled to the sustained tones of the organ keyboard in the same instrument produced the most pleasant and picturesque effects. The performer made excellent use of it.[28]

The Pédalier

Yet another instrument we find Saint-Saëns played in public is the pédalier or pedal piano. Although most pédaliers coupled the piano keys to a pedalboard, Auguste Wolff, a partner in Pleyel & Co., pianoforte makers, had just designed and built a pédalier which was completely independent, having its own strings, hammers and mechanism. Its height allowed the strings to be longer and thicker than usual, and the dimensions of the soundboard, relatively large for an instrument of only two-and-one-half octaves, lent a unique beauty and power to its tone.

---

[23]Dieterlen, *L'Harmonium*, 291.

[24]Letter from Gioacchino Rossini to Alexandre Debain, Paris, 9 May 1856. Quoted in F. J. Fétis, *Rapport du jury: Fabrication des instruments de musique / Exposition de 1855*, p. 1345 (Paris: Napoleon Chaix et Cie, 1857) 1.

[25]The movements are Allegro, Andante and Allegro (Pastorale). (Paris: Régnier-Canaux, 1857).

[26]*Le Ménestrel* (26 November 1854) and *La France musical* (26 November 1854) 386.

[27]*La France musicale* (4 March 1855) 71.

[28]Henri Blanchard, *Revue et Gazette musicale* (18 March 1855) 84.

Plate 5. The Pleyel Pédalier

In the best grand pianos the notes of the bottom octave, especially the lowest five, are somewhat dull and indistinct, but in M. Wolff's pédalier the lowest C is as pure and rich as the finest 16′ flute stop. Just as an 8′ stop is always added to a 16′ stop in the organ, so M. Wolff, to offset the heaviness of the thick strings, has playing simultaneously a set of thin strings sounding the octave above, thus producing a sound of remarkable fullness.[29]

At one of Auguste Wolff's private salons Saint-Saëns played this new pédalier and Henri Blanchard wrote that in the Bach fugue, "It was certainly not saying too little that he played almost as agilely and as intelligently with his feet as with his fingers."[30]

In a concert on 2 April 1866 at Salle Pleyel, with Berlioz, Gounod and Liszt in the audience, Saint-Saëns played two Schumann *Canons* and the *Sketch in F Minor* on the pédalier—the latter was encored.[31]

The Rebuild of the Saint-Merry Organ

The organ of Saint-Merry, had it been in proper working order, was suited to its traditional liturgical demands. By 1855 the only important "modern" organ music that had been written was Schumann's *Six Fugues on B.A.C.H.*, Mendelssohn's *Six Sonatas* and Liszt's *Fantasie und Fuge über den Choral "Ad nos, ad salutarem undam."* However, the gradual awakening of organists to the literature of Bach and the possibilities of their instrument, influenced by the piano and its extended technique, provided the incentive for a modern instrument—one which would inspire a new school of composers writing under the influence of a new aesthetic. No longer a liturgical adjunct, the organ would become a concert instrument, like the piano, with its own technique and its own literature. Saint-Saëns and César Franck were the founders and originators of this "new" organ style (indeed, not only were they the first but, as history has shown, the greatest French composers of their era to write for the organ) which influenced the later nineteenth-century organbuilders and which was in turn influenced by them.

---

[29]Louis Niedermeyer, "Un nouveau pédalier de M. Wolff," *La Maîtrise* (December 1857) 139–40.

[30]Henri Blanchard "Concerts et Auditions musicales," *Revue et Gazette musicale* (15 March 1857) 83.

[31]*Revue et Gazette musicale* (29 April 1866) 130.

Plate 6. Saint-Saëns at 20 in 1855

During Saint-Saëns's first year at Saint-Merry the initial steps were taken to rebuild the organ. Antoine-L. Suret (who had just finished an organ at Sainte-Élisabeth-du-Temple for Auguste Bazille) submitted a proposal for work on the instrument on 11 January 1854. He enumerated a number of improvements specifically requested by the organist, Camille Saint-Saëns. The young organist's demands were in no way eccentric or even original but were the standard changes which would bring a seventeenth- or eighteenth-century classic organ into line with current concepts of organ design.

In spite of his youth Saint-Saëns was completely aware of the organ world about him. His requirements for the rebuilding of the Saint-Merry organ were specific. Suret's proposal[32] enumerates precisely the desired changes of Saint-Saëns.

1. Replace the four keyboards, covering the naturals with ivory and the sharps with ebony.

2. Raise the pitch of the entire instrument to that of the orchestra.

3. Replace the pedalboard "which the organist uses only with difficulty" with a new one in the "German style" and extend the compass upward seven notes to 'C. Add a 16' Bourdon (of wood) of 26 pipes, descending to ravalement „,A.

4. The 16' and 8' Bourdons of the Grand-Orgue and the 8' Montre of the Positif went down only to „G. Saint-Saëns requested that pipes be added to complete their compass down to „C.

5. Add a low „C-sharp to all the stops of the Grand-Orgue and Positif.

6. Replace the Récit and Écho with an enclosed expressive division using existing pipework. The Bourdon, Flûte and Trompette, all 8' ranks, were to be carried down to ‚C but the Cornet and Hautbois were to be left as they were (‚A– '''D) since "they do not usually go below ‚A." The Voix humaine was to be transferred from the Grand-Orgue. He

---

[32]Norbert Dufourcq, *Les Grandes Orgues de Saint-Merry de Paris à travers l'histoire.* (Paris: L'Association de l'Orgue, 1983) 49.

Plate 7. Saint-Merry, Cavaillé-Coll organ console

asked that two new 8' stops be added: a Cor anglais and a Flûte harmonique.

7. The drawstop shanks were to be replaced with new ones of rosewood; porcelain discs, engraved with the name of each stop, were to be inserted into their ends. The porcelain was to be a different color for each manual.

8. Four iron combination pedals were to be placed horizontally above the pedalboard: one to bring on the Tirasse Grand-Orgue, one to take it off, a Positif au Grand-Orgue and a Tremblant.

Nothing ever came of Suret's proposal and the project was temporarily abandoned. Almost a year later, three days before Christmas 1854, the same plan was shown to Aristide Cavaillé-Coll who, in a letter, gave his opinion of the suggested rebuild.[33] While he approved of most of the changes he advised retaining the four manuals but extending them all to fifty-four notes. He pointed out that in raising the pitch of the organ it would not be necessary to add bass pipes for the C-sharp, only one pipe at the top of each rank—"the smallest instead of the largest!" And he recommended converting the Pédale Bourdon 8' to a 16' and the 4' to an 8'. He also felt that having four pédales de combinaisons was completely insufficient by current standards.

Two organs were set up in his erecting room: one for Saint-Nicolas in Ghent and the other for the Cathedral of Carcassonne. The builder invited the Saint-Merry church council to visit his shop and suggested they bring their young organist to demonstrate the organs for them.[34] It is not known if the visit took place (Saint-Saëns did play the Carcassonne organ the following year), but the contract was signed on 19 May 1855.[35]

The renovation of the organ consisted chiefly in rebuilding and modernizing the existing instrument.[36] The console was rebuilt and remained *en fenêtre*, that is, built into the case, instead of detached and reversed like most of Cavaillé-Coll's organs. The number of manuals was

---

[33]Dufourcq, *Les Grandes Orgues de Saint-Merry* (1983) 53.

[34]Ibid. Letter from Cavaillé-Coll to M. Rédier, 25 January 1855.

[35]Work began on the organ about the first of July. In a letter to a friend (Paris, 26 June 1855) Saint-Saëns mentions that *réparation* of his organ begins "next week."

[36]In his Invitation to the Solemn Reception, 25 November 1857, Cavaillé-Coll refers to the instrument "which had just been restored and perfected."

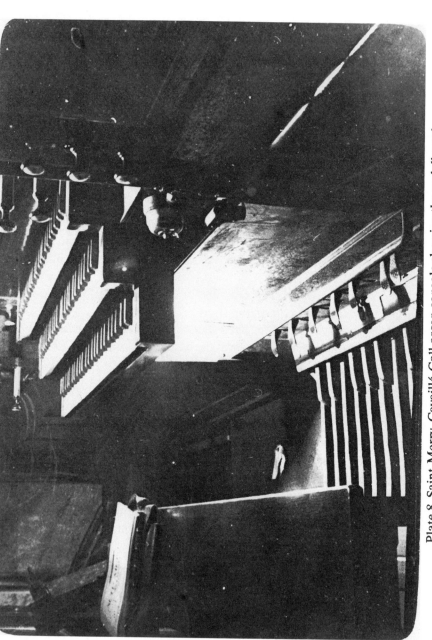

Plate 8. Saint-Merry, Cavaillé-Coll organ console showing the pedalboard

reduced to three, their compass extended to fifty-four notes and a new pedalboard of twenty-seven notes installed. The mutations of the Grand-Orgue were converted into unison stops: the 2 2/3' moved to 8' pitch and the 1 3/5' to 4'. Twelve basses were added to the Deuxième Trompette to make a 16' Bombarde. The Positif was left untouched. The Récit and Écho were combined into a modern Récit; the Cornet and Flûte were eliminated and the Voix humaine of the Grand-Orgue was moved to this expressive division. The Pédale Flûtes were extended downwards to make 16' and 8' stops and the pitch of the entire organ was raised. Finally, eleven pédales de combinaison were added. Norbert Dufourcq[37] felt that it was at Saint-Saëns's insistence that the Cornet of the Grand-Orgue and the mutations of the Positif were retained: "Without him the instrument would certainly have lost its *couleur ancienne* at the hands of the modern builder." Referring to his completed work at Saint-Merry, Cavaillé-Coll wrote:

> In comparing the old specification with the new one a notable increase has been found in the number of heavy stops which give the organ its appropriately majestic character and, on the contrary, there is a reduction in the number of high-pitched shrill stops which give the sound of old instruments a nasal quality little in keeping with the noble harmonies of sacred music.[38]

Saint-Saëns's Organ Playing

It was one year after Cavaillé-Coll began working on the organ at Saint-Merry that one first read of Saint-Saëns's organ playing. Mention was made of two organs set up in Cavaillé-Coll's shop. One of them had been ordered by and built for, but never delivered to, the Cathedral of Carcassonne. Eventually, in 1857 it was installed in the Cathedral of Luçon; in the meantime it stood for a year in the builder's erecting room and was demonstrated at innumerable soirées by various noted organists. The names of both César Franck and Saint-Saëns first appeared in connection with that of Cavaillé-Coll after they had played this organ in 1856.

[37]Dufourcq, *Le Grand Orgue de Saint-Merry* (1947) 33.

[38] Dufourcq, ibid.,attributes this remark to Cavaillé-Coll. It is also to be found, verbatim, in Joseph d'Ortigue's review of the inaugural concert in *La Maîtrise* (15 December 1857) 142.

In the spring of 1857 Henri Blanchard wrote of Saint-Saëns's playing on a pédalier a Bach fugue, certainly the D major, BWV 532, "almost as agiley and as intelligently with his feet as with his fingers."[39] The day after Blanchard's review appeared, Cavaillé-Coll wrote a letter to the treasurer of the church council of Sainte-Madeleine de Tarare submitting a list of names of "the leading Parisian organists" whom he recommended to play at the dedication of their new organ. Since Lefébure-Wély was traveling in Italy and therefore unavailable, Cavaillé-Coll suggested as second choices Pietro Cavallo of Saint-Vincent-de-Paul, Charles Simon of Saint-Denis, Auguste Durand of Saint-Roch, Saint-Saëns of Saint-Merry and the thirteen-year-old Charles-Marie Widor of Saint-François in Lyon. A fee of 500 francs was suggested to cover the expenses of the Parisians and "a modest fee" for Widor."[40] Saint-Saëns did not play the recital.

Inauguration of the Organ at L'Isle-Adam

He did, however, inaugurate his first organ later that year. Cavaillé-Coll had refurbished a one-manual, eight-stop orgue-de-choeur from Losges and installed it in Saint-Martin, the parish church of L'Isle-Adam, a town on the Oise river about thirty-seven kilometers northwest of Paris. Saint-Saëns played at the dedication on 10 October 1857, and Charles Collin (1827–1911), a former student of Lefébure-Wély and the organist of the Cathedral of Saint-Brieuc from 1846 to 1909, related the amusing circumstances:

It was a holiday in that lovely region. The national guard, at ease, the drum corps, led by the band, all mingled together. The latter, sensing the importance of the role they had to fulfill, placed themselves near the organ. There, as elsewhere, when these gentlemen started up, they did so wholeheartedly. Fifes, cornets and trombones blew earnestly; snare and bass drums vibrated spiritedly. The future composer of *Henry VIII*, who undoubtedly had not consulted the program, was there, upset, indignant, but could do nothing. The time came for the organ to be heard. Flustered, he tried to calm his listeners by playing very delicate, soft, refined things.

---

[39]Henri Blanchard, "Concerts et auditions musicales," *Revue et Gazette musicale* (15 March 1857) 83.

[40]Letter of Cavaillé-Coll, 16 March 1857. Quoted in Fenner Douglass, *Cavaillé-Coll and the Musicians*, Vol. I (Raleigh: Sunbury Press, 1980) 363.

Wasted effort! He began again with renewed ardor, lost the battle completely and had to resign himself. The organ lost, the ceremony ended and the instrument and instrumentalist were judged not strong enough.[41]

After Saint-Saëns became famous though, the church was very proud that he had inaugurated its organ and a plaque was erected to that effect.

Premiere of *Mass in G Minor*, Op. 4

The rebuilt organ of Saint-Merry was not completed until June 1857,[42] but it was in use by the middle of March. It was essential to the performance of Saint-Saëns's *Mass in G Minor*, Op. 4, which was given its first performance at Saint-Merry on Saturday, 21 March.[43] Scored for choir, four soloists and orchestra of strings, two flutes, two English horns, three trumpets, three trombones and harp, it also required two organs: Grand Orgue and Petit Orgue.[44]

Saint-Saëns had dedicated the *Mass*, his first sacred work, to the pastor of Saint-Merry, Abbé Gabriel. To repay him for the honor the Abbé sent his young organist on a short trip to Italy.[45] It was perhaps due to this

---

[41]Charles-René Collin, "Souvenirs artistique," *La Flûte Harmonique*, No. 31/32 (1984) 35–36.

[42]Dufourcq, *Les Grandes Orgues de Saint-Merry* (1983) 62.

[43]Bonnerot, 32

[44]Daniel Fallon, *The Symphonies and Symphonic Poems of Camille Saint-Saëns*, unpublished Ph.D. dissertation, Yale University, 1973, 120–129. Fallon has conjectured that this *Mass* was originally written as an entry for a competition. In the fall of 1855 the Société Sainte-Cécile of Bordeaux had announced a competition for a Mass with full orchestra. The Société held an annual competition and the prize included not only a gold medal worth 300 francs but a performance with the orchestra. Each year the prescribed work was in a different genre. It was announced in the fall and the composers were given six months to complete their work. Composers often entered more than once—Saint-Saëns later won the Bordeaux competition twice. Since the records of the competition are missing for that period, it is impossible to know if Saint-Saëns had been an unsuccessful competitor.

Franz Liszt was enthusiastic about the work and wrote to Saint-Saëns: "It is such a great, capital, beautiful and admirable composition that among contemporary works of its kind I know perhaps none so striking, either in loftiness of feeling and religious character or in its sustained, capable, vigorous style and consummate mastery. It is like a magnificent cathedral in which Bach would have his choir." (Rome, 4 August 1869, preserved in the Saint-Saëns Archives, Chateau-Musée de Dieppe. Translated in *Letters of Franz Liszt*, edited by La Mara, New York: Greenwood Press, 1969, p. 149).

[45]Bonnerot, 32.

Plate 9. Saint-Merry, the nave and apse

temporary absence of the organist that the Solemn Reception of the newly rebuilt organ at Saint-Merry was postponed until the end of the year.

This was the first time that Saint-Saëns had an organ of his own to play and he was taking full advantage of his new instrument. One may observe how seriously he took his responsibilities in a charming letter probably written to his friend Jules Cohen, one of his classmates from the Conservatoire.

Thursday, 9 April 1857

Cher ami,

One more chore!

My organ being available, I would like to play for mass Sunday some Bach pieces which I don't know by heart and for which an intelligent page turner is absolutely necessary. Naturally, I thought of you. Isn't that kind!

If it's impossible, let me know so I can worry about another acolyte. Otherwise, I'll count on you. If I were conniving, I would tell you that Madame Petit came by a while ago to say that she's having a dance next Thursday and that I can only take you on the condition that you come Sunday to turn pages for me. But I am so good-hearted that I'll take you anyway.

Yours,

C. Saint-Saëns

Alas!!! Today I am twenty-one-and-a-half years old!!![46]

Fantaisie in E-flat

Saint-Saëns not only played the organ with renewed interest, he began composing for it. In two days, 12 and 13 May 1857, he composed his first organ work—and one that would prove to be his most popular—the *Fantaisie in E-flat*. It was heard for the first time at the public inauguration of the Saint-Merry organ in December. Although no dedication appears on the first edition published by Costallat, the manuscript[47] bears the inscription "à son ami G. Schmitt.[48] This was

[46]Marc Pincherle, *Musiciens peints par eux-mêmes* (Paris: Cornuau, 1939) 152.
[47]Bibliothèque Nationale No. 650.
[48]A subsequent edition brought out in 1878 by Richault et Cie., successors to Costallat, printed "Dediée à son ami Georges Schmitt."

Georges Schmitt, organist of Saint-Sulpice. Cavaillé-Coll had been maintaining the Saint-Sulpice instrument while working on the Saint-Merry organ. As work was being completed on the latter organ, Cavaillé-Coll signed a contract to rebuild the Saint-Sulpice organ and began work 26 March 1857.[49]

Georges Schmitt

A native of Trèves (Prusse rhénane) Georges Schmitt had, at the age of fifteen, succeeded his father as organist of the cathedral. He had achieved fame while quite young, as the composer of a patriotic song which became as popular in Germany as the *Marseillaise* had become in France. He went to Paris in 1844, studied composition with Halévy and received the *conseils* of Spontini and Niedermeyer. Schmitt entered the household of the Queen of Spain as music teacher but in 1848 sailed for America where he became organist of the Cathedral of New Orleans. He stayed briefly, and in 1849 succeeded Louis Séjan as organist of Saint-Sulpice in Paris. In 1857 he was appointed professor of organ at the École Niedermeyer and in 1860 maître-de-chapelle to the Queen of Spain.[50] In April 1863 Schmitt resigned his post at Saint-Sulpice and was succeeded by Lefébure-Wély. More scholar than player, Schmitt's frequent contributions to the *Revue de musique sacrée* testify to his erudition.[51] When the rebuilt organ of Saint-Sulpice was inaugurated in 1862 the reviewers excused Schmitt's obviously embarrassing performance, but his presiding at the largest organ in France elicited harsh words from Cavaillé-Coll:

[49]Grégor Klein, *Le Grand Orgue de Saint-Sulpice* (Paris: La Flûte Harmonique, numéro spécial, No. 20, 1981) 6.

[50]For further biographical details see Louis Roger's article in *Illustration musicale* (1862 or 1863) which includes a biography and lithograph of Schmitt and Alfred Feuillet's "Georges Schmitt," *Revue de musique sacrée* (15 October 1863) 352–55.

[51]For example, the following appeared within a year and a half:

"Essais sur l'origine des séquences ou proses," Ch. I (15 November 1862) 8–3; Ch. II–IV (15 December 1862) 47–51.

"Notices historiques et biographiques sur les Hymnologues de l'Église Catholique" (15 February 1863) 105–10; (15 March 1863) 144–51.

"Étude sur la musique des hébreux" (15 November 1863) 22–29, dated October 1862.

"Étude sur l'orgue hydraulique" (15 June 1864) 210–15.

Many French and foreign organists have visited us at Saint-Sulpice during these holidays. Unfortunately, as you had foreseen there is indeed an organ without an organist; the titular has proven hardly worthy of such an instrument.[52]

Inauguration of the Saint-Merry Organ

The organ was inaugurated by Saint-Saëns on Thursday evening, 3 December 1857 at eight o'clock. Before a large audience he played four organ pieces which alternated with two motets sung by the choir. The organ was first heard in a series of "improvisations on the different stops." Joseph d'Ortigue[53] noted that "a performance whose main objective is to exhibit the technical merits of the instrument could be disastrous—a pitfall skillfully avoided by M. Camille Saint-Saëns with a great deal of feeling." Though he remained "musical, even severe," he was, nonetheless, pleasant and "keenly aroused the interest of his audience upon whom he lavished capricious and ingenious fantasies." He did not for an instant "lose sight of that style best suited to the organ—fugal style." The series of improvisations ended with "a chorus of Voix humaines over which the Flûte played elegant embroideries which, by their lightness, recalled those with which the real flute accompanies the English horn solo in the *William Tell* Overture."

For his second organ solo Saint-Saëns played his recently composed *Fantaisie in E-flat*. Henri Blanchard found it "not 'fantastic' but serious, elegant and religious, all at the same time."[54]

The least appreciated work on the program was what must have been the first movement of Mendelssohn's *Sixth Sonata*—the only movement in D minor, the key by which it is identified in the review. Played "with a magisterial gravity and solemnity," it was described as "somewhat labored" by one critic and "a bit dull" by another.

D'Ortigue called attention to the "cleanliness, ease and precision" the which Saint-Saëns played the Bach *Fugue in D Major*, BWV 532, "a very difficult piece in which the pedal part plays an important role."

[52]Letter from Cavaillé-Coll to Jacques-Nicolas Lemmens, Paris, 1 October 1862, printed in *L'Orgue*, No. 58–59 (January–March, April–June 1951).

[53]Joseph d'Ortigue, "Inauguration des Orgues de Saint-Merry à Paris," *La Maîtrise* (15 December 1857) 142–43.

[54]Henri Blanchard, "Auditions musicales," *Revue et Gazette musicale* (6 December 1857) 394–95.

A. CAVAILLÉ-COLL ✱ & Cⁱᵉ,

Rue de Vaugirard, 94 et 96, à Paris.

GRANDE MÉDAILLE D'HONNEUR, EXPOSITION UNIVERSELLE DE 1855.

RÉCEPTION SOLENNELLE

DU GRAND ORGUE DE L'ÉGLISE SAINT-MERRI

Le Jeudi 3 Décembre 1857, à huit heures précises du soir.

MM. A. CAVAILLÉ-COLL ET Cⁱᵉ vous prient de leur faire l'honneur d'assister à la séance de réception du grand Orgue de l'église Saint-Merri qu'ils viennent de restaurer et de perfectionner. Cette séance aura lieu, le jeudi 3 décembre prochain, à 8 heures du soir, dans l'église Saint-Merri, rue Saint-Martin, à Paris. M. Camille SAINT-SAENS, organiste de cette paroisse, fera entendre l'instrument. Il sera chanté quelques motets pour alterner avec les morceaux d'orgue. *Une quête sera faite au profit des pauvres de la paroisse.*

NOTA. On entrera dans l'église sur la présentation de ce billet, qui servira également à l'admission des personnes de votre société.

Paris, le 25 novembre 1857.

ORDRE DE LA SÉANCE.

1º IMPROVISATIONS SUR LES DIFFÉRENTS JEUX DE L'ORGUE.
   Par M. *Camille Saint-Saëns.*

2º AVE, MARIA . . . . MINÉ.
   Chanté par le Chœur de Saint-Merri.

3º FANTAISIE . . . . C. SAINT-SAENS.
   Exécutée par M. *Camille Saint-Saëns.*

4º O SALUTARIS . . . . CH. GOUNOD.
   Chanté par le Chœur de Saint-Merri.

5º FRAGMENT D'UNE SONATE. . . . . MENDELSSOHN.

6º FUGUE EN *RÉ* . . . . S. BACH.
   Exécutés par M. *Camille Saint-Saëns.*

Plate 10. Cavaillé-Coll's invitation to the inauguration of the recently rebuilt organ of the Church of Saint-Merry

Saint-Saëns, Organist of the Madeleine

Four days later Saint-Saëns was appointed organist of the Madeleine, "Cathedral of the Champs-Elysées" and the official church of the Second Empire. It was not until over a week later that he received official acceptance in the form of a letter from the pastor:

Paris, 16 December 1857

Monsieur:

I have the honor of informing you that the Building Committee, in its meeting on the 7th of this month, in accordance with your request, appointed you organist of the parish.

The committee has maintained your salary commensurate with that of M. Lefébure-Wély (who has resigned),[55] 250 francs per month, to which are added the fortuitous honorariums.

As you begin your duties, the committee, in granting you your predecessor's position, wanted to demonstrate the esteem in which it held your talent and its assurance that you will fulfill all of its expectations and those of the faithful.

The committee asks that you be available for service to the parish the first of January 1858, inclusively. It will count on you for that day. It informs you, moreover, that the organ is at your disposal as of today and that you can use it, become familiar with it, and make all the necessary preparations.

Very truly yours,

(signed) Duguerry
President of the Building Committee
Pastor of the Madeleine[56]

The appointment was no surprise to Saint-Saëns; the letter was a mere formality. The first paragraph mentions that he had applied for the position, but his selection as Lefébure-Wély's successor was predetermined. Previously, he had met the pastor of the Madeleine, Gaspard

[55]He had ostensibly resigned in order to devote himself exclusively to composition (although he did continue to inaugurate new organs). His three-act opera, *Les Recruteurs*, was given at the Opéra-Comique, 11 December 1861. He did not take another church post until he went to Saint-Sulpice, May 1863.

[56]Letter from Gaspard Deguerry to Camille Saint-Saëns, Paris, 16 December 1857. Saint-Saëns archives, Chateau-Musée de Dieppe.

Deguerry, at the home of Frédéric de Reiset, the great art collector and director of the Louvre. "If my organist resigns," he had told Saint-Saëns, "I will hire you."[57]

The resignation of their organist (the first public announcement appeared the week before Christmas)[58] probably came as a surprise to the Saint-Merry parish council, which had just incurred a 29,000 franc debt for the renovation of the organ. For Saint-Saëns at the age of twenty-two, however, it was a professional advancement of the highest order. Aside from the prestige connected with the Madeleine, he now had at his disposal a magnificent new organ built by Cavaillé-Coll, a salary of 3,000 francs a year and the highest wedding fees in Paris.[59]

He succeeded the most famous organist in Europe, Lefébure-Wély, who had held the post at the Madeleine for eleven years, and whose playing was the epitome of the "worldly style" as practiced within sacred precincts. For thirty years, in church and in recital, the "Auber of the Organ" had reigned as "Prince of Organists"—the most prominent, the most universally recognized and certainly the most popular French organist of his day.

Lefébure-Wély

Born 13 November 1817, Lefébure-Wély had studied with his father, who was organist of Saint-Roch in Paris, and played his first Mass at the age of eight. He was nine when his father suffered a paralytic stroke; during his illness he substituted for him, and upon his death in 1831 succeeded him as organist of Saint-Roch. After winning prizes in

---

[57]Bonnerot, 33.

[58]*La France musicale* (Sunday, 20 December 1857) 414.

[59]Its budget was also the highest in Paris. The following random sampling of revenues of Parisian churches in 1867 illustrates this remarkably:

La Madeleine	200,000	francs
Saint-Sulpice	100,000	"
Saint-Roch	100,000	"
Notre-Dame-de-Lorette	80,000	"
Saint-Merry	55,000	"
La Trinité	50,000	"
St-Étienne-du-Mont	45,000	"
St-Denis-du-St-Sacrement	33,000	"

Eugène-Emmanuel Viollet-le-Duc "Les Églises de Paris," *Paris Guide* (Paris: Librairie Internationale, 1867).

piano and organ at the Paris Conservatoire, Lefébure-Wély quickly established his reputation as a virtuoso on the piano, organ, pédalier, harmonium, harmonicorde, melodium, Poïkalorgue and any other new keyboard invention that would spread his fame or line his purse. He specialized in a kind of cheerful musical insincerity which appealed to a wide and uncritical audience. As a composer he was an enthusiastic purveyor of light, elegant and successful music—witty trifles that combined sparkling melodic verve with simplistic rudimentary compositional techniques. (Few pianists of former generations were unfamiliar with *Monastery Bells*.)[60]

His recitals were often family talent exhibitions, with Mme. Lefébure-Wély (a fine singer to whom Gounod in 1855 dedicated his popular song *Sérénade*) singing her husband's songs and his two daughters playing duets written by their father. He would do anything for an effect—having the gaslights turned down during his rendition of a "storm" or running back and forth between the Grand Orgue and a harmonium in the front of the church (as he once did at Saint-Sulpice at the solemn closing of the Month of Mary, before a congregation of 5,000).[61]

While he was at Saint-Roch, Lefébure-Wély was among the organists who inaugurated the new organ at the Madeleine in 1846; soon after, he and Alexandre Fessy, the organist, exchanged posts—Lefébure-Wély going to the Madeleine and Fessy to Saint-Roch. Cavaillé-Coll admired Lefébure-Wély as much for his musical skill as for his ability to sell an organ; the musician was always the first asked to inaugurate Cavaillé-Coll's newest instrument. He described a Requiem for the minister of justice at which Lefébure-Wély played the organ of the Madeleine. The prelude and sortie lasted almost half an hour each.

> The prelude was a genuine funeral symphony . . . the sortie a great, beautiful funeral march . . . Lefébure-Wély shows what a great artist he is

---

[60]The organist of Leeds Town Hall, described Lefébure-Wély as "undoubtedly one of the most clever organists of the day. He wrote some very attractive pianoforte pieces and many popular organ works . . . which have been played by many organists in England . . . and have made his name not only familiar, but famous . . . .Personally, I never met with a more genial, kindhearted Frenchman than Lefébure-Wély. He was the *beau idéal* of a gentleman . . .I hope I have said sufficient to show that Wély was no ordinary character, but a genius of which the musical world is justly proud." (William Spark, *Musical Memories*, London: Sonnenschein, 1888, p. 368–69.)

[61]*Le Ménestrel* (7 June 1863) 216.

Plate 11. Lefébure-Wély

on these solemn occasions. All the orchestras in the world cannot equal, for liturgical purposes, a symphony played by M.Lefébure on the organ of the Madeleine.[62]

Of course, many critics recognized that his style was incompatible with the celebration of the divine mysteries. He was a brilliant organist, it was true, but one to whom "the waltz and the opera overture were the epitome of the Introit and the Offertory."[63] Even Rossini had told him, "You are liked more for your faults than your virtues."

Lefébure-Wély, on the other hand, had no delusions about either his talent or his reputation. He wrote in his journal, May 1865, "I improvised an interminable fugue today. I really hope they will no longer say that I only know how to play polkas."[64] And he complained to Cavaillé-Coll about the tuning of his Voix humaine: "I had a wedding yesterday and I couldn't use the stop, even though that's all I'm paid for."[65] But he captivated musicians as well as laymen. Gioacchino Rossini attended his recital at Saint-Sulpice on Easter Monday, 1864.

After sitting through the player's own *Offertoire in F* and Bach's *Fugue in E Major* [sic], the great man started to leave. Then the storm began.

"A storm!" he cried. "I always enjoy those. I'll stay."

And he did.[66]

---

[62]Letter from Cavaillé-Coll to M. Mercaux of Roncq, 15 November 1857. Quoted in Douglass, I, 1081.

[63]Cellier, *L'Orgue*, 183.

[64]Em. Mathieu de Monter, "Lefébure-Wély," *Revue et Gazette musicale*, (4 January 1870) 11.

[65]Letter from Lefébure-Wély to Cavaillé-Coll, no date, between 1854–1858. Quoted in Douglass, I, 103.

[66]Louis Roger, *Revue de musique sacrée* (15 April 1864) 188.

Rossini's funeral provides a perfect example of liturgical inappropriateness in nineteenth-century church music. For the Requiem at La Trinité, 20 November 1868, the choirs of the Opéra, the Théâtre Italién and the Conservatoire and four of the most celebrated singers of the day sang from the galleries. Various portions of the Mass were set to Rossini's music. The "Dies irae," set to the *Stabat Mater*, was sung by four soloists. "Liber scriptus," set to the "Qui est homo" was sung by Patti and Alboni. "Quid sum miser" was set to the "Pro peccatis" and sung as a bass solo by Jean Baptiste Faure. The "Lacrymosa" was from Mozart's *Requiem*. "Quando corpus" of Rossini's *Stabat Mater* and the "Agnus Dei" was adapted to the "Prayer" from *Moses*. *L'Univers* deplored the irreverent attitude of those in attendance. The church resembled a concert hall or a theater. People entered with their hats on, chatting and laughing. Bravos *(continued)*

His organ technique was typical of the period, "his style better adapted to the piano than to the organ and his pedal playing similar to that of the other French organists who barely even use their left foot."[67] Saint-Saëns was "greatly impressed" by Lefébure-Wély, singled him out as a "wonderful improviser" and mentioned his skill in exploiting various registers, the clearness of his playing and his graceful harmonies. "These fine qualities, of which the music he has published gives no idea whatever, were too frequently marred by a frivolous and secular style."[68]

---

were heard after the solos and once applause even broke out. At the elevation the altar and the body of the deceased were forgotten and everyone turned to watch the quartet in the tribune. (*Revue de musique sacrée*, December 1868, p. 97.)

[67]Cellier, *L'Orgue*, 183.

[68]Saint-Saëns, "Music in the Church," *The Musical Quarterly*, II/1 (January 1916) 7.

CHAPTER III

Saint-Saëns and the Madeleine (1858–1877)

Unlike the other churches of Paris—even, to a certain extent, Notre-Dame—the Madeleine stands alone, unhidden by surrounding buildings. All of its noble proportions are visible as it rises proudly and prominently in one of the finest sections of the city, eclipsing its environment by its stateliness and size. Similarities between the building's detached classical architectural style and the new organist's musical personality are obvious. The church's facade, modeled after the Parthenon, reflects the same feelings of restraint and discipline that permeate all of Saint-Saëns's music.

Although the foundations of the Madeleine were laid in 1764, during the reign of Louis XV, the building was not completed until 1842. The church was originally designed in the form of a Latin cross but, upon the death of the architect thirteen years later, his successor changed it to a Greek cross surmounted by a dome, like the Panthéon. Construction of the new building was suspended in 1789 with the outbreak of the Revolution. In 1806 Napoleon ordered the work to be continued and the edifice prepared as a Temple of Glory to honor the French Army. Thus, with its new design the Madeleine assumed the appearance of a Greek temple with fifty-two fluted Corinthian columns, each sixty-six feet high, forming a colonnade around the perimeter and surmounted by a sculptured frieze. The project for a pagan temple fell with the

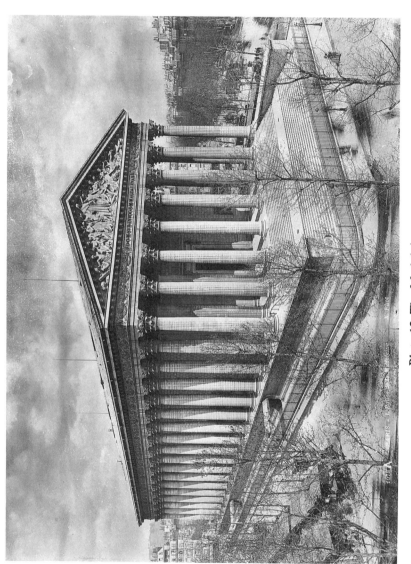

Plate 12. The Madeleine

Emperor, and successive governments returned the monument to the purpose for which it was originally intended. Work was finished in 1842 and the church was consecrated 9 October 1845.

The interior of the Madeleine sparkles sumptuously with every frieze, molding and capital faced or paved with all of the known marbles overlaid with gold leaf, and every flat surface covered with handsomely carved woodwork. Today, the view down the vast, single nave is just as Saint-Saëns saw it except for the large mosaic between the altar and the semicircular fresco of the choir dome which was added after his departure.[1]

The Clergy

The pastor of the Madeleine who had engaged Saint-Saëns was Jean-Gaspard Deguerry,[2] formerly pastor of Saint-Eustache. He had been at the Madeleine since 1848. The vicar, Pierre-Henri Lamazou,[3] a fervent supporter of Cavaillé-Coll, later wrote a book on the organ of Saint-Sulpice and in 1868 was secretary of the commission in charge of the new organ of Notre-Dame Cathedral. He held the former organist, Lefébure-Wély, in high regard and had once defended his style of organ playing:

[1]Critics have by no means unanimously admired the Madeleine. Yvan Christ found the exterior "of less value in itself than in the decorative role it plays in one of the essential perspectives of Paris. . . . An enormous bronze door . . . sculpted by Triqueti, with bas-reliefs inspired by the Ten Commandments, is over thirty-four feet high and weighs 7,045 pounds—the largest ever made. One would have wished for less weight and more talent . . . . The interior consists of a single nave vaulted with three domes set on pendentives which rest on Corinthian columns which, in turn, stand on massive ledges. . . and the nave ends in a great semicircle of Ionic columns. Each bay is made up of Ionic galleries surmounted by triangular pediments. The whole, terribly "rich" and a veritable riot of columns, expresses a desire for extreme ornamental opulence which does nothing to bring life into the vast space and characterizes only too well the decadence of classicism. Such is this temple of grandiloquence and gigantism, a sad and majestic piece of bravura, in which Paris is doomed to pray to the beautiful repentant sinner of the gospel." (*Églises de Paris*, Éditions des Deux Mondes, 1956) 46–47.

[2]Deguerry was born in Lyon, 27 December 1797, and died in Paris, 5 May 1871.

[3]Lamazou was vicar of the Madeleine until 1874 when he was appointed pastor of Notre-Dame-d'Auteuil. He was named Bishop of Limoges in 1881 and then appointed Bishop of Nevers in 1883. He died in the train station at Nevers the day he arrived to take possession of his episcopal seat. (Antoine Kriéger, *La Madeleine*, Paris: Desclée de Brower, 1937) 148. Lamazou is buried in the Chapelle des Morts in Notre-Dame-d'Auteuil. His tombstone is in front of the altar and his marble statue stands to the left. (E. Duplessy, *Paris Religieux*, Paris: Roger et Chernoviz, 1900) 174.

Religious style, whether in music, architecture or rhetoric, is apparently the one that lifts the soul to God and inclines the faithful to prayer and meditation. From this standpoint, M. Lefébure's style is religious in its very essence.[4]

Abbé Lamazou's position was at variance with his new organist's uncompromising definition of what church music ought to be: "Music of a grand style in accord with the elevated sentiments expressed in the liturgy."[5]

Louis Dietsch, Maître-de-Chapelle

Saint-Saëns's associate at the Madeleine was Louis Dietsch,[6] the maître-de-chapelle. After studying for a year at the Paris Conservatoire and winning first prize in double bass, Dietsch was successively organist at the Église des Missions étrangères (before Charles Gounod) and maître-de-chapelle at Saint-Paul-Saint-Louis and Saint-Eustache before going, in January 1850, to a similar post at the Madeleine. In 1840, on Rossini's recommendation, he was appointed chorus master at the Paris Opéra. Dietsch's opera, *The Flying Dutchman*, to a libretto written previous to, and completely independent of Richard Wagner's work, was produced at the Opéra in 1842. A scandal ensued when Wagner accused him of using a translation of his own libretto.

Dietsch taught harmony, counterpoint and fugue at the École Niedermeyer from its founding in 1853, and succeeded Girard as conductor of the Opéra in January 1860. The next year he had a second altercation with Richard Wagner when he conducted incompetently the three notorious Paris performances of *Tannhäuser*.

Another controversy in which Dietsch was involved concerned the famous *Ave Maria* attributed to Arcadelt. In 1842 he presented his arrangement of Arcadelt's three-voice chanson *Nous voyons que les hommes* as a four-voice *Ave Maria* "by Arcadelt" which he had discovered. Saint-Saëns wrote that

---

[4]Pierre-Henri Lamazou, "Les Organistes Français," *Revue et Gazette musicale* (4 May 1856) 140.

[5]Saint-Saëns, "Music in the Church," 5.

[6]See Jeffrey Cooper's entry in *The New Grove*, Vol. II, 470–71.

... the defective prosody had always made me doubt the authenticity of the piece because ancient works are always perfectly written from the point of view of prosody. I was astonished, therefore, when I learned from Dietsch ... that he was himself the composer of the celebrated *Ave Maria* and that its fame was due to fraud.[7]

Liturgy at the Madeleine

Parisians were accustomed to the ceremonial splendor of the Catholic church, but visitors to the Madeleine, particularly Protestants, could not help but be impressed with the liturgy. Not the least of the attractions of the parish was the music, and attention is called to it in each of the descriptions we have of the sumptuous nineteenth-century ritual.

The details of the ornament are in the best style and so are most of the worshipers; for it is one of the fashionable churches of Paris. There, especially at the lazy mass (as the old writer has it, "la messe des paresseux," which was said at "la plus haute heure de matin," at "onze heures"), you see *des mondaines* by the dozen; only the lazy eleven o'clock has become one in the afternoon. What in the world would the old chronicler have said to the swarms of fashionables who just save their souls by hurrying off from a comfortable déjeuner to those one o'clock masses?

But there is a mixture at La Madeleine: old ladies of the *noblesse*, *nouveaux riches*, a few soldiers who like the music, half-a-dozen husbands who go as a duty to their wives, an old Bretonne, gorgeous in chains and muslin and velvet bodice, and two or three black women, charming in the yellow handkerchiefs which swathe their heads.

It is a mixture, and what brings them? Probably the music, for at no church in Paris, and few elsewhere, do you hear such refined, soft, emotional strains as there. Sometimes the boys' voices are not of the best, but the artistic taste with which they sing is always there. There is a special tone about the music of La Madeleine one meets with nowhere else; it aims at raising one's soul from the earth upon which it is supposed to grovel; it certainly never interrupts prayer or disturbs thought. Even on Good Friday, when the old *Passione* by Haydn or the new one by Dubois is performed, refinement, not clatter, is the distinguishing characteristic. All the great masters' Masses are sung at La Madeleine; but you can devote yourself to your own prayers all through them without being disturbed if you so wish. Moreover, one

[7]Letter from Saint-Saëns printed in *The Catholic Choirmaster* and reprinted in *The American Organist* (March 1923) 196.

Plate 13. The Madeleine when Saint-Saëns was the organist

hour suffices in Paris for what in London endures an hour and a half, or more.[8]

Two kinds of "ushers" positioned themselves throughout the congregation. One, the French equivalent of the English beadle, preceded the priest who took up the collection and carried the bag into which, from time to time, the offering was emptied. After Mass he stood at the door of the church soliciting alms for the poor. The *Suisses* were the disciplinarians. They wore cocked hats, carried halberds, and sauntered about leisurely making sure that everyone in the congregation observed proper etiquette. If a worshiper failed to kneel at the appropriate time or feigned a kneeling posture by leaning back and half-sitting on his chair, the Suisse would come up behind him and, shaking the back of his chair, try to jerk him out of it. "And the worst of it is that, although the visitor is innocent of what lies in store for him, we who know the ways of the Suisses anxiously anticipate the fatal moment!"[9]

The Englishman, Sir Francis Head, described the colorful liturgy of the Madeleine in the mid-nineteenth century:[10]

> In crossing the Place de La Madeleine, I stopped for a few minutes to look at the beautiful facade of the church, and as several people were ascending its steps, I followed them into its interior, during the performance of high Mass.[11]

---

[8]S. Sophia Beale, *The Churches of Paris* (London: Allen, 1893) 240. Saint-Saëns appreciated this difference, too: "The demands of English religion . . . are not excessive. The services are very short and consist chiefly of listening to good music extremely well sung, for the English are excellent choristers." And he further noted: "The Anglican Church has a sober and artistic atmosphere which is by no means as overwhelming as our own Catholic church, where the real presence and the confession arouse terror inspired by disturbing mysteries.

[9]Ibid., 242.

[10]Sir Francis Head, *A Faggot of French Sticks; or Paris in 1851* (New York: Putnam, 1852) 102–5.

[11]Elsewhere (op. cit.,144), Sir Francis writes: A tide of well-dressed people, without crushing each other's dresses, were slowly flowing into the church at one door and out of it by another. On entering with the stream, after listening for a few moments to the organ loudly pealing, I observed on both sides of the door, half seated and half kneeling, a lady, dressed in the height of the fashion, to receive (each in a crimson velvet purse bound with gold) contributions on behalf of the poor. One, in mourning, was about forty; the other, nearly thirty, who was endeavouring to make her mouth look as devout and as pretty as possible, was in colours. Both had in their laps splendid prayer books bound in crimson velvet and gold.

On entering I was much struck with the excellent music resounding throughout the building. In England a church organ is very apt not only to be uproarious but tyrannically to overwhelm the audience with its powers. Here it was subservient to the human voice. Sometimes it appeared to be cheering it on—sometimes in silence to be listening to it and only to chime in when absolutely required.

The service was arranged and executed with great science and taste. The best, the shrillest as well as the sweetest voices appeared to proceed from behind the altar but, from wherever they came, they reached the roof as well as every portion of the building.

Before the altar there occasionally stood, with his back towards the congregation, a single priest—then three alongside each other—then two, one before the other. On each side of the altar was a row of young handsome boys, dressed in bright scarlet caps, bright scarlet cloaks, over which were snow-white short surplices, confined round the waist by a broad light-green sash, the ends of which hung at the left side.

The changes wrought in this picture by the simple movement of the scarlet cap had evidently been well studied and produced very striking effects. At a particular part of the service the boy's black shining hair was suddenly displayed, and the cap held in the off hand had apparently vanished. At another moment the blood-red cap was seen, held by both rows of boys on their breasts next to the congregation—then it lay on their white laps—and then, on their rising from their seats, it suddenly appeared again on their heads.

In contrast to these boys there occasionally, from behind the altar, glided into view some pale-looking priests in jet-black gowns, surmounted, like those of the boys, by short white surplices. During these ceremonies and while two powerful assistants in white gowns, jet-black hair and crimson sashes were swinging incense, the shrill notes of a single boy behind the altar were suddenly drowned by a chorus of fine voices, which gradually subsided into the deep double bass notes of one or two priests.

The service was on the whole admirably performed and, to those who have been taught to revere it, must be highly impressive. After the elevation of the host, the wafer was administered to several persons in the front row next to the altar and a large basket of broken bread, in colour and consistency strongly resembling what is commonly called sponge cake, was distributed to the congregation, almost every one of whom partook of it. It was carried throughout the church by a priest, preceded by a person upwards of six feet high, dressed in gold-laced cocked hat, worn cross ways à la Napoleon, an embroidered coat with an epaulette on one shoulder and crimson trappings on the other, a sword, crimson plush knee-breeches ornamented with gold, white stockings and black shoes.

When the service was about three quarters over, a man at one end of the church and a woman at the other, both very gaudily dressed, were seen worming their way to every person present, from each of whom a slight money transaction was taking place. Everybody gave something, and about every third person received back something. When the woman came to me I gave her a franc, upon which she fumbled for some time in her pocket and returned me an amount of cash apparently more than I had given to her. I felt it would not be decorous to decline to take it or proper to inquire of my neighbour— even in a whisper—what was the object of the benevolence. It proved, however, to be a slight payment for the chair I had occupied.

As soon as the service was over, more than three quarters of the congregation left the church and, with a full intention to follow the stream, I was lingering to take a last look at the altar when I observed two or three priests most actively employed in hurrying off every glittering object from it and covering it with black trappings. At a side altar in the centre of the church similar preparations were being made and the alterations were scarcely effected when the great gates of the church were thrown open and a procession of people in mourning, marked with raindrops slowly walked up the aisle. In a few seconds there followed four well-dressed men, bearing, covered with dingy white serge trappings, a coffin on which rested a milk-white wreath of immortelles.

The coffin was deposited in the centre of the church and those of the congregation not seated were gathering around it when I heard a priest say, "There will be another!" The words were hardly out of his mouth when the "rap-a-tap-tap" of a couple of muffled drums was heard outside the great gates, which instantly rolled open to admit about twenty soldiers of the National Guard, followed by a crowd of persons of apparently every condition of life. As soon as all had entered, the corporal in command gave the word of command— "Order arms!"—on which the butts of the muskets reverberated against the hard pavement. After a few minutes, the word "Shoulder arms!" was given, in compliment to the coffin which now entered the church.

On its lid were the scarlet epaulettes, the drawn sword and empty scabbard, the one crossed over the other, of its inmate, and the body, guarded by its comrades proceeded towards the little altar, before which it halted.

Plate 14. The Madeleine, the rear wall

52

While the rich man's requiem was resounding from the great altar, the soldier's funeral was going on at the little one. There were the same words, the same gestures, and the same holy ceremonies. Candles were burning round each of the two corpses and while the service of the rich one was dignified and continuous, that of the soldier was interrupted not only by little words of command from the corporal but, on the elevation of the host, by the sudden roll of the two muffled drums. It was striking to see the power and authority of the army existing within the walls of the church, and the stiff, motionless, upright attitude of the soldiers, who during the whole ceremony wore their shakos, was strangely contrasted with the varied obeisances and white and black vestures of the bare-headed priest.

The Organ

The organ of the Madeleine was one of the earliest built by Aristide Cavaillé-Coll. Inaugurated in October 1846, it was distinguished by being that builder's second largest instrument (forty-eight stops) and containing his first Voix céleste. The organ case, however, was one of Cavaillé-Coll's least favorite and he later wrote that it was not to be cited "as a good model to follow [because] its divisions are too uniform to give the instrument its true character, although the general effect of the organ combines well with the interior portico of woodwork, giving it all a rather monumental aspect."[12]

Organist of the Madeleine

As *organiste titulaire* of the Madeleine, Saint-Saëns played every Sunday of the year, with the exception of Advent (the four Sundays preceding Christmas) and Lent (the six weeks before Easter). During these two penitential seasons organ music was forbidden save for the third Sunday of Advent, known as "Gaudete Sunday," and the fourth Sunday of Lent, "Laetare." He played three services each Sunday. The most elaborate of the week's Masses was the eleven o'clock high Mass when the choir was present and usually sang special settings of the Ordinary. At the one o'clock low Mass or "organ Mass," the organist played throughout, stopping only during the sermon. Vespers were at 2:30 and

---

[12]Aristide Cavaillé-Coll, "De l'Orgue et de son architecture," *Revue Générale de l'Architecture* (1872) 8.

the organ alternated with the choir during the singing of numerous psalms and hymns.

High Masses on holy days of obligation (Ascension Thursday, All Saints Day, the recently declared Feast of the Immaculate Conception and Christmas) were celebrated with more elaborate musical programs than on ordinary Sundays. For instance, the musical program for Christmas Day 1867 included:

Kyrie	from *Messe du sacré*	Luigi Cherubini
Gloria	from *The Imperial Mass*	Franz Joseph Haydn
Credo		
Offertory	Motet: *Adeste fideles*	
Sanctus	from *Messe du sacré*	Luigi Cherubini
Elevation	*O Salutaris*	Jean-François Le Sueur
Agnus Dei	set to the melody of an old Noël	Louis Dietsch

Equally solemn services were held for Perpetual Adoration during the first two weeks of February: Corpus Christi, celebrated on both the Thursday after the first Sunday and on the second Sunday after Pentecost, was one of the great religious attractions of Paris. During the eleven o'clock Mass a great procession made up, in part, by the children who had received their first communion, carried the Blessed Sacrament under the galleries outside the church to the accompaniment of martial music played by the Saint-Nicolas School students' band. Every day during May—the Month of Mary—there were services in all of the churches and for the closing, on 31 May, great services with processions were held.

The twenty-second of July was the feast day of the patron saint of the Madeleine—Saint Mary Magdalen—but it was celebrated on the following Sunday. The Feast of the Appearance of Our Risen Lord to Saint Mary Magdalene fell on the second Sunday after Easter and, although a secondary feast of the patron saint, it was celebrated more solemnly and a special panegyric of Sainte-Madeleine was given at Vespers.

The order of music for a typical Sunday high Mass was as follows:

Entrée. The organist began to play as soon as the celebrant left the sacristy and continued until he reached the altar. This entrance procession could include the priest and as few as two acolytes or a large retinue of acolytes, clergy and choir. When the priest began the prayers at the foot of the altar, the organist stopped and the choir sang the

Introit. If the Ordinary of the Mass was a choral setting, it was accompanied by the orgue-de-choeur and orchestra. When unaccompanied plainchant was sung, the organist alternated with the choir.

Kyrie. The choir began and the organist improvised verses in place of the second Kyrie, first and third Christes and the second of the last three Kyries.

Gloria. The priest intoned "Gloria in excelsis Deo" and the organist improvised the first verse. The choir sang the even numbered verses and the organist improvised every odd numbered verse.

Gradual. This was sung by the choir only.

Tract. It followed the Gradual immediately and replaced the Alleluia during penetential seasons and in the Requiem Mass.

Alleluia. Sung during Eastertime. The organist alternated with the choir. On feast days, when there was a Sequence, the organist played an improvised interlude between the Alleluia and the Sequence.

Sequence. The organist alternated with the choir—the choir always beginning.

Credo. This was sung entirely by the choir. It was the only part of the Ordinary in which the organ never interpolated versets.

Offertory. The organist played from the end of the Credo until the "Orate fratres"—his first opportunity to play anything longer than two minutes.

Sanctus. The organ alternated with the choir. As Saint-Saëns once wrote in a note to Gabriel Fauré, "When the choir-boys start, the organ stops. The organist endures!"[13]

Elevation. A solemn piece was either played or sung while the priest consecrated the bread and wine and raised the host and chalice. The practice of singing an "O Salutaris" at this point in the Mass dated from the end of the reign of Louis XII (1514)[14] but other motets in honor of the Blessed Sacrament were also appropriate and it was to fulfill this liturgical lacuna that Saint-Saëns included an "O Salutaris" in his *Mass,* Op. 4, Gabriel Fauré a "Pie Jesu" in his *Requiem,* and César Franck a "Panis angelicus" in his *Mass.*

Agnus Dei. The organ alternated with the choir.

Communion. The organist played alone.[15]

Ite missa est. After the priest intoned the dismissal, "the organ responded with a prelude (pianissimo)" and gave "the notes for the choir's response, 'Deo gratias.' "[16]

Sortie. This postlude accompanied the procession as it moved from the altar and returned to the sacristy, continuing as the worshipers left the church. Saint-Saëns considered the fugue to be the form ideally suited to the Sortie: "As the voices enter, the people leave. When all the voices have entered, all the people have left!"[17]

The organist adjourned for lunch but had to return in the afternoon for Vespers. At this service five psalms, an office hymn and the

[13]Camille Saint-Saëns and Gabriel Fauré, *Correspondance, soixante ans d'amitié* (Paris: Heugel, 1973) 44. Letter from Saint-Saëns to Fauré written sometime after Easter around the year 1875.

[14]Adrien Gros, "Des morceaux chantés pendant la célébration du service divin," *Revue de musique sacrée* (15 September 1862) 376.

[15]L. C. Laurens ("Des fonctions du grand orgue pendant les offices," *Revue de musique sacrée,* 15 August 1864, pp. 290–96) warned organists of a "deplorable" practice which was limiting their participation in the ceremonies: some maîtres-de-chapelle were using the Offertory as a time for a motet and the Elevation for an "O Salutaris" or a "Benedictus." Their duties were thus being reduced and organists were cautioned to discourage this practice before they found themselves unemployed!

[16]Saint-Saëns–Fauré, *Correspondance,* 44.

[17]Bernard Gavoty, *Louis Vierne* (Paris: Albin Michel, 1943) 279.

Magnificat were sung by the choir while the organist improvised alternate verses. There was little romance connected with the honor of being organiste titulaire du grand orgue and the artistic satisfaction gained from providing musical "interruptions" was slight indeed.

Artistic reward was, however, offset by what Abbé Deguerry, in his letter to Saint-Saëns informing him of his appointment to the Madeleine, had referred to as "fortuitous honorariums." Wedding fees made up a substantial part of the organist's income. The Madeleine being as great a center of the latest fashions as the grandstand at Longchamp or the annual horse show in the Champs Élysées, lent itself quite naturally, both inside and out, to lavish displays at the most extravagant weddings. Such was the wedding of the Prince de Polignac and Mlle. Mirès on 5 June 1860. The Madeleine was "richly decorated."

> The ceremony was attended by an enormous crowd of persons involved in politics, administration, finance, the arts, letters and *the* most prominent people.
> When the Bishop of Marseille, who officiated at the Nuptial mass, entered the church, M. Saint-Saëns played a very beautiful solemn march which made a profound impression on the congregation.
> All the music for the mass was composed by the Prince Edmond de Polignac, the youngest of the four brothers of this illustrous family. The work was quite remarkable and testified to the composer's serious studies .... The performance of this mass by musicians from the orchestra of the Opéra and by the choir of the Madeleine under the direction of M. Dietsch left nothing to be desired.[18]

The Perfect Organist

Saint-Saëns was the outstanding example of his own definition of "The Perfect Organist": "a virtuoso hardened to every difficulty and an ingenious improviser."[19] He held distinct views on most subjects, including what type of music was appropriate in church. He played *some* written music—probably at weddings (for instance, he mentioned playing Lizst's *Saint Francis of Assisi Preaching to the Birds*[20])—and he had

---

[18]*Revue et Gazette musicale* (10 June 1860) 213.
[19]Saint-Saëns, "Music in the Church," 5.
[20]Ibid., 7.

Plate 15. Saint-Saëns at the organ: a self-portrait, c. 1875

played some of Bach's music while at Saint-Merry. Whether he played Bach at the Madeleine we do not know, but he later wrote that he considered Bach's organ music to be out of place in the liturgy of the Catholic church. The chorale preludes were "the very essence of Protestantism and, with few exceptions, his preludes and fugues, fantaisies and toccatas are pieces in which virtuosity holds first place."[21] "They are concert pieces which bear no relation whatsoever to the mass and which inspire neither a meditative nor a prayerful mood; beyond the comprehension of the congregation to which they address themselves, they can interest but a few rare listeners familiar with them."[22]

For the most part Saint-Saëns improvised—as the necessities of the service required—although he might just as well have played from music for, from all accounts, his improvisations were indistinguishable from composed music, either his own or that of other composers. Charles-Marie Widor wrote that

At the organ he developed plainchant themes in a form and a style which disavowed neither Bach nor Mozart nor Mendelssohn. Performance difficulties do not exist for such an artist. The conception and the interpretation amount to the same thing: a written piece is no different than one which is improvised.[23]

Through his playing the organ assumed the role it would later be assigned by Pius X. "Through him the mass became a symphony."[24] His style, so different from that which one had been accustomed to hear at the Madeleine, was noted and, according to the taste and motives of the listeners, praised or criticized. After a Cherubini *Mass* had been sung at the Madeleine, Adolphe Batte commented that "the parish organist, M. Saint-Saëns, was appreciated for the quiet, fine, polished taste and the correct and severe manner which characterizes his talent."[25]

Those who enjoyed and admired that quiet, refined taste and serious style hardly suspected the circumatances under which they were wrought:

---

[21]Saint-Saëns, *École Buissonnière*, 166.
[22]Saint-Saëns, "Music in the Church," 8.
[23]Charles-Marie Widor in *L'Éstafette* (9 July 1877), quoted in Georges Servières, *Saint-Saëns* (Paris: Alcan, 1923) 100.
[24]"Un organiste [Jean Huré], 'L'Orgue laïque,'" *L'Orgue et les Organistes* (February 1925) 24.
[25]Adolphe Batte, *Revue et Gazette musicale* (25 November 1860) 406.

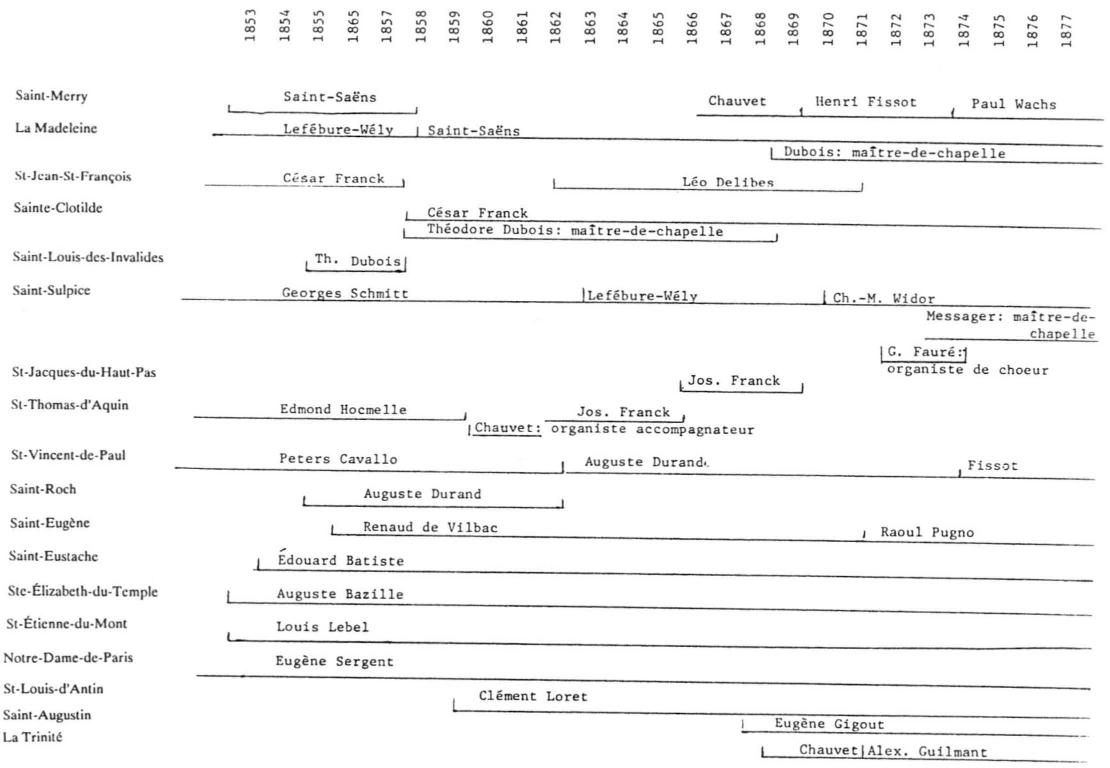
1853 1854 1855 1865 1857 1858 1859 1860 1861 1862 1863 1864 1865 1866 1867 1868 1869 1870 1871 1872 1873 1874 1875 1876 1877
Saint-Merry
Saint-Saëns
Chauvet
Henri Fissot
Paul Wachs
La Madeleine
Lefébure-Wély
Saint-Saëns
Dubois: maître-de-chapelle
St-Jean-St-François
César Franck
Léo Delibes
Sainte-Clotilde
César Franck
Théodore Dubois: maître-de-chapelle
Saint-Louis-des-Invalides
Th. Dubois
Saint-Sulpice
Georges Schmitt
Lefébure-Wély
Ch.-M. Widor
Messager: maître-de-chapelle
G. Fauré: organiste de choeur
St-Jacques-du-Haut-Pas
Jos. Franck
St-Thomas-d'Aquin
Edmond Hocmelle
Chauvet: organiste accompagnateur
Jos. Franck
St-Vincent-de-Paul
Peters Cavallo
Auguste Durand
Fissot
Saint-Roch
Auguste Durand
Saint-Eugène
Renaud de Vilbac
Raoul Pugno
Saint-Eustache
Édouard Batiste
Ste-Élizabeth-du-Temple
Auguste Bazille
St-Étienne-du-Mont
Louis Lebel
Notre-Dame-de-Paris
Eugène Sergent
St-Louis-d'Antin
Clément Loret
Saint-Augustin
Eugène Gigout
La Trinité
Chauvet
Alex. Guilmant

Plate 16. Organists of Parisian churches during Saint-Saëns's tenure at Saint-Merry and the Madeleine

Saint-Saëns arrived at the last minute, raced up to the organ gallery four steps at a time, threw himself on the bench, worn out and frightfully pale, hurriedly pulled out his stops and began in a calm, solemn style in such seamlessly perfect form that, had there been a way of transcribing his improvisation, it could have been sent to the engraver without emendations.[26]

Saint Saëns's Views on Sacred Music

Saint-Saëns had an active interest in sacred music, certainly, and composed over twenty motets and the *Oratorio de Noël* during his years at the Madeleine. Listening to a choir over which he had no control (nor did he wish to have)—particularly after it had been taken over by Théodore Dubois—he formulated strong opinions regarding church music. He was keenly aware of the appropriateness of the music as well as the setting of the words to the music, and was not hesitant in condemning whatever did not meet his standards.

He was particularly annoyed by the common practice of excerpting movements from several different masses "instead of performing one mass in in its entirety and thus presenting an ensemble of uniform style."[27]

He was obsessive in his condemnation of three kinds of sacred choral music and said that, had he the power, he would ban: 1. "motets written by composers ignorant of Latin, in whose works the setting and repetition of the words makes no sense"; 2. works in popular style, particularly those of the Jesuit priest, Louis Lambillotte, "who was probably a holy man but whose pitiful music is strangely out of place under the sacred vaults. In art, holiness is not enough: talent, as well as style, is necessary"; 3. "music, even that of the great masters, which was not composed to sacred texts but, on the contrary, to which words were more or less successfully adapted. Such pieces are artistic crimes. Nothing justifies them, given the prodigious amount of music specially written for the Church between the sixteenth century and now."[28] Saint-Saëns felt so strongly about these "adaptations" that in his will he forbade the singing at his funeral of the universally popular *Air* by Stradella to which the words of the "Pie Jesu" had been set![29]

[26]Bonnerot, 36.
[27]Saint-Saëns, "Music in the Church," 5.
[28]Saint-Saëns, *École Buissonnière*, 166.
[29]Bonnerot, 217.

Harmonium Works: *Trois Morceaux* and *Six Duos*

The Madeleine occupied a considerable part of Saint-Saëns's time, but he continued to devote several hours each day to composition. The publication of his first works after he went to the Madeleine, the *Trois Morceaux*, Op. 1, for harmonium, and the *Six Duos*, Op. 8, for harmonium and piano, was announced in November 1858.[30] If it seems strange that the first publications by the new organist of the most prestigious church in Paris should be for the harmonium, we must remember that the instrument was then at the height of its popularity. Debain, Alexandre, Mustel, and even Cavaillé-Coll could hardly keep up with the orders for its manufacture. Music especially composed for it was in short supply and great demand. While the registration for the *Trois Morceaux* is adaptable to any of the harmoniums, Saint-Saëns specifically registered the *Six Duos* for the Debain instrument.[31] The publisher, E. Girod, bought them for 500 francs and the twenty-two-year-old composer, an amateur astronomer, used the money to buy a telescope.

Composed in April and May 1858 and dedicated to Lefébure-Wély, *Six Duos* are possibly the finest contribution to ensemble music with harmonium. They not only testify to the young composer's contrapuntal skill but to his understanding of the sonorities of the two instruments and the ingenious way in which he took advantage of them. The movements are:

> Fantasia e Fuga
> Cavatina
> Choral
> Capriccio
> Scherzo
> Final

The *Fuga* (whose subject is the theme of the *Fantasia* in diminution) was Saint-Saëns's first published fugue; six for organ and eleven for piano

---

[30]*Revue et Gazette musicale* (14 November 1858) 382.
[31]Saint-Saëns, *École Buissonnière*, 330.

were to follow. But it is to the Romantic epoch, rather than to the Classical, that the *Cavatina* belongs. Its sumptuous harmonies anticipate *Samson et Dalila* by a decade. The *Choral*, marked Agitato, is an etude in double notes for the piano into which the harmonium interjects several statements of the German chorale version of a Gregorian psalm tone, the "Tonus Peregrinus." The initial four-part harmonization is from Bach's Cantata No. 10, *Meine Seele erhebt den Herren*. Of all German chorales this was probably the one most familiar to Saint-Saëns. To the Tonus Peregrinus was set "In exitu Israel," the fourth psalm sung every Sunday afternoon at Vespers. The repeated notes of the elegant *Capriccio* and the grace and ease of the Mendelssohnian *Scherzo* (really a tarantella) display the aristocratic polish that marks all of Saint-Saëns's works. What he referred to as his "6 petits Duos"[32] last over a half hour.

Professor of Piano

It was in the spring of 1861 that Saint-Saëns became the piano teacher at the École Niedermeyer.[33] It was the only teaching post he ever held and, except for serving on the juries of the Paris Conservatoire, this was the only school with which he was ever connected. The school had been founded in 1853 by Louis Niedermeyer, an enthusiastic, prolific, but rather unsuccessful, opera composer, whose *Pater noster* enjoyed great popularity in Catholic churches for many years. His École de musique religieuse, known as the École Niedermeyer, was a boarding school for boys. Its purpose was to train organists and choristers in an attempt to raise the standards of church music in France, and its success can be measured by the reputations of some of the musicians who received their training there: Gabriel Fauré, Eugène Gigout, Albert Périlhou and André Messager.

Louis Niedermeyer, who had studied with Ignaz Moscheles (a friend of Beethoven and one of Mendelssohn's piano teachers), taught piano at the school; Clément Loret, organist of the Niedermeyer family's parish church, Saint-Louis-d'Antin, taught organ and plainchant; and Louis Dietsch, *maître-de-chapelle* at the Madeleine, taught harmony and composition. Niedermeyer died on 14 March 1861, at which time the

---

[32]Ibid.

[33]For an interesting history of the school see Maurice Galerne's *L'École Niedermeyer* (Paris: Éditions Margueritat, 1928).

school became the property of his son Alfred, who, having little interest in music, appointed Dietsch director. Now in the middle of its second term, the school was bereft of a piano teacher. Dietsch undoubtedly persuaded Saint-Saëns to fill in until graduation. This perhaps temporary arrangement lasted for the next four years.

At the distribution of prizes on 22 July 1861, eleven of Saint-Saëns's students received awards, three of whom were to become famous names in the organ world: Gabriel Fauré won a repeat of his first prize from the year before, Eugène Gigout won the first prize and Albert Périlhou won the second prize.

Saint-Saëns was a popular teacher with his piano class.[34] Young and enthusiastic, he exposed his pupils to modern music—Schumann, Wagner and Liszt—composers little known or played in France at the time.[35]

When he played the piano, which he often did, it was a joy to hear him. Quite apart from the technical problems on which he was very strict—purity of execution, care for sonority, quality of sound, pianistic color, phrasing, correct accents and the style best suited to each composer—he enjoyed opening up our minds to all that was worthy of interest, even outside music, and stimulated our imagination by leading us on to the other arts and arousing our curiosity about everything.[36]

Saint-Saëns fondly remembered his days as professor of piano at the École Niedermeyer and remained close with several of his students throughout his life. Around 1914, when the name of Eugène Gigout came up in conversation with Jean Huré, Saint-Saëns said, "Gigout? He was my little 'Cent-six' (106)!" And he went on to explain. "Yes, I promised him a fine reward if he would play Beethoven's 'Hammer-Klavier' Sonata, Op. 106, by heart. He did it very well, hence the name I gave him. The reward? I took him to Faust." ("Faust," Gigout often told Huré, "was our Pelléas.")[37]

Appendix C lists the prizewinners of the annual examinations of the École Niedermeyer during the years of Saint-Saëns's association with

---

[34]"Discipline at the École Niedermeyer was strict, comfort was unknown and working conditions were something of a paradox—the piano was studied in groups, with fifteen instruments playing at the same time!" (Marguerite Long, At the Piano with Gabriel Fauré (New York: Taplinger Music Co., 1891) 20.

[35]Gabriel Fauré, "Camille Saint-Saëns," Le Revue Musicale (February 1922) 97.

[36]James Harding, Saint-Saëns, 86.

[37]Jean Huré, "Eugène Gigout," L'Orgue et les Organistes (15 December 1925) 5–6.

the school. A number of his works were dedicated to these former students.[38]

For the first two years, Saint-Saëns taught all of the piano students—the First Division for the advanced pupils and the elementary Second Division. Beginning with the 1862–63 term Allaire-Dietsch taught the Second Division.

Louis Dietsch died unexpectedly on 20 February 1865. Gustave Lefèvre, the fiancé of Alfred Niedermeyer's eldest daughter, Eulalie, was appointed director.[39] (They were married on 4 April 1865 at Saint-Louis-d'Antin.) Saint-Saëns resigned about this time for, at the distribution of prizes on 28 July 1865, while his name was among those on the jury, Louis-Désirée Besozzi was listed as professor of piano for the First Division.

The Société Académique de Musique Sacrée

In an attempt to raise the standards of church music further, Saint-Saëns lent his support to the Société Académique de Musique Sacrée. This organization, made up of musicians, music lovers, clergy and laity in

---

[38]The first six prizewinners in the 22 July 1861 class received dedications of his piano arrangements of six Bach works:

1. Cantata 28, Overture	Gabriel Fauré
2. Cantata 3, Adagio	Eugène Gigout
3. Cantata 8, Andantino	Adolphe Dietrich
4. Violin Sonata No. 2, Bourée	Adam Laussel
5. Violin Sonata No. 3, Andante	Émile Lehmann
6. Cantata 35, Presto	Albert Périlhou

To other students, Édouard Marlois (later a professor of the London Academy of Music), he dedicated the "Prélude" of Six Études, Op. 52 (1877), and to Julien Koszul (later director of the Conservatoire of Roubaix), he dedicated the Polonaise for two pianos, Op. 77 (1886). Saint-Saëns returned to his three favorites throughout his life, however. To Fauré he subsequently dedicated the Trois Rhapsodies sur des Cantiques Bretons, Op. 7 (1866), the Prélude et Fugue in D Minor, Op. 109, No. 1 (1898), for organ, and the ten songs in La Cendre Rouge, Op. 146 (1915). Gigout received the Prélude et Fugue in E-flat, Op. 99, No. 3 (1894), and the Sept Improvisations, Op. 150 (1917). The Prélude et Fugue in G, Op. 109, No. 2, was dedicated to Périlhou in 1898.

[39]F. de Ménil, "L'École de Musique Niedermeyer," Musica (July 1903) 149.

and around Paris, was founded on 6 December 1861 "to contribute, to maintain and to develop religious and classical musical art by an intelligent restoration and performance of plainchant and by the thorough study and performance of the works of the great masters." By November 1862 the membership included more than two hundred Parisians alone—including Auber, Rossini and Ambroise Thomas. Georges Schmitt, organist of Saint-Sulpice, was one of the joint music directors who assisted the president in conducting the meetings. Saint-Saëns was the official organist and he and his vicar, Abbé Lamazou, were among the ten committee members.[40]

Saint-Sulpice Organ Inauguration

It was not until five years after the inauguration of the Saint-Merry organ that Saint-Saëns again participated in the inauguration of another organ. On Tuesday, 29 April 1862, he, together with four other organists, took part in the inauguration of Cavaillé-Coll's largest instrument—indeed, the largest organ in France—that of the Parisian church of Saint-Sulpice.

The program played after the blessing of the organ can be reconstructed as follows:

Offertoire	Georges Schmitt
Méditation, Op. 20, No. 1	Alexandre Guilmant
Fantaisie in C	César Franck
Improvisation	Camille Saint-Saëns
Pastorale "Storm"	Auguste Bazille
Improvisation on a theme from *Judas Maccabaeus*	Georges Schmitt

What must have been an embarrassing exhibition of pedestrian musicianship by the organist of Saint-Sulpice, Georges Schmitt, was excused by one writer as an excess of modesty and by another as "a display of great sangfroid in not trying to show off all of his expertise by putting into play all the resources of the organ but in playing purely and simply and exquisitely a graceful piece, developed enough to do justice to the

[40]*Revue de musique sacrée* (15 November 1862).

instrument."⁴¹ Schmitt was a source of great frustration to Cavaillé-Coll. With him presiding over the instrument it could never be shown to advantage—a situation which changed a year later with the appointment of Lefébure-Wély as organist.

Alexandre Guilmant, a young twenty-five-year-old organist from Boulogne-sur-Mer, who on the advice of Cavaillé-Coll had been sent to Brussels to study with Jacques Lemmens, was the organbuilder's "discovery" who featured in this concert his own *Méditation* "which recalled the naïve grace of Haydn" and combined an "expressive style with the most elevated erudition."⁴² Three days later he gave a solo recital which was enthusiastically praised in the music journals.⁴³

While Antoine Elwart dismissed César Franck's contribution as "severe without pedantry,"⁴⁴ Louis Roger mistook his performance of his *Fantaisie in C* for an "improvisation which left the audience with the impression that he had played a well worked-out piece!" Had he but known that Franck had been "working it out" for the last six years! "Its opening had the fullness of those powerful harmonies reminiscent of *Fingal's Cave*," and "the foundation stops had as much poetry as could be given them. The improviser had only one shortcoming: he did not end soon enough."⁴⁵

Roger then leveled the same criticism at Saint-Saëns:

More than anyone, M. Camille Saint-Saëns deserved this reproach. Taking a motif which, under his talented fingers proved to be very interesting and, wanting to distill its very essence, it resulted in one of those long-winded pieces in which the ear cannot follow the laborious development. He can sustain this criticism all the more since we don't need this instance to be convinced of his fine talent. Written or improvised, his piece had its faults but the man still has a great ability.⁴⁶

⁴¹Louis Roger, "Inauguration du Grand Orgue de Saint-Sulpice," *Revue de musique sacrée ancienne et moderne* (15 May 1862) 230.
⁴²Ibid., 31.
⁴³*L'Univers musical* (8 May 1862) 147–48 completely ignored the inauguration of the organ but devoted an entire page to its "Deuxième audition," and mentioned Franck, Renaud de Vilbac, Joseph d'Ortigue and Lebeau among the artists in the audience.
⁴⁴Antoine Elwart, *Revue et Gazette musicale de Paris* (11 May 1862) 155–56.
⁴⁵Roger, op. cit., 231.
⁴⁶Ibid.

Plate 17. Saint-Sulpice, the organ

Elwart found his playing "profound without obscurity,"[47] while Charles Colin wrote that he "displayed the qualities of a remarkable mechanism in a broad- scaled piece full of originality."[48]

Auguste Bazille's style and taste in organ playing was similar to that of Lefébure-Wély's. He had, as a matter of fact, played the organ for the wedding of the latter's daughter, Marie Lefébure-Wély, in August 1868.[49] A composite description of his performance informs us that he was "endowed with a charming imagination" and "improvised a ravishing pastorale in the middle of which he skillfully introduced storm effects." He knew just how to show off the organ's timbres "from the pastoral oboe to the Pan flute."[50] All those present were grateful even though he had compromised his musical integrity to bring them a storm complete "with whistling wind, heavily rumbling thunder, a chorus of imploring voices, lightning and rain."[51]

Storms and the Organ

The improvisation of a storm was de riguer on every organ recital program. The first pédale de combinaison on practically every organ was the "Orage," a pedal which depressed several of the lowest pedal notes and gave a very successful imitation of thunder. The portrayal of thunderstorms in music had long been a favorite device with composers. Had not Haydn included one in *The Seasons*? Beethoven's *Pastoral Symphony* was soon followed by musical storms by Berlioz, Rossini, Liszt, Tchaikowsky, Debussy and Sibelius. In the organ world Lemmens and Lefébure-Wély were accomplished in the art of reproducing meteorological phenomena, and each composed one.[52] Indeed, the number of recitals

---

[47]Elwart, op. cit., 155.

[48]Charles Colin, "Réception du Grand Orgue de Saint-Sulpice," *La France musicale* (4 May 1862) 137–38.

[49]*Revue de musique sacrée* (September 1868) 71. Marie had fallen deeply in love in 1864 with Pablo Sarasate, the Spanish violin virtuoso. After a three year courtship they were engaged to be married. The wedding was arranged but Sarasate returned from a concert tour to find Marie engaged to someone else! (Margaret Campbell, *The Great Violinists*, Garden City: Doubleday & Co., 1981, p. 89.)

[50]Colin, loc. cit.

[51]Roger, op. cit., 230.

[52]For those who didn't have a "thunder pedal" or who wanted to play storms on their harmoniums, Lefébure-Wély gave an "Exercise for imitating thunder": "Hold several low notes down at the same time—C, D, D-sharp, and E—and make them louder*(continued)*

Plate 18. Saint-Thomas d'Aquin, the organ

one played was in proportion to the quality and realism of the storms one played or improvised.[53] Those whose playing was characterized as "severe"—César Franck, Saint-Saëns, Chauvet and later, Guilmant and Widor, played more fugues than storms. Contrapuntal severity was certainly one of the reasons for the few public appearances of César Franck.

Saint-Thomas-d'Aquin Organ Inauguration

Two weeks later, on 15 May 1862, Saint-Saëns inaugurated another of Cavaillé-Coll's rebuilt organs, that of Saint-Thomas-d'Aquin. The only review of the program, written by a priest, Abbé Jouve, was given over to the history of the choir's selections and followed by the complete text of the vicar's homily! The musical portion of the ceremony was as follows:

Improvisation	
Played by Camille Saint-Saëns	
Benedictus	Franz Joseph Haydn
The Choir	
Sermon	Abbé Alix
Tantum ergo	Thoinot-d'Arbeau
Ave Maria	de Winther
The Choir with solos by M. Quesne	
Fugue	J. S. Bach
Played by Camille Saint-Saëns	

Father Jouve arrived too late to hear any but the very end of the "magesterial improvisation" with which Saint-Saëns began, but he did note in the performance of "a Bach fugue an aplomb and a surety hardly

---

and softer with the expression pedal." (Lefébure-Wély, *Méthode Théorique et Pratique pour le Poïkilorgue*, Op. 9, Paris: Canaux et Nicou-Choron, 1839.)

[53]Organists who played storms were included among the seven descriptions of organists in an article on "Organs and Organ Playing" in the English magazine *The Orchestra* (3 May 1872) 73–75:

The sensationalist who creates unpleasant perturbations of the viscera and nausea in nature's chemical furnace with undreamt of inversions, creeping chromatics, inaudible echoes and ear-stunning crashes.

Plate 19. Notre-Dame-de-Saint-Dizier, the organ

appreciated, especially when it is such elaborate instrumental music as that of the illustrious German composer.[54]

Notre-Dame-de-Saint-Dizier Organ Inauguration

In August Saint-Saëns went to Saint-Dizier, a town 200 kilometers east of Paris, to inaugurate a three-manual organ just rebuilt by Cavaillé-Coll. An extended account of this recital appears in a book about the new organ and, in spite of its literary shortcomings, it is invaluable as the only description of Saint-Saëns's improvisations.

INAUGURATION OF THE ORGAN OF
NOTRE-DAME-DE-SAINT-DIZIER

22 August 1862

Improvisation
Blessing of the Organ

I.

Improvisation
The Ascension   Luigi Bordese
                         Choir

Improvisation, "Pastorale"
Cantique de Noël   Adolphe Adam
                 Sung by Abbé N . . .

          Accompanied by M. Saint-Saëns

Improvisation

II.

Improvisation
Improvisation on Voix céleste and Unda maris

Ave Maria   Luigi Cherubini
          Sung by the organist of Notre-Dame

Improvisation, "Storm"
Lauda Sion   Gregorian
                         Choir

Prelude in E-flat, BWV 552   J. S. Bach

[54]Abbé Jouve, "Inauguration de l'Orgue de la Paroisse Saint-Thomas-d'Aquin," *Revue de musique sacrée* (15 June 1862) 260–61.

The ceremony began with a soft improvisation which "modulated into the minor." After the blessing:

The organist set off the Flûte and Bourdon with a very rhythmical motif played on all the accompanimental stops which gradually increased from piano to forte in an effortless modulation. Charmed at first by the sweetness of the sounds, you were soon seized by the fullness and power attained.

The second improvisation, a Pastorale, featured the Viole de gambe and other stops of the same family. A veritable string quintet was heard: violins, violas, cellos and double basses. All participated. Their effect was imitated with a truly incredible realism.

Saint-Saëns accompanied a priest who sang "O Holy Night." In his next piece

... solos on the Hautbois, Basson, Flûte and Clarinette answered one another in charming phrases appropriate to the character of each, realized with a magisterial knowledge possessed in the highest degree by the eminent organist. The Trompettes and Bombardes made an appearance in the brilliant harmony. The deep and majestic sounds of the Bombarde contrasted pleasantly with the melodious tones of the Basson and Trompette harmonique. Even the harp blends into the harmonies of this symphony. O how happy M. Saint-Saëns should be to have under his fingers an instrument which so humbly translates his brilliant inspirations.

The second part of the concert opened with a Flûte solo. Listen! ... What agility! What spirit! The trills ... the octave runs ... nothing is missing. It is our great flutist, Tulou,[55] playing the most graceful variations. You are surprised and captivated by such perfection—how such a great organ can produce such delicate, suave sounds! The giant is made a child for your pleasure!

Listen again! ... the violin tunes ... mi, la, ré, sol ... The music lover is transported—the connoisseur smiles. And if at such perfect imitation, the one sees only a special effect on the Viole de gambe, the other surely tells himself that this must be the last word in art. To further impress us with the riches of the instrument which he holds in his strong grasp, M. Saint-Saëns carries us on admirable modulations which defy our knowledge and study into a new harmonic world.

[55]Jean-Louis Tulou (1786–1865) was a noted French flutist and composer.

74

After this piece, the indefatigable organist gives us a slow and solemn improvisation on the delightful stops of M. Cavaillé-Coll's invention: the Voix céleste and the Unda maris. Heavenly voices are heard singing a soft prayer on the waves of the sea . . . .

The organ recital continued after a vocal solo by the regular organist of the church.

The piece was sung . . . A strange noise is heard! A storm seems imminent. It is still in the distance but it seems to be approaching . . . Lightning flashes and thunder rolls in the expanse . . . and soon the unchained elements, battling one another, no longer seem to obey the voice which holds them captive. The storm bursts—the wind blows violently under the vaults of the church. We are all witnesses to one of nature's great cataclysms and are transported under the spell of the artist's prodigious talent. He controls the storm . . . He holds the lightning! . . . His rage subsides! Hear the prayer which ascends to heaven! You who have heard these marvelous phenomena, these frightening effects, tell us if it is possible to translate this magnificent improvisation into words!

The concert lasted for more then two hours during which time Saint-Saëns "captivated his audience and held it constantly under the charm of his brilliant and varied improvisations."[56]

In October, all of Cavaillé-Coll's favorite organists were to be found at the atelier of his rival, Merklin-Schütze & Cie, to hear the recently set-up organ built for the Cathedral of Arras. Guilmant, Batiste, Renaud de Vilbac, Lefébure-Wély, Hocmelle and Chauvet played the four-manual, fifty-two-stop organ; Saint-Saëns, Eugène Vast and François Benoist were in the audience.[57]

Alexis Chauvet and the Saint-Merry Organist Competition

In November 1863 Benjamin Darnault, who had succeeded Saint-Saëns as organist of Saint-Merry, resigned upon his appointment as organist of Saint-Roch. The new organist of Saint-Merry was to be chosen

---

[56](Chanoine) A. Bourdon, *Notice sur le grand orgue de Notre-Dame-de-Saint-Dizier, construit par M. Cavaillé-Coll.* (Bar-le-Duc: Numa Rolin, 1863) 40–47.
 Other accounts in *Revue et Gazette musicale* (2 November 1862) 358 and *Revue de musique sacrée* (15 November 1862) 20–22 reprint a quote from *L'Union de la Haute-Marne* that "the learned organist of the Madeleine held the large audience under the spell of his brilliant improvisations for more than two hours."
[57]Georges Schmitt, *Revue de musique sacrée* (November 1862) 34–35.

Plate 20. Alexis Chauvet

through a competition. Just how important the post was regarded is indicated by the celebrity of the jury appointed to oversee the selection: François Benoist, professor of organ at the Paris Conservatoire, was chairman and the five judges were Saint-Saëns of the Madeleine, Charles Simon of Saint-Denis, Darnault, organist, and Charles Vervoitte, maître-de-chapelle of Saint-Roch, and François Delsarte, Georges Bizet's uncle, whose singing class at the Conservatoire Saint-Saëns had attended as a youth. Alexis Chauvet was one of the four competitors and won the post. There seems to have been little doubt that Saint-Saëns was influential in his young friend's nomination, and Adrien Gros, maître-de-chapelle of Saint-Germain-des-Près, accused the jury of partiality and favoritism and insinuated that the post would have been awarded to Chauvet even without a competition.[58]

If the allegations were true it was just as true that Chauvet was the most qualified man for the post. Two years younger than Saint-Saëns, Alexis Chauvet had won first prize in Benoist's organ class in 1860 and had been organist accompagnateur at Saint-Thomas-d'Aquin, then organist of Notre-Dame-de-Bonne-Nouvelle and Saint-Bernard-de-la-Chapelle. He was quite the Bohemian, with his frock coat flapping at his calves, his long hair, and his top hat pushed back on his head.[59] He was a remarkable improviser and, playing more Bach than any other Parisian of his day, he was nicknamed "le petit père Bach." Unfortunately, his promising career was cut short, for he died of a lung ailment at the age of thirty-three.

Adrien Gros's description of the organ competition is all the more interesting for the light it sheds on the hiring practices of the Parisian churches of the 1860s. As had been announced, each of the candidates was required to play:

1. An organ piece, either prepared or improvised;
2. An improvisation on a given theme: Saint-Saëns provided a phrase in F major;
3. An accompaniment to a piece of plainchant: the "Alma redemptoris," transposed down a fifth.

---

[58]Adrien Gros, "Letter to the Editor," *Revue de musique sacrée* (15 February 1864) 122–23.
[59]Cécile Cavaillé-Coll. Quoted in Norbert Dufourcq, *La Musique d'Orgue Française de Jehan Titelouze à Jehan Alain* (Paris: Librairie Floury, 1949) 161.

77

The evening before the competition each organist had received a letter informing him that he would also be required to play a fugue with pedals! Gros objected strongly (and rightly) to this last-minute requirement—"How well could a fugue with pedals be prepared the night before a competition?"—and suggested that an unpublished sight-reading piece could have been given or they could have just as well sight-read a fugue. He further pointed out that no practice time had been given to the organists to familiarize themselves with the instrument and that although the competitors were assembled at 4:30 in the afternoon (the specified hour for the competition), the jury did not arrive until five o'clock. The competitors drew numbers to determine their playing order but, even though a curtain had been hung on either side of the tribune so the players could not be seen, Gros pointed out how easy it was to identify who was playing: "'Style is the man,' as Buffon said, is perhaps even truer in music than in literature."

Each organist improvised on the theme and then played the "Alma redemptoris." The first man played Lemmens's *Prière* but, by not playing a fugue, disqualified himself. Chauvet, the second contestant, played his own *Grand Choeur* and Bach's *Fugue in G Minor*, BWV 542. The third played either an improvised or composed piece and the fugue from Hesse's *Fantaisie in D*; the fourth improvised and played a fugue of his own composition on the first notes of the "Ave maris stella."

Adrien Gros suggested that the jury knew the identity of the players and that, if the players had known the makeup of the jury, it would have influenced their choice of pieces. Obviously, Chauvet's performance of the great Bach fugue delighted Saint-Saëns; undoubtedly, Chauvet was the most gifted of the four organists. The organbuilder, Cavaillé-Coll, must have been pleased by his appointment: Chauvet had just had installed and inaugurated a new Cavaillé-Coll organ in his former church, Saint-Bernard-de-la-Chapelle, and was now titulaire of his 1857 rebuilt organ at Saint-Merry. When he left in 1869 it was to become organist of yet another new Cavaillé-Coll instrument—at the new church of La Trinité.

The Prix de Rome, 1864

In 1864 Saint-Saëns again competed for the Prix de Rome and again was unsuccessful. He lost to Victor Sieg, who, after his return from Rome, became organist of Notre-Dame-de-Clignancourt and a singing inspector in the Paris public schools.[60] While it is true that many of the great names in French music have won the Prix de Rome: Berlioz, Gounod, Bizet, Massenet and Debussy, numerous lesser composers, many of whom were organists also won the First Prize: François Benoist, Renaud de Vilbac, Théodore Dubois, Henri Busser and Marcel Dupré. Édouard Batiste, Auguste Bazille, Théodore Salomé and Gabriel Pierné won the Second Grand Prix. None of the other two dozen or so organists, whose names are too obscure to mention, ever attained the achievements of Camille Saint-Saëns, and it must have been a source of extreme aggravation throughout his life as he watched so many inferior talents win the prize and leave for their three-to-five-year sojourn in Rome. And he must have been enraged when he read Sieg's obituary which, recounting the only important event of his life, noted that Sieg "obtained the Grand Prix de Rome in 1864—the same year that C. Saint-Saëns won a Second Prize."[61]

The Soirées: Pauline Viardot and Princess Mathilde

The social life of the young organist of the Madeleine centered around soirées, or evening musicales, held in private homes on different nights of the week. Saint-Saëns was much sought after in social circles and a constant participant at the most elegant soirées in the French capital. He entertained in his own home on Monday evenings. Two hours of music were followed by refreshments served by his mother and great-aunt.

Pauline Viardot,[62] the celebrated singer, held her soirées on Thursday and Sunday evenings.

From the salon . . . which was devoted to ordinary instrumental and vocal music, we went down a short staircase to a gallery filled with valuable paintings, and finally to an exquisite organ—one of Cavaillé-Coll's masterpieces. In this temple dedicated to music we listened to arias from the oratorios of Handel and Mendelssohn . . . I had the honor to be her regular accompanist both at the organ and the piano.[63]

---

[60]Bonnerot, 43.
[61]*Le Monde Musical* (15 May 1899) 211.
[62]She had created the rôle of Fidès in Meyerbeer's *Le Prophète* in 1849.
[63]Saint-Saëns, *École Buissonnière*, 220.

Plate 21. Pauline Viardot's Salon

After the musical portion of the evening a game of charades was often played—a time relished by the most frequent participant: Camille Saint-Saëns. Romain Bussine, Gabriel Fauré and Paul Joanne usually went to the Madeleine on Sunday mornings "and in the tribune, during mass, worked out in whispers the details of the evening's charades."[64] It was at one of these informal evenings in Madame Viardot's salon that Saint-Saëns appeared as Marguerite in a costume which included a blue and white bonnet over two thick plaits of fair hair, and sang the "Jewel Scene" from Gounod's *Faust!*[65]

His most impressive social conquest was his attendance at the salon of Princess Mathilde Bonaparte Demidoff, first cousin of the Emperor, Napoleon III. Princess Mathilde was the most distinguished hostess of Second Empire Paris and during the thirty years she lived on in the Republic, she presided over what the Goncourts called "the true salon of the nineteenth century."[66] In 1860 the Princess had used her political influence to have Saint-Saëns exempted from military service—by reason of his indispensable duties as organist of the Madeleine. Later, when it was suggested that she might use her influence to help him mount an opera, she replied, "What! He isn't satisfied with his position? He plays the organ at the Madeleine and the piano at my house! Isn't that enough for him?"[67]

It was to Princess Mathilde that Saint-Saëns dedicated his *Sérénade*, Op. 15, for piano, organ, violin and viola or cello. It was premiered at a soirée given by the Prince of Hohenzollern on 7 January 1866. The composer played the organ and Julien Sauzay the piano. Saint-Saëns set the *Sérénade* as a song (to words by L. Mangeot) in 1866 and twenty years later arranged and published it as a piano solo.

The number and variety of his concerts during this period were typical of Saint-Saëns's schedule which would continue for the next sixty years. During the winter of 1864 he played a series of concerts at Salle

[64]Pauline Viardot, "La Jeunesse de Saint-Saëns," *Musica* (June 1907) 83–84.
[65]Paul Viardot, "Saint-Saëns Gai," *Le Guide du Concert* (Numéro Saint-Saëns 1914/1922) 13.
[66]Joanna Richardson, *Princess Mathilde* (London: Weidenfeld & Nicholson, 1969) 8.
[67]Saint-Saëns, *École Buissonnière*, 23.

Pleyel which included the trios, duos and concertos of Mozart. In 1865 he organized with Pablo Sarasate a series of chamber music concerts which featured Beethoven's quartets and trios by Félicien David and Henri Litolff. In March 1865 at Lyon, Saint-Saëns gave a series of three concerts featuring not only his own music but also that of Schumann, Liszt, Wagner, Mendelssohn and Bellini. And in April he took part in a concert in Dijon to help raise money for the erection of a monument to Rameau.

During the summer of 1865 Saint-Saëns's third organ work was published: *Élévation ou Communion*, Op. 13. It was included in *La Chapelle au Couvent*, a collection of sacred music for women's voices. Louis-Désirée Besozzi, his successor at the École Niedermeyer, was coeditor of the volume and it was, doubtless, at his request that Saint-Saëns contributed this piece.[68]

Élévation ou Communion, Op. 13

Two manuscripts of the work are preserved in the Bibliothèque Nationale. The first, perhaps dating from as early as 1856, is the third of *Cinq pièces inédits pour orgue ou harmonium*, Ms 914[a-e]. Its title, *Communion ou "O Salutaris,"* suggests that it may be either an organ reduction or a first draft of a motet. The piece which follows it is entitled "Ave verum" and is indeed a keyboard reduction of the four-part motet for mixed voices (published a semitone lower, in E-flat), dedicated to Dietsch. Of the "O Salutaris," however, no vocal setting exists.

In *La Chapelle ou Couvent* the piece is printed on two staves, but the indication "2 Claviers et Pédale" and the registration, "Voix humaine ou Voix céleste," leaves no doubt that the work is for organ, not harmonium. A footnote further directs that the first left-hand note is to be played by the pedal and held throughout the entire measure.[69]

A second manuscript (Ms 654) is on three staves and may have been the copy prepared by the composer for Durand's 1880 edition. At that time the *Élévation ou Communion* was issued in two separate editions: one for organ, the other for harmonium. Saint-Saëns evidently

---

[68]It was reviewed by Adolphe Batte in *Revue et Gazette musicale* (10 September 1865) 295.

[69]An unauthorized three-stave version was brought out by G. Schirmer in New York in 1876. Samuel P. Warren, organist of New York City's Grace Church, was the editor.

thought enough of the piece to transcribe it later for piano solo. This arrangement was published by Choudens in 1886.

Élévation ou Communion is dedicated to Alexis Chauvet who repaid Saint-Saëns's compliment by dedicating to him *9 Offertoires de caractères gradués destinés au Temps de l'Avent et au Temps de Noël*, for organ or harmonium.[70] Saint-Saëns was not alone in his admiration of Chauvet's talents: César Franck dedicated his *Fantaisie in C* to him.

At the end of 1865 Saint-Saëns composed his *Psalm 18* for choir, soloists and orchestra. It was performed at the Madeleine at Christmas Eve midnight Mass.

Among the unique concerts in which Saint-Saëns took part was a varied program which he played on 2 April 1866 at Salle Pleyel before an audience which included Berlioz, Gounod and Liszt. On the pédalier (pedal piano) he played two Schumann Canons and the *Sketch in F Minor*. On the piano he played Liszt's *Legend, "Saint Francis of Paola Walking on the Waves."* He then accompanied his *Suite*, for piano and cello, and his *Sérénade*, Op. 15, for piano organ, violin and viola or cello.[71]

Saint-Maclou-de-Rouen Organ Inauguration

Saint-Saëns inaugurated his first organ not built by Cavaillé-Coll in the summer of 1866. A competitor, the firm of Merklin-Schütze, had just rebuilt the organ of Saint-Maclou in Rouen. The organist was Aimabale Dupré, Marcel Dupré's grandfather; he was joined in the dedicatory concert by Aloys Klein, organist of Rouen Cathedral, and several musicians brought up from Paris. These included Saint-Saëns of the Madeleine; Auguste Bazille, organist of Saint-Éisabeth-du- Temple (who had been among those organists who dedicated the organ of Saint-Sulpice four years earlier); Renaud de Vilbac, organist of Saint-Eugène; and Charles Vervoitte, maître-de-chapelle of Sàint-Roch (where a new Merklin-Schütze organ had been inaugurated on 15 May 1861), who brought his tenor soloist, M. Hayet, and two choirboys, MM. Renaud and Tarkin. With them came Antoine Prumier (père), professor of harp at the Paris Conservatoire. On Thursday, 26 July 1866, each organist

---

[70]*Four Offertoires* were published by Durand in 1867. Five additional ones were added and the complete set brought out in 1869.

[71]*Revue et Gazette musicale* (29 April 1866) 130.

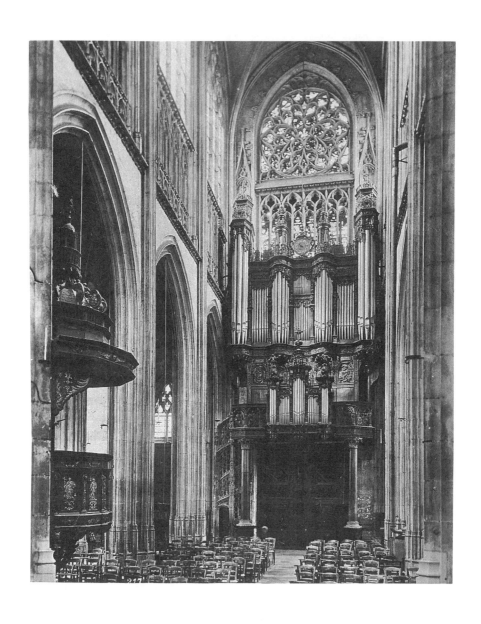

Plate 22. Saint-Maclou-de-Rouen, the organ

84

played one piece, and between them singers performed solos and duets composed by their director, Charles Vervoitte, accompanied by organ, harp and cello.

The reviewer for the Rouen paper all but ignored Saint-Saëns, finding his playing "tedious," but was enthusiastic over the performance of the Rouen Cathedral organist, Aloys Klein, of Renaud de Vilbac, "an extraordinary composer and virtuoso,"[72] and of Auguste Bazille, "who reproduced the howling wind, driving rain and chorus of voices of those in distress in his representation of a thunderstorm."[73]

Trois Rhapsodies sur des Cantiques Bretons

In August 1866, Saint-Saëns went on an excursion to Brittany with four painters, among whom was his friend, Henri Regnault.[74] They were joined by Gabriel Fauré who, since January, had been organist of Saint-Sauveur in Rennes, and together they made a pilgrimage to the shrine of Sainte-Anne-la-Palud. During this trip Saint-Saëns composed three *Rhapsodies Bretonnes*, Op. 7, loosely constructed fantaisies on Breton hymns, and dedicated them to his former piano student, Fauré.

Since he had just played the new organ at Saint-Maclou in Rouen, it seems to have been this well-designed, traditional, two-manual, 23-stop Merklin instrument, rather than the one at the Madeleine, that Saint-Saëns had in mind when registering the *Trois Rhapsodies*. The latter organ lacked a Gambe, Hautbois and Cromorne on the Récit and a 16' Bourdon on either the Positif or the Grand-Orgue. Although "Tirasse du II clavier" (indicated the twenty-first measure before the end of the first *Rhapsodie*) could apply to the Grand-Orgue (it being the second manual on the Madeleine organ—the Positif being the lowest), the Saint-Maclou instrument had a Récit (or II) tirasse. The Merklin organ

---

[72]Renaud de Vilbac (1829–1884) won first prize in Benoist's organ class at the Paris Conservatoire and the Grand Prix de Rome at the age of fifteen. He was organist of Saint-Eugène where he rivaled Lefébure-Wély in improvisation and equaled him in execution (wrote Gustave Chouquet in the 1935 edition of Grove's *Dictionary*). Known as a salon piano composer and an arranger of operatic potpourris for amateurs, he became almost blind in his last years and died in poverty. He made a piano transcription of Saint-Saëns's song, *Danse macabre*, for the publisher, Enoch, in 1874.

[73]*Revue et Gazette musicale* (5 August 1866) 247.

[74]A letter written by Regnault 22 October 1866 states that he did not leave for Bretagne until 4 September (Henri Regnault, *Correspondance de Henri Regnault*, recueille et annotée par Arthur Duparc. (Paris: Charpentier & Cie., 1884) 34.

had all the right stops in all the right places except for the Voix céleste on the first manual but, since it was intended to be under expression, the composer's intentions could not have been realized at the Madeleine either. That same year he composed his *Romance*, Op. 27, for violin, piano and organ (or harmonium), which he dedicated to Gustave Doré, the famous illustrator.[75]

Samson et Dalila

With the poet Fernand Lemaire, a young Creole from Martinique who had married the cousin of one of his cousins, Saint-Saëns discussed making an oratorio out of the biblical story of Samson.[76] "An oratorio!" exclaimad Lemaire. "No," he replied, "we will make an opera!" The two set to work and at one of Saint-Saëns's Monday soirées in 1867 excerpts from the second act of the new opera, *Samson et Dalila*, were sung. The listeners' reactions were mild. But some time later, when Henri Regnault was home from school in Rome, Saint-Saëns had him sing Samson; Augusta Holmès, Dalila; and Romain Bussine, the high priest. The reaction this time, while not enthusiastic, was less reserved.[77]

Les Noces de Prométhée

In 1867 the Universal Exposition was held in Paris. An imperial commission was set up to choose a cantata to be performed by orchestra, chorus and soloists. The first competition was for a text, and the seventeen-year-old Romain Cornut won with his *Les Noces de Prométhée*; the second contest, for a musical setting of the words, brought out 102 composers. Saint-Saëns won, but his cantata, *Les Noces de Prométhée*, was not performed. For "unexplained" reasons (attributable to political intrigue) Rossini's cantata, *Hymne à l'Empereur*, was given by 1,200 performers in the huge Palais de l'Industrie. Saint-Saëns received only half of the 5,000-franc prize money, made up the remainder out of his own

---

[75]A contemporary review describes it as a "Romance for violin with accompaniments for the other instruments . . . No passages are written for mere display; and there is a continuity of design in this piece which will recommend it beyond compositions of far more pretension." (*The Musical Times*, November 1869, p. 275).

[76]Bonnerot, 52.

[77]Bonnerot, 54.

pocket and produced his cantata at the Cirque de l'Impératrice. It was performed for the first time on Sunday, 1 September 1867, with Jean-Baptiste Faure singing the baritone part.[78]

During the Exposition, throughout the month of August, every afternoon between three and five, Merklin-Schütze organs were demonstrated. Saint-Saëns was one of the organists who played. The others included: Batiste, Bazille, Cavallo, Chauvet, Dubois, Durand, Guilmant, Schmitt, de Vilbac, and Widor. The organ could be heard from quite a distance, but "unfortunately it was in the middle of incessant and deafening noise made by all kinds of machines. . . . and it was difficult to appreciate the artistic qualities" which were exhibited.[79]

Notre-Dame-de-Paris Organ Inauguration

Early the next year Saint-Saëns was one of the seven organists chosen by Cavaillé-Coll to inaugurate his newly rebuilt organ at Notre-Dame, the Cathedral of Paris. (Pierre-Henri Lamazou, the vicar of the Madeleine, was secretary of the commission in charge of the new organ.) The solemn inauguration took place at eight o'clock, Friday evening, 6 March 1868. The program:

| Improvisation on the foundation stops | Eugène Sergent |
| Laudate Dominum (sung in faux bourdons) | Gregorian |

Choir and organ
Félix Renaud, maître-de-chapelle

| Prelude and Fugue in E Minor | J. S. Bach |

Played by Clément Loret

| Fantaisie in F | Auguste Durand |
| Ave Maria | Luigi Cherubini |

Sung by Félicien Renaud

---

[78]Bonnerot, 49–51. The jury of the Exposition of 1878 made amends when, at the first official concert inaugurating the Salle des Fêtes of the Trocadéro, Édouard Colonne gave a beautiful performence of *Les Noces de Prométhée*.

[79]Prosper Sain d'Arod in *Revue de musique sacrée* (October–November 1867) 67. Guilmant played the Grand Orgue in the French section, Monday, 10 August, for three-and-a-half hours. On Wednesday, 4 September, Lefébure-Wély demonstrated the Orgue-Mustel for two hours and his two charming daughters played their father's remarkable symphonic duos on Pleyel-Wolff pianos.

Plate 23. Inauguration of the new organ of Notre-Dame Cathedral, Paris, 1868

Introduction et Noël	Alexis Chauvet
Marche from the Cantata for the Exposition	Camille Saint-Saëns
Pater noster	Louis Niedermeyer
Sung by M. Bollaert	
Fantaisie in C	César Franck
Marche funèbre et chant séraphique	Alexandre Guilmant
Agnus Dei	Franz Joseph Haydn
Baritone solo sung by M. Florenza accompanied by the choir	
Improvisation	Charles-Marie Widor
Domine salvum	Gregorian
Laudate Dominum	Ambroise Thomas
Choir and organ	
Sortie, Improvisation	Eugène Sergent

The cathedral was filled, and the noisy crowd, "more curious then attentive . . . disturbed the imposing effect of the solemnity and the sonority of the instrument."[80] For the first time Cavaillé-Coll was able to bring together a group of fine organists (with the exception of Eugène Sergent, the cathedral organist who could not be excluded). One can only wonder what César Franck and Saint-Saëns thought when they read the opening words of E. Repos's review in the *Revue de musique sacrée:*

> . . . everyone deeply regretted not seeing on this program the names of such highly respected artists as MM. Bazille and Batiste and, above all, such great organists as MM. Lefébure-Wély and Georges Schmitt, whose reputations are as great abroad as in France.[81]

Chauvet's *Noël* and Saint-Saëns's *Marche* were singled out by all three reviewers as the best pieces on the concert. E. Repos included Franck's "Impromptu" and Marie Escudier included Guilmant's *Marche funèbre:* "We don't believe we will offend the eight talented organists by stating

---

[80]"Concerts et Auditions Musicale de la Semaine," *Revue et Gazette musicale* (18 March 1868) 85.
[81]E. Repos, "Chronique," *Revue de musique sacrée ancienne et moderne* (March 1868) 24.

that the general consensus was that Chauvet, Saint-Saëns and Alex. Guilmant had the most taste."[82]

As at the inauguration of the organ of Saint-Sulpice in 1862, Guilmant again attracted the most attention:

> We do not want to say, as was purported in one of the papers, that M. Guilmant, organist of Boulogne-sur-Mer, was the most inspired in this recital. We are the first to recognize that this organist evidenced real merit but we can say, after having heard sixteen [sic] organ pieces played almost in succession by a group of talented artists, what would be said after having heard twelve speeches given by as many eminent orators at the same meeting of the Academy or the legislature: the last heard would undoubtedly win the general approval. We will add that our organists were all admirable just as we would no doubt have found all twelve orators to have been eloquent.[83]

A week later Saint-Saëns again played at Notre-Dame. A half hour of organ music at a Mass on 15 March preceded a lecture by the famous Jesuit preacher, Father Félix.

> In that short half hour, M. C. Saint-Saëns was able to charm and hold the interest of serious musicians and, at the same time, the general audience which appreciates the result even more than the thought behind it.
>
> An improvisation in a severe style, in which the composer developed a simple hymn in a most original, skillfull and varied way, and the beautiful *Marche* from his prize-winning symphonic cantata written for the Universal Exposition comprised the serious musical portion.
>
> Between these two pieces was heard a *Storm*, an excerpt from one of Liszt's piano works—*Saint Francis of Paola Walking on the Waves*. We don't like storms very much—even less in church—but we had to admit that the effect under the old cathedral's vaults was frighteningly real. Even the cloud-covered sky contributed to the illusion, letting nothing but the gloomy day penetrate the interior. As for the almost insurmountable difficulties present in the performance of this work of Lizst, we should say that, as everyone knows, for M. C. Saint-Saëns it is no more difficult on the organ than on the piano.[84]

---

[82]Marie Escudier, "Actualités," *La France musicale* (15 March 1868) 83.

[83]E. Repos, *Revue de musique sacrée* (March 1868) 24.

[84]*Journal des villes et des compagnes* (17 March 1868). Reprinted in *Revue de musique sacrée* (April 1868) 32.

Saint-Pierre-de-Dreux Organ Inauguration

The second-smallest Cavaillé-Coll organ Saint-Saëns ever inaugurated was the two-manual, twenty-two-stop organ at Saint-Pierre in Dreux. On Wednesday, 12 August 1868 he "charmed for more than two hours the large select audience that attended the interesting religious and artistic ceremony."[85] As was customary, organ pieces alternated with choral works, the latter being sung by students of the friars' boarding school. Among other pieces Saint-Saëns played were his *Marche* from *Les Noces de Prométhée* and an Allegretto by Mendelssohn (probably that of the *Fourth Sonata*). He ended with a fugue by J. S. Bach.[86]

Théodore Dubois

In November 1868 Théodore Dubois was appointed maître-de-chapelle of the Madeleine.[87] He had served the previous ten years at Sainte-Clotilde as organiste accompagnateur when César Franck was first appointed maître-de-chapelle and organist and, after the new Grand Orgue was finished, as maître-de-chapelle when Franck assumed his duties as organiste titulaire. Dubois spent five years in Italy (from 1861 to 1866) after he won the Grand Prix de Rome, and returned to Sainte-Clotilde where, on Good Friday 1867, he presented for the first time his oratorio, *Les Sept Paroles du Christ*. This and his other church music, both organ and choral, are composed in a style best described by the Anglo-American term "Victorian"—a style far more pleasing to the clergy and congregation of the Madeleine than the formal classicism and fugal improvisations of their titular organist, Camille Saint-Saëns. One of the priests of Sainte-Clotilde had compared Dubois's playing to that of César

[84]*Journal des villes et des compagnes* (17 March 1868). Reprinted in *Revue de musique sacrée* (April 1868) 32.

[85]"Nouvelles Diverses," *Revue et Gazette musicale* (16 August 1868) 263, and "Chronique," *Revue de musique sacrée* (August 1868) 63–64.

[86]Didier Decrette, *Histoire du Grand Orgue de l'Eglise Saint-Pierre-de-Dreux* (Vernouillet: Les Vignes de la Brosse, 1977).

[87]*Revue de musique sacrée* (November 1868) 88. He succeeded Charles Trévaux, doyen of maîtres-de-chapelle of Paris," to whom Saint-Saëns dedicated his *Tantum Ergo*, Op. 5. The work for eight-part choir was written in 1856 but published in 1868. Trévaux probably succeeded Dietsch as maître-de-chapelle of the Madeleine in 1865.

Plate 24. Church of La Trinité

Franck: "Ah! M. Franck was very boring! He always played as though he were dead tired. But M. Dubois—he delighted us![88]

Dubois's *March of the Magi Kings*, in which a high B is sustained throughout to represent the eastern star which guided the three kings to Bethlehem, and his *In paradisum* are of less than elevated style and compositional skill, but their unctuous novelty brought them great popularity in the organ world for many years.

La Trinité Organ Inauguration

Toward the middle of March 1869 Cavaillé-Coll's new organ in the new church of La Trinité was inaugurated. Gioacchino Rossini lived in the parish and had been a member of the organ commission (as he had been the previous year for that of Notre-Dame). His *Petite Messe solennelle*, originally composed with an accompaniment of harmonium and two pianos, had been rescored for full orchestra and had been premiered at the Théâtre Italien just two weeks before. Alexis Chauvet, the new organist of La Trinité, planned to open the dedicatory recital with the Offertoire from the *Petite Messe solennelle*, feeling thet the contrast between the church's great organ and the little organ at the Théâtre Italien would be all the more striking. Moreover, Chauvet had "carefully prepared it according to the tradition preserved by Georges Mathias who had interpreted it for the first time at Comte Pillet-Will's [at whose house the first performance had been given on 14 March 1864] under the eyes and with the indications of Rossini."[89]

Bagier, the director of the Théâtre Italien, however, obtained a court injunction forbidding the performance of the Offertoire on the grounds of a conflict of interest. "So, the Offertoire was not performed and, in view of the importance which it had on the program, M. Chauvet did not want to substitute anything for it." The program continued with each of the six organists playing his own work.

[88]Cellier and Bachelin, *L'Orgue*, 188.
[89]Concerts et auditions musicales de la semaine," *Revue et Gazette musicale* (16 March 1869) 101.

93

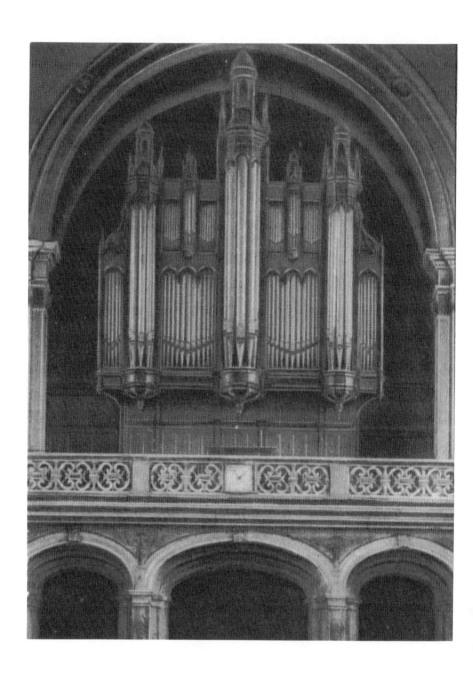

Plate 25. La Trinité, the organ

Méditation religieuse	Henri Fissot
Andante	Charles-Marie Widor
Scherzo	
Bénédiction nuptiale	Camille Saint-Saëns
Fantaisie Pastorale	Auguste Durand
Improvisation	César Franck
Sortie en forme de marche	Alexis Chauvet

As usual, several choruses and vocal solos alternated with the organ pieces.

Henri Fissot, who had just succeeded Chauvet as organist of Saint-Merry, played his *Méditation religieuse*—a piece "of sober effects but of great serenity and with beautiful character."

The twenty-five-year-old Charles-Marie Widor was still living in Lyon where his father, François Widor, was a great friend and exact contemporary of Cavaillé-Coll. Widor was assisting at Saint-Sulpice during what was to be Lefébure-Wély's last illness. He "displayed great technical skill" in his two pieces. Saint-Saëns's *Bénédiction nuptiale*, written ten years before, was dismissed as "a piece of little effect and few ideas—this is not to say that the composer lacks talent." Auguste Durand was organist of Saint-Vincent-de-Paul and at the end of the year would found his famous publishing firm. The reviewer found his piece "entirely too derivative." César Franck of Sainte-Clotilde played "a vigorous well-developed improvisation in which he sought to point up the greatest possible number of sonorities." Years later Widor recalled that "the themes, their development and execution were equally admirable. He never wrote better!"[90]

The concert ended with Chauvet playing "a brilliant *Sortie en forme de marche* in which he introduced the theme of Rossini's Offertoire, forbidden to the church and monopolized by the theater—an ingenious protest which received general approval."[91]

Each year theaters and opera houses were closed during Holy Week and the temporarily unemployed artists traditionally devoted their time and talent to charity concerts. The Société Académique de Musique

[90]Raugel, *Les Grandes Orgues de Paris*, 220.
[91]*Revue et Gazette musicale* (16 March 1869) 101.

Sacrée mounted a spectacular benefit at the Cirque de l'Impératrice on the Champs-Elysées on 27 March 1869. Three hundred performers appeared before an audience of 3,000. Saint-Saëns, still organist for the Société, played the Merklin-Schütze organ. For this concert Jean-Baptiste Faure composed what was to be one of his most famous songs, *Charité*, and Saint-Saëns accompanied him in it and his own *Ave Maria* (in E—dedicated to Théodore Biais).[92]

Also during this year the organ of the Madeleine, then twenty-five years old, was in need of serious work, and 13,867.50 francs were spent on repairs, overhauling and general tuning. On 19 December the orgue-de-choeur was taken back to the Cavaillé-Coll shop and a new one delivered.[93]

Death of Lefébure-Wély

On New Year's Eve, at the stroke of midnight—a dramatic gesture of which he would have approved—Lefébure-Wély died. A swollen joint and his feverish activity had led to consumption from which he rapidly succumbed. His requiem was attended by all of the notable musicians including Ambroise Thomas and Charles Gounod. Thomas, in a eulogy at his tomb, said that Lefébure-Wély "had taken his place among the most eminent organists—not only of his own time but of all periods and of all schools."[94] Widor, who had been playing at Saint-Sulpice for most of the

---

[92]H. Moreno, "La Semaine Sainte et les Concerts spirituels," *Le Ménestrel* (4 April 1869) 139-40.

[93]Gilbert Huybens, *Aristide Cavaillé-Coll: Liste des travaux exécutés* (Orgelbau-Fachverlag Rensch: ISO Information, 1985) 18–19.

[94]*Le Ménestrel* (9 January 1870) 45. *Le Ménestrel* immediately set about collecting contributions for a monument to the memory of Lefébure-Wély and by July 1870 6,671 francs had been raised. Well-known contributors included:
100 francs each given by Ambroise Thomas, Victor Mustel, Alexandre Debain and the Pleyel-Wolff firm;
50 francs given by Charles Gounod;
25 francs given by Charles-Marie Widor;
20 francs each given by Francis Planté, Édouard Batiste, Leo Délibes, and Clément Loret;
10 francs each given by J.-L. Battmann, Auguste Durand, and Pablo Sarasate.
Conspicuously absent were the names of those composers who had dedicated organ works to Lefébure-Wély: Alkan, César Franck, and Saint-Saëns. The intervention of the Franco-Prussion War postponed the project a few years, but eventually a monu-

last year, was appointed interim organist—a post he held for the next sixty-four years!

The Franco-Prussian War

Germany declared war on France on 19 July 1870. The roster of the National Guard read like a future "Who's Who of French Music." Saint-Saëns served in the Fourth Battalion and others who enlisted included Gabriel Fauré, Charles-Marie Widor, Vincent d'Indy, Alexis de Castillon, Henri Duparc, and Arthur Coquard. France's lack of allies and an ill-prepared army contributed to its inglorious campaign ending with the capitulation of the Sudan and the eventual loss of Alsace and Lorraine. The French nation blamed its emperor for the humiliating defeat and on 4 September 1870 deposed him. Thus the Second Empire ended and the Third Republic was established.

The Siege of Paris

By the 19th of September Paris was surrounded by the Germans and for the next nineteen weeks the city was under siege. No supplies were allowed to enter the capital and provisions were eventually depleted.

During the siege some 700 horses were slaughtered daily for food and their flesh sold at 1.50 francs per pound, whilst dog's flesh was retailed at two francs per pound. Cats and rats also became the food of starving Parisians. The animals in the zoological gardens were shot and their carcasses sold to the leading restaurateurs in the city. A slice of elephant's flesh as big as one's hand cost 30 francs, the flesh being very tender and not at all badly flavoured.[95]

Everywhere store windows displayed extraordinary provisions: rat patés, mock calves brains made from bones, and elephant sausage. Newspapers and almanacs offered unexpected recipes: rabbit stew made from cats, chat au chausseur, horse à la mode, horsesteaks and gigot de chien rôte (roasted dog's shanks!).[96] Rats were bought and cooked and according to

---

ment designed by Baltard and executed by H. Chevalier was erected in Père Lachaise cemetery and blessed on Wednesday, 2 July 1873. (*La Chronique musicale* October–November 1873).

[95]Harold P. Clunn, *The Face of Paris* (London: Spring Books, c. 1960) 12.

[96]George Cain, *Travers Paris* (Paris: Flamarion, 1909) 63–65.

witnesses they tasted remarkably like terrapin—one restaurant was accused of serving them as such!

Saint-Saëns was quartered at the Palais de l'Industrie when he received a letter notifying him that his friend, the painter Henri Regnault, had been shot and killed.[97] As soon as he was relieved, he returned home and for three days wept inconsolably and would speak to no one. Regnault's funeral was held at Saint-Augustin on 27 January 1871 and Saint-Saëns played the organ. During the Elevation he played the theme of his *Au Cimetière*,[98] which the painter had sung only a few days before.

The next day, 28 January, after 131 days of siege and on the brink of starvation, France was forced to surrender. The same day, Alexis Chauvet, organist of La Trinité, who had long suffered from tuberculosis and whose condition had been aggravated by the ordeal, died.

The Société Nationale

Social life quickly returned to normal as the nation tried to forget its humiliating defeat. The new generation of composers gatherd to found the Société Nationale on 25 February 1871. Under the motto *Ars Gallica* its aim was "to favor the production and diffusion of all serious works, published or not, of French composers." The officers were:

Romain Bussine, president
Camille Saint-Saëns, vice-president
Alexis de Castillon, secretary
Jules Garcin, under-secretary
Charles Lenepveu, treasurer

and the other founding members were:

Louis-Albert Bourgault-Ducoudray   César Franck
Henri Duparc   Ernest Guiraud
Théodore Dubois   Paul Taffanel
Gabriel Fauré   Jules Massenet
Henri Fissot

---

[97]Bonnerot, 60.
[98]This is the fifth of the *Mélodies persanes*, Op. 26. The fourth, *Sabre en main*, is dedicated to Regnault.

The Commune

Before the new society could arrange its first concert, civil war broke out. The unrest in the city was further aggravated by the disbandment of the highly paid National Guard. The soldiers, with no other means of support, were resentful and sprung to violent action. The Guard had not been disarmed and it succeeded in raising an army of 100,000 to overthrow the provisional government. The city, now in the hands of the Communists, was besieged by government troops and was soon in ruin. Although the Communists took money from the Bank of France and from other state institutions there was almost no pillaging of private homes.

> The Commune fought against the Government but, with the exception of priests who were objects of its special enmity and of young men who refused to serve in its regiments, very few private individuals were molested.[99]

Saint-Saëns was one of those young men who, although not an active member of the insurgents, had been in the National Guard, and was placed in a particularly precarious political position. It was necessary for him to flee to England.

In London his several hundred francs were soon spent and he faced real destitution until a fellow-countryman, Félix Lévy, loaned him enough to live on until he could earn some money.[100] One of the directors of the Crystal Palace offered him ten guineas to play the organ while the hall resounded to the workers' hammers, and he earned money from Novello and Boosey with whom he published some songs and piano reductions.

Meanwhile, back in Paris, two generals had been shot by Communist soldiers on 18 March and two days later Abbé Deguerry denounced the murders from the pulpit of the Madeleine. He continued to speak out against the insurrectionists and refused to flee the city as he had been advised by his parishoners. The Madeleine, usually full during Lent, was almost empty. "Paris is a volcano, right now," wrote Abbé Deguerry. "We hear a moaning like that of a turbulent sea. The city is

---

[99]F. Adolphus, *Some Memories of Paris* (New York: Holt, 1895) 141–42.
[100]Bonnerot, 62.

more and more deserted and I think the emigration has taken on even greater proportions than it did with the approach of the Prussians.[101]

> Such a spectacle ... had never before been recorded in history, namely the utter abandonment by a government of its capitol because a section of the populace had risen in arms and made themselves masters of a few important positions.[102]

The Communists had taken over Sainte-Geneviève, dedicated it to Marat, and pulled down the cross which rose above the pediment. On Palm Sunday, 2 April, at the sermon and at the one o'clock mass, Deguerry raised his voice in indignation against the vandals' crime. The Communist leaders, having heard of his protests, arrested him

> the night of 4 April, Tuesday of Holy Week, and incarcerated him first at the Conciergerie, then at Mazas and finally at the prison at La Roquette.
>
> On 23 May Abbé Lamazou was also imprisoned at La Roquette. He had courageously stayed at his post at the Madeleine during the captivity of his pastor and continued his ministry until 18 May, Ascension Day, when the church was closed.[103]

On 25 May six hostages, including Abbé Deguerry and Georges Darboy, Archbishop of Paris, were shot before a firing squad. Three days later (on Sunday morning), government troops took command of the city. The Madeleine was opened in time for Vespers, and Abbé Lamazou, who had been released from La Roquette that morning, informed his parishoners of the fate of their pastor. Their organist, Saint-Saëns, returned to Paris the following week and probably played for his martyred pastor's funeral at the Madeleine on Friday, 9 June.

Organ Recital at Royal Albert Hall, London

In July 1871, Saint-Saëns returned to London for his first professional engagement in the country which would honor him, almost annually, for the next half century. A series of recitals was arranged by six European organists to demonstrate the new Willis organ at the Royal Albert Hall. Those who played were Saint-Saëns of Paris, Mailly of Brussels,

---

[101]Krièger, *La Madeleine*, 147.
[102]Clunn, op. cit., 13.
[103]Krièger, op. cit., 148.

Anton Bruckner of Vienna, Löhr of Budapest, Heintzen of Stockholm and Lindemann of Norway. Among the pieces Saint-Saëns played was the "Church Scene" from Gounod's *Faust*,[104] and *The Orchestra* devoted an entire page to a review of his performance, describing him as "an exceptional and distinguished performer. . . the effect was most marvellous."[105] Less enthusiastic was William Thomas Best, the great English organist, who had opened the organ 18 July and who, when asked what he thought of the distinguished foreign organists, replied that they "just pulled out all the stops and wallowed in it."[106]

First Concert of the Société Nationale

The Société Nationale finally got under way and its first concert in Paris on 17 November 1871 opened with César Franck's *Trio de salon in B-flat*. Two of Saint-Saëns's new works were premiered in December: his first symphonic poem, *Le Rouet d'Omphale* on the seventh, and *Marche Héroïque,* dedicated to Henri Regnault, played by the orchestra of the Concerts Populaires on the tenth. On the sixteenth he was in Bordeaux where, at the Cercle Philharmonique, he played his *Piano Concerto in G Minor* and some organ solos on the three-manual organ.[107]

César Franck's Appointment to the Conservatoire

On 1 February 1872 César Franck was appointed professor of organ at the Paris Conservatoire. Responsibility for the prestigious appointment has variously been assigned to Théodore Dubois, Aristide Cavaillé-Coll and Saint-Saëns; the case presented by the latter is as plausible as that of the others.

In a letter to Léon Vallas (23 November 1915) Saint-Saëns stated that the organ post was offered to himself but he had refused it and recommended that it be given to César Franck.[108] "Franck had great ability and it was I who took steps (in nominating him) to find room for it

[104]Bonnerot, 63.

[105]James Harding, *Saint-Saëns and his Circle* (London: Chapman & Hall, 1965) 116. The author has been unable to find any reference to Saint-Saëns's recital at the Royal Albert Hall in *The Orchestra* for the year 1871.

[106]John Levien, *Impressions of W. T. Best* (London: Novello, 1942) 31.

[107]"Nouvelles Diverses," *Revue et Gazette musicale* (24 December 1871) 370.

[108]Léon Vallas, *César Franck* (New York: Oxford University Press, 1951) 137.

to flourish by giving him the chance to stop wasting his time in mere teaching and to devote himself to composition. Genius needs more than just talent to develop."[109]

Saint-Saëns later wrote that

> Jules Simon, then minister of education, had consulted me on the choice of a professor of organ at the Conservatoire and I strongly recommended César Franck so that he, with the help of the salary granted by the state, might not find himself compelled to waste in giving piano lessons the time he could more profitably devote to composition.[110]

On 2 February 1872 Saint-Saëns played for the installation of his new pastor at the Madeleine: the former vicar-general, Almyre Le Rebours. Coincidentally, years before, as a parish priest, he had taught catechism to the children of the parish of Saint-Sulpice and had prepared Saint-Saëns for his first communion.[111]

Later in the year he composed his *Sonata*, Op. 32, for cello and piano. The Andante was the "outcome of an improvisation at the organ of Saint-Augustin. The first and last pages of the piece reproduce literally what I had improvised."[112] Henri Busser's arrangement of this movement (published by Durand) for organ solo leaves one with the impression that just such an improvisation has been transcribed, so naturally does it lie under the fingers and feet and assume the qualities of an original organ work.

From the early 1870s there was a decided upgrading in the quality of organ music played in France; the style of the Second Empire and Lefébure-Wély, its foremost exponent, was no more. The churches of Paris would now be identified by the organists who would make them famous. Saint-Saëns was still at the Madeleine, and César Franck at Sainte-Clotilde, but the Third Republic had brought with it a whole new school of organ playing: one formed by the Belgian pedagogue Jacques-Nicolas Lemmens. Eugène Gigout, who had been trained at the École Niedermeyer by Clément Loret (a Lemmens student), was now organist

---

[109]Ibid., 138

[110]Saint-Saëns, *Les idées de Vincent d'Indy* (Paris: Lafitte, 1918). Translated by Fred Rothwell and included in *Outspoken Essays on Music* (Boston: Small, Maynard, 1922) 46.

[111]Bonnerot, 86.

[112]Bonnerot, 69.

of the new church of Saint-Augustin. Widor had succeeded Lefébure-Wély at Saint-Sulpice, and Guilmant had succeeded Chauvet at La Trinité.

Chapel of the Palace of Versailles Organ Inauguration

One of the first organ concerts indicative of this new aesthetic in the French organ world was the inauguration of the organ in the chapel of the Palace of Versailles. Cavaillé-Coll had "entirely restored and modernized" the 1736 Clicquot instrument and on Friday, 21 February 1873, Saint-Saëns performed a Bach prelude and fugue and Charles-Marie Widor played one of his new organ symphonies. The Baronne de Caters sang Niedermeyer's *Pater Noster* and was joined by the Russian contralto, Mlle. Bellocka, in the duet from Rossini's *Stabat Mater*.[113] Henri Lambert, organist of the Cathedral of Versailles, and Émile Renaud, who was to be the last organist of the chapel (it was closed permanently in 1906) assisted.[114]

Demonstration of the Organ for Albert Hall, Sheffield

By May 1873 Cavaillé-Coll had set up in his shop the largest organ he would ever build for Great Britain (and his first with sixty-one-note manuals)—to be installed in the Albert Hall, Sheffield. William Thomas Best came to Paris and played a concert in Cavaillé-Coll's atelier for invited guests, Saturday, 3 May. Saint-Saëns and Widor shared a program the following Wednesday.[115]

Organ Jury at the Paris Conservatoire

In July Saint-Saëns sat with Georges Bizet and Jules Massenet on the organ jury at the Paris Conservatoire as César Franck's students

[113]The next month the same two singers participated in one of the first of Édouard Colonne's Concert National. At a "Concert Spirituele" on Holy Thursday, 10 April 1873, they performed Franck's *Rédemption* and Saint-Saëns's *Psalm 18 "Coeli enarrant."* The Psalm was dedicated to the Baronne de Caters (née Lablanche).

[114]"Nouvelles Diverses," *Le Ménestrel* (2 March 1873) 111. Widor saved two of the original Clicquot keyboards and these were incorporated into Victor Gonzalez's completely new organ in 1939. See Cecil Clutton's "Modern French Organbuilding," *The American Organist* (September 1939) 295–99.

[115]Alexandre Guilmant played the following Saturday. An excellent study of this organ is found in Reginald Whitworth's "The Cavaillé-Coll in Albert Hall," *The American Organist* (December 1937) 415–17.

competed for the annual prizes. No first or second prizes were awarded; Joseph Humblot and Jean Tolbecque given the first accessits.

Algiers

Since childhood Saint-Saëns had a fragile constitution. Advised by his doctor that a warmer climate would improve his lungs, he made in October 1873 the first of what were to be his annual winter trips to Algiers.

Marriage and a Publisher

In February 1875 Saint-Saëns committed himself to two relationships: one with a wife, the other with a publisher. On 3 February he married Marie-Laure-Emilie, the nineteen-year-old sister of his friend Jean Truffot. She was less than half his age. Little is known of their relationship and Saint-Saëns later discouraged discussion of the marriage. The couple lived with his mother—not a situation to promote marital bliss—and soon had two boys: André and Jean-François.

On the twenty-second of February Saint-Saëns signed a five-year contract with Auguste Durand stipulating that he was to be Saint-Saëns's exclusive publisher and would pay the composer 500 francs every three months. A ten-year contract was signed 1 April 1880 which stated that Saint-Saëns "was to receive five percent commission but was guaranteed 2,000 francs each year." A final contract, signed 6 March 1889, specified that Saint-Saëns was to receive 4,000 francs annually.[116]

His Resignation from the Madeleine

By January 1877 Saint-Saëns had been organist of the Madeleine for nineteen years and had made it the world's most celebrated organ gallery. Only Olivier Messiaen, another universally admired musician, has brought as much prestige to a similar post—La Trinité. All of the famous musicians passing through Paris called on Saint-Saëns in his tribune: Clara Schumann, Robert Franz, Pablo Sarasate and Franz Liszt. Anton Rubinstein improvised one day and Saint-Saëns played his *Ocean*

---

[116]Daniel Fallon, *The Symphonies and Symphonic Poems of Camille Saint-Saëns*, Ph.D. dissertation (Yale University, 1973) 28–30. This information has been extracted from Yves Gérard's Contract Notes.

Symphony on the organ for him.[117] So well known was Saint-Saëns as the great organist of Paris' illustrious church, that the music world was surprised to receive in the second week of April the announcement of his resignation.[118]

There were several reasons for his decision to resign. He was well known throughout Europe, not only as a pianist and organist but also as a composer. He began appearing in the role he would assume for the rest of his life—composer, conductor, pianist, and organist. Weekends then, as now, were the best time for concerts. To fulfill his responsibilities as organiste titulaire of the Madeleine on Sunday, he had to give up lucrative concert engagements and opportunities for advancing his career and promoting his music. Traveling time was far longer in the 1870s than today and it was often necessary for Saint-Saëns to be absent for months at a time—times not usually compatible with the liturgical seasons. For example, he toured Russia during the entire Christmas season of 1875–76.

But now that he was supporting himself and his family with income derived from other sources, he felt more keenly the humiliation of the organist's traditional frustration: insensitive clergy. Abbé Lamazou had been transferred three years before—as pastor of Notre-Dame-d'Auteuil. Abbé Deguerry's successor, Almyre Le Rebour, had not the same appreciation as his predecessor for the elevated style of church music. The clergy of the parish had considered the *Oratorio de Noël* "a work without rhyme or reason."[119] and, far from being proud of their organist's success, deplored the fact that his name was so often seen on concert posters.[120] They found fault with his austere taste and with his uncompromisingly rigid standards. He enjoyed telling of the day when

> . . . one of the parish priests undertook to instruct me on this point. The congregation of the Madeleine, he said, was composed, for the most part, of wealthy persons who frequently attended the Opéra-Comique. There they formed musical tastes which ought to be respected.

---

[117]Bonnerot, 37.

[118]*Revue et Gazette musicale* (15 April 1877) 118.

[119]Cécile et Emmanuel Cavaillé-Coll, *Aristide Cavaillé-Coll* (Paris: Fischbacher, 1929) 96.

[120]Bonnerot, 86.

Plate 26. Saint-Saëns at the organ

"Monsieur l'Abbé," I replied, "when I hear the dialogue of the Opéra-Comique spoken from the pulpit, I will play appropriate music; but not before."[121]

Another time, after I had played at a wedding the delightful *Saint Francis of Assisi Preaching to the Birds* of Liszt, the officiating priest called me into the sacristy to tell me that "it sounded as if I were tuning the organ and that if I went on that way they would engage another organist."

"I will go whenever it may be desired," was my answer.

But I did not go until I myself desired.[122]

This last story was no doubt the source of the reproach leveled at Cavaillé-Coll who was blamed for "his great folly" in supporting "this village fiddler who makes his organ an intolerable serinette."[123] Saint-Saëns later attributed much of the bad taste which prevailed in French churches "to the fact that the clergy receive no musical education whatever in their seminaries."[124] He felt that the only way that the routine mediocrity could be overcome was by educating the clergy and advocated the introduction in seminaries of courses, not only in music, but in all the branches of the arts.

---

[121]Saint-Saëns, *École Buissonnière*, 176. This was, obviously, Saint-Saëns's most often repeated anecdote. Widor related it:

Vicar: "Monsieur Saint-Saëns, you play very severe music. Don't forget that many of our parisioners are subscribers to the Opéra-Comique."

L'organiste: "When you speak from the pulpit, Monsieur l'Abbé, as they speak on the stage, I will play what is played at the Opéra-Comique."

(Ch.-M. Widor, *Notice sur la Vie et les Oeuvres de M. Camille Saint-Saëns*, Paris: Firmin-Didot, 1922, p. 19).

Frederic B. Stiven (*In the Organ Lofts of Paris*, Boston: Stratford, 1923, p. 24) quotes Saint-Saëns: "When I see one of the ballet dancers from the Opéra-Comique dancing on the steps of the altar, then I shall be glad to play the airs from the opera for you in church, but until then I shall continue to perform what I believe to be suitable music for the worship of God."

Armand Vivet (*L'Orgue et les Organistes*, 15 February 1926, p. 25) writes that Saint-Saëns had replied to one of the notables of the parish: "When the pastor reads a page from *Labiche* from the pulpit, I will play light music for you."

[122]Saint-Saëns, "Music in the Church," 7.

[123]Cavaillé-Coll, 96.

[124]Saint-Saëns, "Music in the Church," 5.

One often complains of what little artistic taste is evidenced by the clergy. How could it be otherwise? Artistic feeling is rarely natural among us; it is ordinarily developed by education. And when a priest, supreme authority in his church, lacks such an education, how could the most disastrous consequences not result?[125]

It has been stated that Saint-Saëns was able to resign from the Madeleine because he had inherited 100,000 francs. He did indeed receive a bequest of such an amount but not until after he had left his post. His friend, Albert Libon, died the 29th of May.[126] His will, written the year before, left the legacy to Saint-Saëns "to free him from the slavery of the organ of the Madeleine and to enable him to devote himself entirely to composition." Saint-Saëns had known of Libon's illness for several weeks but when he went to see him he had been told that Libon had left. "Libon had denied himself the consolation of his friend's visit so that rumors could not be circulated that he had courted him in his last hours."[128] Saint-Saëns read of Libon's death in the newspaper which he picked up upon leaving church after Vespers.

Libon had originally asked that Saint-Saëns write a requiem in his memory to be performed on the anniversary of his death, but in a codicil to his will (19 May 1877) he exempted the composer from this obligation. Nevertheless, Saint-Saëns did not forget his friend nor his desire for a requiem, and a year later, on Wednesday morning, 22 May 1878, at Saint-Sulpice with Widor at the organ, he conducted its premiere. It was repeated the following year on exactly the same date.[129]

At the age of forty-one Saint-Saëns's career as a professional organist was ended, and he would never again play the organ in church on a regular basis. Twenty-five years had been enough.

---

[125]Saint-Saëns, "Musique religieuse," *École Buissonnière*, 6.

[126]Albert Libon had been the Postmaster General of Paris and one of Saint-Saëns's oldest friends. It was to Libon that he dedicated his first piano pieces in 1855—the *Six Bagatelles*, Op. 3—and his second opera, *Le Timbre d'Argent*, which had just been given its first performance at the Théâtre Lyrique on 23 February 1877.

[127]Bonnerot, 87.

[128]Ibid.

[129]Bonnerot, 91.

CHAPTER IV

Saint-Saëns, 1878–1897

The Trocadéro

The Universal Exposition held in Paris in 1878 provided Saint-Saëns with the opportunity to be heard as composer, in a performance of his cantata *Les Noces de Prométhée*, and as organist—the first time he had been heard as recitalist in France since the inauguration of the organ of La Trinité in 1869. Both concerts took place in the Salle des Fêtes of the Palais du Trocadéro.

The Trocadéro was a gigantic pseudo-Byzantine structure built on the right bank of the Seine opposite the Champ-de-Mars, the site upon which the Eiffel Tower was later erected for the 1889 Exposition. The great sloping expanse, known as Chaillot Hill, had been designated as the site for a monument to commemorate the 1823 capture by the French army of a small Spanish fort, the Trocadéro, on the Bay of Cadiz. Although none of the projects ever got beyond the planning stage the area came to be referred to as the Trocadéro. Then in April 1876 a commission was named to study and draw up plans for a building to be used for the Universal Exposition two years hence—a permanent headquarters in which all future events of this nature could take place.

The completion of so large an edifice within a few months was a miracle of modern engineering. In fact, the construction outdistanced the planning. The central building of the palace was an enormous, 5,000-seat

Plate 27. Le Palais du Trocadéro

circular auditorium, the Salle des Fêtes, 197 feet in diameter and 164 feet high.[1] Cavaillé-Coll's original bid of 200,000 francs to build an organ had been rejected.[2] Then, at the last minute, when the organ committee changed its mind, it was too late to build an organ large enough to fill so vast a space in time for the opening of the Exposition. The enterprising builder added a fourth manual and some pedal stops to an organ already set up in his shop and moved it to the stage of the great Festival Hall.

Saint-Saëns's 1868 prize-winning cantata, *Les Noces de Prométhée*, was to be performed at the first concert of the Exposition. The composer attended most of the rehearsals at the Trocadéro and it was upon returning home from one of them, a little before dinner, that he was greeted at the door by his cousin with the news of an appalling tragedy: his son was dead.

[1]Jacques Hillairet, *Colline de Chaillot* (Paris: Editions de Minuit, 1977) 77–80. A description of the hall appeared in *The New York Times* and was reprinted in *Dwight's Journal of Music* (June 1878) 264.

The ensemble of the structure is imposing. On the ground floor, arranged as a parquet—here called orchestra stalls—there are 1,500 seats. In the first row there are 42 boxes, in the form of *baignoires*, with pilasters of black and gold supporting the balcony, which is divided into 50 opera boxes. The appearance of the pilasters is melancholy and funereal, and is not sufficiently relieved by the hangings of dark crimson velvet. Above the balcony is a vast amphitheater for 2,000 persons. Pierced in the wall, like the windows above which they are placed, are nine spacious tribunes. On the right and left of the stage, which is double the size of that of the Grand Opera, are two large proscenium boxes, one intended for the president of the Republic, the other for the minister of agriculture and commerce. The ornamentation of the hall is showy, if you except the black and gold pilasters. On the ceiling is a rose, divided into twelve parts by alternate branches of palm and laurel, with an immense "R.F." in the center. From the cupola extend gilded newels, each ending in a sphinx supported on a bracket, decorated with a scroll bearing the names of Bach, Handel, Haydn, Mozart, Beethoven, Cherubini, Weber, Mendelssohn, Berlioz and Félicien David. At the extreme end of the hall are two triumphal columns surmounted by statues of Fame distributing crowns, with escutcheons entwined in laurel leaves and inscribed with "Honneur aux Sciences! Gloire aux Arts!" These are the work of the sculptor, Carrier Belleuse, as those on the other side of the proscenium boxes are due to the genius of Mr. Blanchard, who has taken for his subject "Law" and "Strength." The frieze above the stage, painted by Charles Lameyre, represents France summoning to her throne all the nations of the earth.

[2]Cavaillé-Coll, 117.

Plate 28. The jury examining scores submitted for the City of Paris' first musical competition, 13 February 1878. Saint-Saëns is playing the piano, César Franck is the seventh figure standing from the left, and Guilmant, who replaced Massenet at the last moment, is the fifth figure from the right.

On Tuesday, 28 May 1878, the elder of his two sons, André aged two and a half, was running around the apartment about three in the afternoon. His mother was in her room getting ready to go out and his grandmother was in the dining room. The maid was doing the wash in a room next to the kitchen and had opened the window to let in some air. The child, hearing the happy shouts of his playmates, ran to look out of the window, leaned out, lost his balance, and fell four stories to the court below.[3]

Six weeks later his seven-month-old son, Jean-François, died of a childhood illness.

Les Noces de Prométhée

Edouard Colonne conducted Saint-Saëns's cantata on 6 June 1878; a correspondent from *The New York Times* described the event:

[At the opening concert] the male choristers occupied the organ tribune and the left of the proscenium; the soprani and contralti were on the right. Black coats were de rigueur for the tenors and basses. . . and the ladies had black gowns with flame-colored ribbons as ornaments. All the instruments were new, the harps were brilliant with fresh gilding and the bass viols shone with a fine red glare.

[The first work was Félicien David's *Le Désert* and after it]. . . came a new cantata by Saint-Saëns. It was for solo, chorus and orchestra, and is an allegorical allusion to the work of civilization where, under the title of the *Nuptials of Prometheus*, this mythological prototype of inventors is delivered from his legendary vultures— Tyranny and Superstition—by Humanity, whom he forthwith espouses.

The score is scientific but not particularly melodious, with, however, some striking passages. The overture begins with a sad, monotonous chant of violins, gradually working itself into a triumphal march and winding up with a marriage hymn. The air of the tenor, Warot, "Aux confins du viel universe," was artistically sung, and Mme. H. M., an amateur, who personified Humanity, received quite an ovation. Melchissédec was applauded as a Titan, and the final chorus, "C'est le jour de gloire de l'humanité," brought down the house. . . Mr. Colonne's 350 instrumentalists kept well together; their execution was perfect.[4]

[3]Bonnerot, 92.
[4]As reprinted in *Dwight's Journal of Music* (June 1878) 264.

Plate 29. La Salle des Fêtes

The Trocadéro Organ Recitals

It was another two months before installation of the organ was completed. Alexandre Guilmant inaugurated it on 7 August, and for two months afterwards, twice a week at three o'clock in the afternoon on Tuesday and Saturdays, fourteen organists were heard in hour-long recitals. César Franck composed his *Trois Pièces (Fantaisie in A, Cantabile* and *Pièce héroïque)* for this series and premiered them on 1 October. Charles-Marie Widor premiered his *Sixth Symphony* on his Trocadéro recital and Saint-Saëns gave the first performance outside of Germany of Liszt's monumental *Fantasy on Ad nos, ad salutarem undam.*

This recital series at the Trocadéro was of great importance in the history of the organ in France, for it was the first time a large concert organ had been installed in a secular hall. No longer would people listen to the solemn tones of the organ only as they rolled beneath Gothic arches in dim light filtering through centuries-old stained glass. Instead, they sat in the great ovoid-shaped room and before them stood the four-manual, sixty-six-stop Cavaillé-Coll organ, its case—with thirty-two-foot towers at either end—dominating the stage.

Admission was free and, as this was the only time the general public could get in to see the celebrated hall without having to pay to attend a concert, the organ recitals drew larger audiences than any other music program at the Trocadéro during the Exposition. Although there was a large turnover in the audience which came and went, a nucleus of music lovers, estimated at between 1,500 and 2,000 persons, who came to hear, not just see, stayed for the entire recital. This was particularly phenomenal, as the organist was hidden from view. Just as in church, the console was reversed so that the organist faced into the auditorium, a wooden screen seen in the very center of the case concealed the player.

Saint-Saëns's Organ Recital at the Trocadéro

Saint-Saëns was the twelfth player to be heard. On Saturday, 28 September, he presented the following program:[5]

Trois Rhapsodies sur des Cantiques Bretons	Saint-Saëns
Prélude du *Déluge*	Saint-Saëns
Prelude and Fugue in E-flat, BWV 552	J.S. Bach
Légende, "La Prédication aux oiseaux de Saint François d'Assise"	Franz Liszt
Grande Fantaisie et Fugue sur le Choral du *Prophète* "Ad nos, ad salutarem undam"	Franz Liszt
Introduction	
Adagio	
Fugue	
Finale	

A large crowd, including all of the illustrious artists of Paris, "the 'elite minority' which reserves itself for great occasions," came for what had become "unfortunately, one of the rare opportunities of hearing the young French master of the organ." At the conclusion of the *Rhapsodies Bretonnes*, "gems of the fine registration and charm of execution,"[6] the audience was warmly enthusiastic and "numerous cries for an encore were heard."[7] The Prelude to *The Deluge* had been added to the original program and "the composer interpreted it very tastefully and skillfully and the organ's various timbres produced a charming effect." Saint-Saëns was given such an ovation that "this time he yielded to the demands of the audience" and played it again.

---

[5]*L'Art Musical* (26 September 1878) 311, listed the Liszt *Légende* between the *3 Rhapsodies Bretonnes* and the Bach *Prelude and Fugue in E-flat*, the *Ad nos Fantaisie* making up the entire second half of the program.

[6]Louis Kelterborn, "A Few Reminiscences of Camille Saint-Saëns," *The Musician* (May 1906) 250.

[7]"Nouvelles Musicales de l'exposition," *Revue et Gazette musicale* (6 October 1878) 321.

He concluded the first half of the recital with "a very beautiful and artistic" performance of Bach's *Prelude and Fugue in E-flat.* One critic observed:

> We only would have wished for fewer heavy manual stops in the *Prelude*— 16-foot tone made the playing a bit confused given the size and acoustics of the hall. Besides, the *organo pleno* in Bach's time was not what it is today and the 16-foot reeds, especially, did not have the intensity of our modern stops on high pressure. On the contrary, the organs were rich in high-pitched stops, mixtures, etc. Above all, clarity of execution is necessary in the *Prelude* which is often written in five parts in a low, rather than high, register.[8]

The second half of the program was devoted to music by Franz Liszt. Saint-Saëns was not only the first to play the *Fantasy on Ad nos* in France, but he was a champion of Liszt's piano music and was the sole French pianist to play any original works of Liszt during his lifetime.[9] The friendship between the two men surpassed their mutual admiration as instrumentalists, and evidenced itself in their devotion to each other's music.[10] Liszt had made his famous transcription of *Danse macabre* in 1876, was responsible for the first performance of *Samson et Dalila* in Weimar in 1877, and had dedicated his second *Mephisto Waltz* to Saint-Saëns in 1881. In 1886 Saint-Saëns dedicated his *Third Symphony* to the Weimar master. He had played both of Liszt's *Légendes (Saint Francis of Assisi Preaching to the Birds* and *Saint Francis of Paola Walking on the Waves)* on the organ. His organ transcription of the first *Légende* was published by Rozsavölgyi & Co. in Budapest (and Leipzig in 1899) and, curiously, the Breitkopf & Härtel edition of Liszt's complete works reprints the first seven pages of Saint-Saëns's organ transcription instead of Liszt's original piano version.

[8]Ibid.

[9]Letter from Franz Servais, Villa d'Este, 20 December 1869 (*Letters of Franz Liszt*, ed. La Mara, tr. Constance Bache, New York: Greenwood Press, 1969) II: 191.

[10]See: Rollin Smith, "Franz Liszt and the Organ," *The American Organist* (July 1986) 67– 73.

Liszt was delighted with the effect of his piece on the organ[11] and wrote Saint-Saëns:

I am still quite struck with wonder at your *Prédication aux oiseaux*. You use your organ as an orchestra in an incredible way, as only a great composer and a great performer like yourself could. The most proficient organists in all countries have only to take off their hats to you.[12]

By his performance of the *Fantasy on Ad nos* Saint-Saëns certainly fulfilled Liszt's description of him as "the most eminent and extraordinary king of organists."[13] The work, composed in 1850, was one he was to play frequently for the rest of his life. Saint-Saëns described it as:

... the most extraordinary organ piece in existence. It lasts forty minutes and the interest does not lag for a moment. Just as Mozart in his *Fantaisie* and *Sonata in C Minor* foresaw the modern piano, so Liszt, writing this *Fantaisie* more than half a century ago, seems to have foreseen today's instrument of a thousand resources.[14]

When Saint-Saëns brought these two works before the general public in 1878 they were still contemporary music, and then, as now, they were criticized as being too pianistic. One reviewer wrote that "It would take nothing less than the great talent of this eminent artist to make us accept these two virtuoso pieces, the second of which, although written for the organ... seemed to rely chiefly on pianistic devices."[15]

But the writer for *Le Ménestrel* concluded that:

It is futile to speak of M. Saint-Saëns playing. It is simply prodigious. As for his registration, it is a reflection of the orchestral palette of the composer of the Symphonic Poems. M. Cavaillé-Coll, who attended the recital, stated with satisfaction that, after numerous hearings of the organ, it was still possible to draw new effects from his superb instrument.[16]

[11]The priests of the Madeleine, however, were not. It was his playing of the *Légende* that caused them to accuse him of making their instrument sound like a "bird organ." (Cavaillé-Coll, 96.)

[12]Letter from Franz Liszt to Saint-Saëns, Weimer, 14 May 1882 (Chateau-Musée de Dieppe).

[13]Letter from Franz Liszt to Mason & Hamlin Co. in Boston, Weimar, 12 June 1883 (*Letters of Franz Liszt*, II: 438).

[14]Saint-Saëns, "L'Orgue," *L'Echo de Paris* (1 January 1911). Reprinted in *École Buissonnière—Notes et Souvenirs* (Paris: Lafitte, 1913) 173.

[15]*Revue et Gazette musicale* (6 October 1878) 321.

[16]E.G., "Concerts et soirées," *Le Ménestrel* (6 October 1878) 363.

There was disappointment only in not hearing Saint-Saëns improvise. After so many illustrious musicians had made the long trip to the Madeleine to hear his improvisations, "for no apparent reason, none found a place on the very meaty program of this recital."[17]

To thank all of those involved in the Trocadéro organ recital series, Cavaillé-Coll gave a banquet in the great hall of his factory. In addition to his numerous personal employees and workmen, he invited Saint-Saëns, Franck, Guilmant, Widor and Gigout, who each during the course of the evening, played one of the organs set up in the hall and spoke briefly.[18]

Election to the Institut

In November, elections were held at the Institut de France to fill the seat left vacant by François Bazin. From the first ballot the contest was between Saint-Saëns and Jules Massenet. On the third ballot Massenet won by an absolute majority—eighteen to thirteen—and, ever the gentlemen, he sent Saint-Saëns a telegram which read: "My dear Colleague: The Institut has just committed a great injustice."[19] Saint-Saëns replied by return mail, "I quite agree!"

Saint-Saëns finally won a seat in the Académie des Beaux-Arts, one of the five academies which compose the Institut de France, on 19 February 1881. Significantly, it was that of Henri Reber, a professor of composition at the Conservatoire to whom he had dedicated *La Lyre et la Harpe* in 1879. He was tied with Léo Delibes on the first ballot, but won twenty-two to nine on the second. Membership in the Académie was a source of great pride to Saint-Saëns and he had engraved on his *carte-de-visite* and on all of his published works:

Camille Saint-Saëns

de l'Institut

He religiously attended the Académie's Thursday afternoon meetings whenever he was in Paris.

---

[17]Ibid.
[18]*Le Ménestrel* (10 November 1878) 404.
[19]Bonnerot, 94.

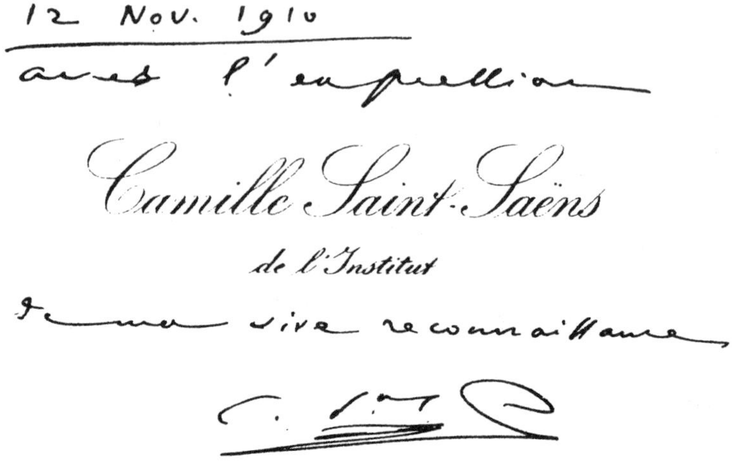

Plate 30. Saint-Saëns's *carte-de-visite*

No longer organist of the Madeleine, Saint-Saëns's concert schedule increased and he had numerous opportunities to be heard on the organ as well as the piano. When he was engaged by the Royal Philharmonic Society of London to play his G-minor Piano Concerto in Saint James's Hall on 2 July 1879, he took advantage of the Gray & Davison organ and played Bach's *Prelude and Fugue in A Minor*, BWV 543.[20] Between 20 and 23 May 1880 he attended the annual festival of the Association of German Musicians held in Baden-Baden. In a church concert he played one of his *Rhapsodies Bretonnes* "on the organ in his inimitable masterly and charming way. In the same concert, also, an organ sonata by Guilmant made a particularly fine impression."[21]

Domestic Problems

In July 1881 Saint-Saëns and his wife, Marie, went to Bourboule for a vacation. On the morning of 28 July he disappeared from the hotel

---

[20]Myles Birket Foster, *History of the Philharmonic Society* (London: 1912) 369. Foster says that the organ "was known amongst organists of the day as 'The Beast.'"
[21]Kelterborn, op.cit., 250

where they were staying, and a few days later Marie received a letter announcing his decision not to return. They never saw one another again and never had a legal separation.[22] In a letter written some fifty years later Mme. Saint-Saëns remembered:

> He left me three years after the deaths of my children and not very kindly, but through some whim that has never been explained. I asked people to look for him throughout the countryside. . . and found that he had taken the train to Paris. For several days, ill and deserted, I was left on my own. Then Henri Duparc (who was staying at my hotel) took me back to Paris. There I fell into the arms of my mother-in-law, thinking to find shelter, but I realized that she was the one who had *caused all the trouble*. I suffered many injustices through the capricious character of my husband, but he had good qualities, too.[23]

That there was some contact between the couple is evident from a remark in a letter written ten years later in which Saint-Saëns compared his wife to his former organblower at the Madeleine: "They are both alike: unemployed and miserable."[24] Marie Saint-Saëns returned to her family and died near Bordeaux at the age of 95 on 30 January 1950.

When the Association of German Musicians met in Zurich in July 1882, Saint-Saëns was again invited. At the cathedral on a gloomy, rainy afternoon, with Franz Liszt in the audience, Saint-Saëns ". . . revealed his supreme powers as an organ virtuoso by a highly impressive and masterly performance of Liszt's *Prophète Fugue.*"[25]

On another occasion, in Basel:

> . . .we had an opportunity to enjoy Saint-Saëns's wonderful powers as an interpreter of his own works or those of classic masters on the piano or organ . . . His technique was extremely brilliant, clear in the finest details, rich in colors, wonderfully refreshing in rhythmic life, elegant and graceful, yet always virile, absolutely free from sentimentality and an excess of rubato, which so many modern virtuosi seem to hold indispensable for an exhibition of "taste or feeling"; and so was his interpretation always that

---

[22]Bonnerot, 93.
[23]Harding, *Saint-Saëns and His Circle*, 156.
[24]Letter from Saint-Saëns to an unknown correspondent, 3 July 1891.
[25]Kelterborn, op. cit.

Plate 31. Saint-Saëns in 1883

of a superior artist who was intimately acquainted with the individual style of every master. Thus his readings of Bach were marvels of lucidity and refinement, combined with strength and grandeur.[26]

The "Organ" Symphony

The origin and progress of the *Symphony in C Minor*, Op. 78, have been reconstructed by Daniel Fallon through correspondence between Saint-Saëns and Francesco Berger, who between 1885 and 1910 was Honorable Secretary of the Royal Philharmonic Society in London.[27]

It was noted in minutes of the Philharmonic Society on 4 July 1885 that "an invitation to compose a new orchestral work for next season be sent to Gounod; if refused, to Delibes or Massenet or Saint-Saëns."[28] Nothing further is recorded, but an entry for 1 August 1885 states that it was "resolved . . . that Saint-Saëns be invited to play a concerto at one of the concerts, either his own or not, as he prefers." Berger sent the invitation in a letter on 3 August 1885 and offered five dates between March and June 1886. Saint-Saëns chose 19 May and suggested two possible programs: his *Fourth Concerto* and *Rhapsodie d'Auvergne*, or Beethoven's *Fourth Concerto* and his own *Septet*, for trumpet and strings. He would play a number of piano solos at either program, asked for a fee of forty pounds and closed by saying that he would be pleased if the Society would include a symphony of his on one of its programs.

Berger replied by saying that the Society was "an Art institution" and not involved in "private speculation with the object of making money. All the great artists who have appeared at these concerts have been generous in their arrangements and you may, upon reflection, be willing to imitate their example and accept "a somewhat smaller honorarium, say of thirty pounds." Saint-Saëns, "not wanting to appear uncompromising," accepted the thirty pounds.

The fee established, Berger next asked if he would "be able to compose some symphonic work expressly for next season instead of recommending one that is not new?" Saint-Saëns replied that "Without making a formal commitment I can promise you that I will make every effort to

---

[26]Ibid.

[27]Daniel Fallon, *The Symphonies and Symphonic Poems of Camille Saint-Saëns*, Vol. 2, Appendix II, 449–459.

[28]Ibid., 361.

123

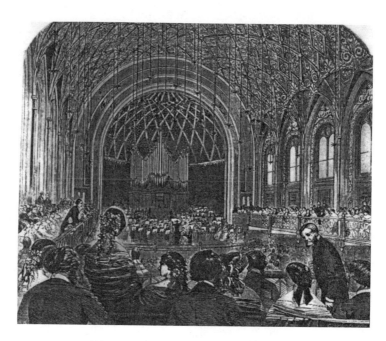

Plate 32. St. James's Hall, Piccadilly

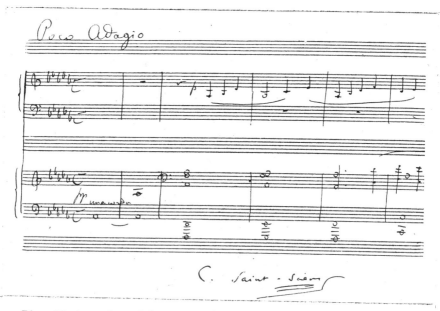

Plate 33. A portion of the manuscript of the Adagio of Saint-Saëns's *Third Symphony*

respond to your wish and to write a new symphony for the sake of the Philharmonic Society."

Saint-Saëns worked on the symphony throughout the winter and completed it at the end of April 1886. The inclusion of an organ part is due, no doubt, to the availability of the 1858 Gray & Davison organ in Saint James's Hall, Piccadilly—the home of the Royal Philharmonic Society. Saint-Saëns was familiar with the instrument as he had played it in concert in 1879. Its specification is known to us only through a Gray & Davison shop-book preserved in the English Organ Archive.[29]

Although a Swell division is penciled in, the instrument was probably a very large one-manual and pedal organ: nineteen stops on the Great and four in the Pedal. As is obvious from the engraving of the hall, the organ was ideally placed on the stage and spoke unimpeded into the room. It must have been a great surprise to Saint-Saëns when he arrived at Saint James's Hall[30] in May 1886 to conduct his new "Organ" Symphony to discover that the fine Gray & Davison organ had been removed in 1882 and replaced with an instrument built by Bryceson Brothers & Ellis. This new organ, with fewer stops spread over its two manuals (each of which was enclosed) than had previously been available on one, boasted a three-rank mixture on the Great and an 8' Horn in place of 16', 8' and 4' chorus reeds. How disappointingly ineffective the great organ chords in the last movement must have sounded to the composer as he conducted the premiere of his new symphony on 19 May.[31]

[29]See page 269, Appendix E, for the specification. This information, together with details of the instrument, was furnished by Dr. Michael Sayer, Honorary Archivist of the English Organ Archive. The particulars of the Bryceson Bros. & Ellis instrument in Saint James's Hall were provided by the Rev. B. B. Edmonds of Suffolk. We are indebted to Mr. Austin Niland who recommended these two scholars to us and to Mr. Niland himself, who lent invaluable assistance in researching these two organs.

[30]Saint-Saëns had last been in Saint James's Hall in June 1880 for a benefit concert (Bonnerot, 103).

[31]According to Alexandre Cellier, Saint-Saëns specifically told him that organists should observe exactly what he had written in the score at the entrance of the organ in the Adagio. The Pedal does not enter until the third measure. Cellier felt that "In omitting this indication, the extraordinary mysterious effect of the entrance of the very melodious 8 foot stops is destroyed. It would be a mistake, as well, to bring in the 32 foot from the beginning; indeed, the 16 foot Soubasse suffices. As Saint-Saëns indicated it, the roundness of the 32 foot only imposes itself at the re-entry of the theme played by the full orchestra (rehearsal letter V) and, although the composer did not notate it clearly, I think that the Voix céleste should not be left on until the end. It is preferable to return to the delicate color of the beginning with the 8 foot manual Bourdons accompanied by the 32 foot. (Fritz Morel, "Camille Saint-Saëns, organiste," L'Orgue 160/161 (October–December 1977) 111.

The *Symphony in C Minor*, Op. 78, was well received in London and also in Paris where Jules Garcin conducted it for the first time on 9 January 1887. With this work Saint-Saëns climaxed his artistic and creative life. "I have given all that I had to give. . . What I have done I shall never do again."

Saint-Saëns had been active in the Société since its inception, playing in its concerts and assuming a participatory role in policy-making. A younger generation was beginning to be heard, and that generation appeared, particularly to Saint-Saëns, to be led by César Franck and his loyal disciple, Vincent d'Indy, who since 1876 had performed, with Henri Duparc, the joint duties of secretary of the organization. In this capacity d'Indy not only recorded the proceedings of meetings and kept the Société's records in order, but he began a movement within the organization to lift its ban on foreign (particularly German) music. The two sought "to raise the standard of their nation's Art" by putting on a series of concerts in which French works could be heard with and compared to modern works of other national schools.[32]

The proposal elicited a cool response from Saint-Saëns. And when the plan broadened to include excerpts from Richard Wagner's operas, little heard in Paris and, according to Duparc, "the mainspring of the enterprise," Saint-Saëns's brow would darken and, pushed to the limit by the insistence of the two young men, he would cry, "But the day Wagner is played in Paris, what will become of us?"[33]

> The anecdote is believable. Saint-Saëns was jealous of the overbearing power of the great German master. He had a vested interest: the legitimate concern for the future of his own works. . . Vincent d'Indy, a passionate disciple of Franck, carried away by youthful enthusiasm and placed above material concern by his financial security, was incapable of the slightest compromise. He was an absolute artist! With neither hesitation nor regret, he ostracized from his musical world an eminent composer whose talent he had always admired but whose taste and character he could no longer respect.[34]

[32]Léon Vallas, *Vincent d'Indy* (Paris: Michel, 1950) I: 240.
[33]Ibid.
[34]Ibid., 240–41.

In November 1886 d'Indy introduced and was successful in getting passed a resolution which allowed the introduction "on the programs of the Société Nationale works of real interest and still unknown in France, as well as important selections from the masterpieces of Bach, Rameau, Gluck, etc., restored to their original editions." The adoption of this resolution, contrary to the purpose of the Société's founders, had the precise effect desired by d'Indy: Saint-Saëns and Romain Bussine resigned. Years later Saint-Saëns responded (in what Léon Vallas described as "grossly exaggerated terms") to a published lecture of Vincent d'Indy in which he described how Franck "gradually became the moving spirit of the new Société Nationale and then took the leading part in the movement."[35]

> César Franck, whose works were then mostly unheard, seized the propitious moment to emerge from the shadows of obscurity and hurry off to the proper office to become a naturalized Frenchman in order that he might be eligible to join the Société. He was welcomed therein with open arms, and I myself, as President of the Société, often gave him my help and cooperation in getting his works performed.
>
> No long time passed before I began to be aware of the underground work going on with a view to sapping my influence and substituting for it that of Franck and his pupils. By a continued series of petty annoyances they succeeded in causing the resignation of their most troublesome opponents, like Bizet and Massenet. At committee meetings César and his pupils formed an exclusive circle of their own, plotting in low voices in dark corners. In short, the situation became such that I, in my turn, handed in my resignation. From that moment on the Césarean and Wagnerian party had imperial power and the Société became what it is now: a closed shop whose value and aims I know nothing of and which is entirely out of touch with the intentions of the founders.[36]

Saint-Saëns and César Franck

From our distant perspective it is apparent that the animosity between Franck and Saint-Saëns was generated by Franck's circle of pupils.

[35]Vincent d'Indy in *La Renaissance* (12 June 1915).
[36]Saint-Saëns in *La Renaissance* (4 September 1915). Quoted in Vallas, *César Franck*, 193.

All through the early years of the Société Nationale (before d'Indy's influence began to be felt) we find Saint-Saëns frequently playing Franck's works. He was quite aware that he "was one of the first to give them a hearing, at my own risk and at a time when the public still disregarded them."[37] At the first concert of the Société Nationale in 1871 he had played Franck's B-flat Trio. He played the *Third Trio* in 1872 and the *First Trio* in 1873, 1874, 1877 and 1878.[38] On 17 January 1880 he played the piano part in the first performance of Franck's *Quintet* at a Société Nationale concert and much has been read into Saint-Saëns's having "walked off the platform at the conclusion of the work and left standing on the piano the manuscript which Franck had adorned with a dedication to Saint-Saëns himself."[39] It was never the custom for a performer to carry the music back and forth with him as he acknowledged the audience's applause and what later became a valued manuscript was then just the score of another new and unpublished piece. The two colleagues' most bizarre collaboration was surely at one of the Concerts Danbé when Bourgault-Ducoudray conducted the choir and orchestra in a performance of Handel's *Alexander's Feast*. "M. Saint-Saëns and César Franck vigorously sustained the voices with the piano and organ."[40] Saint-Saëns was even one of the pallbearers at Franck's funeral[41]—further evidence that his

---

[37]Saint-Saëns, *Les idées de Vincent d'Indy* (Paris: Lafitte, 1918).

[38]Vallas, *Franck*, 153.

[39]Ibid., 167.

[40]*La Chronique musicale* (April–June 1874) 33.

[41]An interesting letter from Eugène Gigout (who played the organ at Franck's funeral at Sainte-Clotilde) to Saint-Saëns is to be found in the Saint-Saëns archives in Dieppe. In it he asks his former teacher's help in having him appointed Franck's successor at the Paris Conservatoire:

Paris, 9 November 1890

Mon cher Maître et ami,

Do you think that I might be of service as head of the organ class at the Conservatoire?

The succession to César Franck is a heavy burden.

In any case, I would be obliged for whatever is within your power to do for me in this circumstance and for your advice regarding this matter.

I think I will be supported readily enough on the side of the Beaux-Arts which subsidizes my organ school.

But M. Ambroise Thomas, although very friendly towards me, hardly knows me as teacher and as musician.

You alone can be, towards him, the deus ex machina.

Engène Gigout

quarrel was not with Franck himself but, rather, with his disciples and proselytizers.

In later years Saint-Saëns was reserved in his opinion of Franck's music. For instance, in 1904 he told an interviewer that he felt Franck to be a "little over-rated today,"[42] and he wrote the young Francis Poulenc in 1917 that he did not agree with those who would make Franck's great talent a genius but that his opinion was unimportant because the verdict "is up to posterity. It is she who, in the last resort, will judge and award the gold or silver palm which is due him."[43]

The Saint-Saëns Archives

Saint-Saëns's mother, with whom he had lived all his life, died at the age of 79 in December 1888. He spent most of the next year away from Paris, and in September 1889 moved out of his apartment in the rue Monsieur-le-Prince. A distant cousin, Léon Letellier, was librarian in Dieppe and through him Saint-Saëns deposited his papers and furniture with the city of Dieppe. Letellier opened a small museum on 18 June 1890 and from then until his death

> Saint-Saëns regularly sent to his own museum a large number of new items: paintings, engravings, portraits, photos, sketches of his works, autograph manuscripts and *all* the letters he had received.[44]

In 1923 the municipal museum was transferred to a 15th-century castle built on a cliff overlooking the English Channel. This Chateau-Musée now houses the largest single collection of Saint-Saënsiana, which includes about 20,000 letters addressed to Saint-Saëns.

The Final Period

The final period of Saint-Saëns's life—the last thirty years—really began on 23 November 1891 with the premiere of *Samson et Dalila* at the Paris Opéra. Although composed long before and premiered at Weimar in 1877, it had been slow in winning a hearing in Paris and, indeed, was first heard only the year before at the Théâtre Lyrique. Saint-Saëns was now in his mid-fifties and from this period on he was regarded

[42]*Le Courrier Musical* (1 December 1904) 644.

[43]Francis Poulenc, *Emmanuel Chabrier* (Paris: La Palatine, 1961) 113.

[44]Yves Gérard, *Saint-Saëns and the Problems of 19th-Century French Music Seen Through the Saint-Saëns Archives* (Paris: unpublished pamphlet, December 1969).

Plate 34. Saint-Saëns in 1890

as an institution: the celebrated French musician; famous composer of piano concerti, symphonies, symphonic poems, songs and operas, as well as the renowned Organ Symphony; distinguished pianist and organist. Each season, musical organizations throughout the world arranged Saint-Saëns programs for which he was engaged to appear as composer who conducted his own works, played the piano and, if available, the organ.

Doctor of Music, Cambridge

In June 1893 Saint-Saëns, Tchaikovsky, and Boito journeyed to Cambridge, England, to receive honorary degrees from the University. Saint-Saëns vividly describes the proceedings before the investiture. The ceremony began

> ... by our dressing up in full silk gowns with ample sleeves, half-red and half-white, and putting on our heads mortarboards of sable bullion velvet with golden tassels. So appareled we walked in procession through the town beneath a burning sun. At the head of the group of Doctors marched the King of Bhaunagar,[45] a golden turban sparkling with fabulous jewels on his head and a necklace of diamonds round his neck. Dare I confess that, as an enemy of the drab and commonplace nature of modern clothes, I was delighted with this little adventure.[46]

After the ceremonies Saint-Saëns went into Trinity College Chapel to try out the organ. "It is an excellent instrument and easy to handle—fortunately so, in view of the large numbers who had gathered there."[47]

Charles Gounod's Funeral

Charles Gounod died on 18 October 1893. His widow arranged the music for the funeral with Gabriel Fauré, maître-de-chapelle of the Madeleine. Fauré sent Saint-Saëns the following letter:

[45]Sir Frederick Bridge, then organist of Westminster Abbey, who was in attendance, wrote in his *Westminster Pilgrim* (London: Novello, 1918, p. 306):

> I must confess to being unable to trace this potentate, nor do I remember having seen him at the ceremony. He is probably a figment of the versatile Doctor's imagination.

[46]In reality, *The Daily Graphic* (Wednesday, 14 June 1893, p. 8) distinctly mentions "the Maharajah of Bhaunager" as among those receiving honorary degrees.

[47]Saint-Saëns, *Portraits et Souvenirs*, 133.

Plate 35. Saint-Séverin, the organ

21 October 1893

Mon cher Camille:

Mme. Gounod asked me to ask you to play the organ for Gounod's funeral at the Madeleine next Thursday at noon. She understood that it was impossible to exclude Dubois and she hopes that one of you could play the Entrée and the other the Sortie.

She also asks that you both take themes for improvisation only from *Mors et Vita* or *Rédemption*. Perhaps inadvertently, she didn't mention *Gallia*.

She pointed out especially and asked particularly for you to use the theme in the third part of *Rédemption*.[48]

Saint-Saëns at Saint-Séverin

Saint-Saëns's renewed interest in the organ was due in large measure to Albert Périlhou. His former piano student from the École Niedermeyer had been appointed organist of Saint-Séverin in January 1891. The original 14th-century organ had been rebuilt by Thierry (1673), Claude Ferrand (1745), Pierre Dallery (1807), and completely rebuilt by John Abbey and inaugurated on 3 December 1890.[49] Abbey had retained some of the old stops: the Positif Cromorne, Récit Hautbois and some mutations. The combination of Saint-Saëns's delight in the organ and his affection for Périlhou brought him to the tribune of Saint-Séverin for the eleven o'clock mass every Sunday he was in Paris, "dazzling his hearers with the magic of his magnificent improvisations."[50] He usually arrived at Saint-Séverin near the end of the high mass and

---

[48]*Saint-Saëns et Fauré, Correspondence*, 54.

Théodore Dubois, the organiste titulaire of the Madeleine, could not have been more hospitable. He wrote on either 19 or 20 October 1893:

Mon cher Saint-Saëns:

I understand that the obsequies of our dear Gounod will take place at the Madeleine Thursday.

I came to see you and to put my organ at your disposal in the event that you would want to pay this last artistic homage to your dear and illustrious friend and colleague.

[49]*Le Monde musical, Spécial numéro*, 1890.
[50]Félix Raugel, *Les Grandes Orgues de Paris*, 103.

133

... would seat himself at the end of the tribune against the iron guard rail and wait attentively until Périlhou finished the mass. He always seemed to be quite cold because he wrapped a wide scarlet silk scarf around his head—an eccentricity which did not go without arousing the curiosity and ready indignation of those faithful who saw it. Every time he arrived during the high mass he sat in that place and the ritual scarf appeared from his overcoat pocket. But at the eleven o'clock mass this extravagant and even scandalous coiffure disappeared the very moment the maître's female admirers came up to the tribune.[51]

Gabriel Fauré, the maître-de-chapelle at the Madeleine, often joined Périlhou and Saint-Saëns for what became the prelude to their traditional Sunday afternoon luncheon. The three would take turns improvising.

The tribune rarely received visitors, but one Sunday during an improvisation the attention of the three friends was drawn to the strange appearance of a person standing on the top step of the stairway, not daring to come forward, who was surprised by the new and unexpected sight of an organist sitting at the console manipulating the keyboards, pedals and stops.

Noting the visitor's astonishment piqued Périlhou's ever-ready sense of humor and, calling Fauré over to sit beside him, Périlhou asked him to take over the improvisation without interruption. Leaving his friend to continue, he left the console and stood away from the organ.

As the spectator's surprise increased, Fauré asked Saint-Saëns to substitute for him under the same conditions and so, without interruption, the three artists took turns on the organ bench, one only leaving when the hands of the other had taken over the chord.

I don't know how long this exercise lasted but the visitor left the tribune certainly convinced that that instrument required a very complicated contest![52]

---

[51]J. Ermand Bonnal, "Saint-Saëns at Saint-Séverin," *Bulletin Trimestriel des Amis de l'Orgue*, 24 (December 1935) 7.

[52]F. Lauth, "Une anecdote sur A. Périlhou (1895)" *Bulletin Trimestriel des Amis de l'Orgue*, 29 (March 1937) 17–18.

Saint-Saëns delighted in communal improvisations. When he was still at the Madeleine, Julius Schulhoff, the Czech pianist and composer whose concerts were patronized by Chopin, came to improvise on the organ. "He began extemporizing and Saint-Saëns, standing behind him, accompanied him in the bass. Then, sitting down, Saint-Saëns began to improvise on Schulhoff's improvisation." (Bonnerot, 37).

Louis Vierne

When Périlhou needed an assistant, Widor recommended his young student, Louis Vierne. They became good friends and in 1892 he introduced Vierne to Saint-Saëns. Vierne recalled that although Saint-Saëns was

> . . . sometimes a difficult personality, he nevertheless was always extremely kind and tolerant towards me. He had known and liked my Uncle Colin—his mother and my aunt had been close acquaintances and had seen each other often.
>
> He enjoyed having me improvise the Sortie at the end of mass and laughed until he cried at my dreadful harmonic mistakes: "Very good! You don't expect it but it is very musical, youthful and earnest and the counterpoint does not get lost. You will go far, young man, when you are a little older and, through experience, will have lost some useless things. In the meantime, sow your wild oats; I see nothing wrong with that. What is important will show itself."
>
> When Périlhou spoke to him about my becoming a composer, "Does he feel like becoming a martyr?" he responded. "If yes, he shouldn't be embarrassed about it—he certainly has something to say."[53]

Two years later Saint-Saëns distributed the diplomas at the Paris Conservatoire and, as he handed Vierne his first prize in organ, said, "Great organist! Excellent musician!"[54]

Saint-Saëns at Carnot's Funeral

When the president of France, Sadi Carnot, was assassinated in June 1894, Saint-Saëns was delegated to play the organ at Notre-Dame for the state funeral. The organ was being overhauled and Saint-Saëns asked Widor to send two students to pull stops for him. Vierne was one of them.

> There were still sixteen reed stops missing; the rest was in place and newly tuned. Being used to managing the pneumatic combinations at Saint-Sulpice I was entrusted with the ones at Notre-Dame, which were identical but placed on the bottom row of stops. Cavaillé-Coll had sent me the list

[53]Louis Vierne, *Journal* (Paris: Les Amis de l'Orgue, 1970) 167.
[54]Ibid., 172.

of stops that were in so that Saint-Saëns was able to play with ease, confident that when he wanted certain colors they would be ready for him. I must not get sidetracked here on my memories of Saint-Saëns as an improviser. At Notre-Dame he was magnificent. He pointed out the pure timbre of the foundation stops, the clarity and bite of the mixtures, the nobility and smoothness of the few reeds that were in order. He deplored the fact that the organ was heard largely under conditions most unfavorable to bringing out its true worth, and he added to that regret some rather harsh comments on the poor incumbent who, after all, was really a good man, although very jealous of his organ loft, which he did not willingly open to his colleagues.[55]

Later Concerts

Saint-Saëns spent most of his life in the concert hall. If he was not playing or conducting a musical performance, he was attending one. His calendar for June 1896 was typical of his busy schedule. On the second of that month he played a concert at Salle Pleyel to commemorate the 50th anniversary of his first concert—6 May 1846.

On 11 June he attended a concert at the Trocadéro in which he heard Louis Vierne as organ soloist in the premiere of Widor's *Third Symphony* for organ and orchestra. Widor then played the organ for the Trio from the *Oratorio de Noël*, and Harold Bauer was piano soloist in Saint-Saëns's *Concerto in G Minor*.

The next evening, Friday, 12 June, Eugène Gigout hosted a soirée at his studio for a number of Saint-Saëns's friends. A concert of the maître's works, played by Gigout's students, preceded the reunion:

Fantaisie in E-flat	J. Rousse
Communion	P. Levatoise
Trois Rhapsodies	Mlle. G. Ziégler
Fantaisie, Op. 101	J. Deneau
Bénédiction nuptiale	P. Verdeau
Final Chorus from *L'Oratorio de Noël*	A. Kunc
Trois Préludes et Fugues	Mlle. Germaine Moutier

[55]Louis Vierne, *Mes Souvenirs* (Paris: Les Amis de l'Orgue, 1970) 84.

Albert Geloso played the *Sonate*, Op. 75, for violin and piano, three singers sang *Rêverie*, *Sérénité* and the first performance of a duet, *Vénue*, with words also by Saint-Saëns. Then, for a finale, they sang the Trio from the *Oratorio de Noël* accompanied by Gigout at the organ and Saint-Saëns at the piano.[56]

Saint-Saëns followed with keen interest the events and political intrigues at the Paris Conservatoire, even more so after Gabriel Fauré became connected with it. In 1896, upon succeeding Ambroise Thomas as director of the Conservatoire, Dubois resigned both his composition class at the Conservatoire and his post as organist of the Madeleine. Fauré succeeded to the latter. Jules Massenet, who had coveted the directorship, resigned his composition class. Two vacancies were thus created. Widor, then professor of organ, expected to take over Dubois's composition class. Fauré hoped for the other composition class, but Saint-Saëns advised: "In your position, I would let Widor succeed Massenet and I would take the organ class. It hurt neither Widor nor César Franck."[57]

Fauré responded that the three composition classes had been combined into two, that Widor was sure to be named to one of them, and that Guilmant would get the organ class. "I will never undertake teaching students who don't even know harmony how to improvise fugues."[58] When the faculty appointments were finally settled, Fauré took over Massenet's composition class.

Organ Tour of Switzerland

As if to announce his reawakened passion for the organ, Saint-Saëns toured Switzerland between 23 September and 3 October 1896. With Mlle. Baldo, a noted singer, he appeared in churches and cathedrals in Winterthur, Zurich, Berne, La-Chaux-de-Fonds, Neuveville, Vévey, Neuchatel, Lucerne and Geneva. For the most part the programs were composed of Saint-Saëns's works:[59]

---

[56]*Le Monde musical* (30 July 1896) 72.

[57]Letter from Saint-Saëns to Gabriel Fauré, 4 (or 11) August 1896. In *Correspondance*, 57–58.

[58]Ibid. Letter from Gabriel Fauré to Saint-Saëns, 24 August 1896.

[59]"Concerts: Camille Saint-Saëns en Suisse," *Le Monde musical* (30 October 1896) 209.

Plate 36. Saint-Saëns at the organ of Saint-Séverin

Prélude et Fugue in E
Bénédiction nuptiale
Fantaisie, Op. 101
Rhapsodie Breton
Berceuse, Op. 105
Prélude et Fugue in E-flat

and Liszt's *Grande Fantaisie et Fugue sur le choral du Prophète*. He accompanied Mlle. Baldo in:

Deus Abraham	Saint-Saëns
Panis angelicus	Franck
Jésus de Nazareth	Gounod

Brussels Exposition

Saint-Saëns attended the Brussels Exposition in October 1897. On the 13th he gave an organ recital in the Grande Salle des Fêtes, and the next day a Saint-Saëns festival was held in which he conducted his *Third Symphony* and played the organ in *Le Lyre et la Harpe*.[60]

Saint-Vast-d'Armentièrs Organist Competition

Although he did not teach, except for a few private pupils (Reynaldo Hahn and Isadore Philipp studied piano with him), Saint-Saëns served on the juries at the Conservatoire, judged various compositions and, with Gigout, presided over a jury to choose an organist and maître-de-chapelle for the church of Saint-Vast-d'Armentièrs. The competition was held at Saint-Vincent-de-Paul in Paris, Tuesday, 19 October 1897, and the candidate was required to play Bach's *Fugue in G Minor*, BWV 578, a well-developed improvisation on a subject given by Saint-Saëns, to accompany a piece of plainchant, and to play an organ work of his own choice.[61]

[60]*Le Ménestrel* (17 October 1897) 333.
[61]*Le Ménestrel* (3 October 1897) 319.

Honorary Organist of Saint-Séverin

In appreciation of his voluntary services for so many years the parish council of Saint-Séverin, at the request of Albert Périlhou, made Saint-Saëns "Honorary Organist" of the church. He received the following citation from the pastor:[62]

Monsieur Camille Saint-Saëns à Paris:

I am happy to have the honor of informing you of the decision just reached by the Conseil de Fabrique of the Church of Saint-Séverin.

The Conseil, in recognition of the generosity with which you have continuously favored our Parishioners with your splendid talent, is pleased to bestow on you the title of

Honorary Organist of Saint-Séverin.

Plays Before Queen Marie-Christine of Spain

Later in November Saint-Saëns went to Madrid to play before the Spanish royal family.

After Queen Christine had heard me play the piano, she expressed a desire to hear me play the organ. An excellent instrument of Cavaillé-Coll was chosen [in the Church of San Francisco]. The day was fixed for this ceremony, which, naturally, was to have been of a private nature, when some great ladies lectured the indiscreet queen for daring to go to a sacred place for any purpose other than to take part in a divine service. The queen was displeased by this remonstrance and she responded by coming to the church, no longer incognito but in great state, with the king (then very young), her ministers and court, while cavalrymen stationed at intervals along the way played fanfares.

I had written a religious march especially for the event and the queen kindly accepted its dedication. I was a little flustered when she asked me to play the too-familiar melody from *Samson et Dalila* which begins "Mon coeur s'ouvre à ta voix." I had to improvise a transcription suited to the organ—something I had never dreamed of doing.

[62]Letter from the pastor of the church of Saint-Séverin to Saint-Saëns, Paris, 8 November 1897. In the Saint-Saëns Archives, Chateau-Musée de Dieppe.

During the performance the queen leaned her elbow on the organ, her chin resting on one hand and her eyes upturned. She seemed rapt in ecstasy which, as may be imagined, was not precisely displeasing to the author.[63]

The march to which Saint-Saëns refers is his *Marche religieuse*, Op. 107, which was published by Durand the following year and was dedicated to Queen Marie-Christine.

[63]Saint-Saëns, *École Buissonnière*, 16–17.

Plate 37. The dedicatees of the *Trois Préludes et Fugues*, Op. 99 (left to right): Charles-Marie Widor, Alexandre Guilmant, and Eugène Gigout. The Paris Conservatoire's 1903 organ jury is gathered in Widor's apartment in the rue des Saint-Pères, December 1903.

CHAPTER V

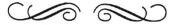

Later Organ Works

During the 1880s, Saint-Saëns recovered from his discouragement with the organ world and his disappointments as organist of the Madeleine through his activities at Saint-Séverin. From the 1890s until the end of his life, even if not preoccupied with the organ, he maintained a constant interest in it.

In the summer of 1894 he composed his first works for solo organ since completing the *Rhapsodies Bretonnes* in 1866. *Trois Préludes et Fugues*, Op. 99, were dedicated in chronological order (though he could not have known of Gigout's eventual appointment) to César Franck's successors as professors of organ at the Paris Conservatoire: Charles-Marie Widor, Alexandre Guilmant and Eugène Gigout.

In 1895 Saint-Saëns composed his *Fantaisie*, in D-flat, Op. 101, and dedicated it to Queen Elisabeth of Rumania, better known under her literary nom de plume, Carmen Sylva.

The second set of *Trois Préludes et Fugues*, Op. 109, was completed in February 1898 at Las Palmas. These were dedicated to Gabriel Fauré, organist of the Madeleine; Albert Périlhou, organist of Saint-Séverin; and Henri Dallier, since 1879 organist of Saint-Eustache, who was to succeed Fauré at the Madeleine in 1905. When Fauré received the just-published volume, he wrote to his former teacher and friend:

Upon my return from London I found the superb *Préludes et Fugues* for organ which I will never be able to play properly, and I had the great joy of seeing my name at the head of one of them. I thank you a thousand times for this pleasant and flattering surprise.[1]

Barcarolle, Op. 108, a chamber work for violin, cello, harmonium and piano, was composed on 7 March 1898, and Saint-Saëns received 800 francs from Durand upon its publication in May. The work was premiered at a concert by La Trompette, a chamber ensemble, on 18 May 1898, with the composer playing the harmonium. Another *Barcarolle*, scored for the same combination of instruments—except that the organ replaced the harmonium—had been written one year before, but was never published.[2]

Transcriptions

Not only was Saint-Saëns engaged in composing new organ works, but throughout the 1890s he enthusiastically arranged and re-arranged many of his works for other instruments and combinations of instruments. In 1891 he made an orchestral arrangement of themes from the first and third *Rhapsodies* of Op. 7. It was published in 1892 as *Rapsodie (sic) Bretonne* in F, Op. 7bis.

In 1898 he transcribed for two pianos four of his *Six Duos*, Op. 8, originally written for harmonium and piano. He included the *Fantaisie et Fugue, Choral, Scherzo,* and *Final*, omitting the *Cavatina* and *Capriccio*. The incentive for these arrangements was Pleyel's new Piano-Double, a

---

[1]Letter from Gabriel Fauré to Saint-Saëns, in *Correspondance*, 60. Saint-Saëns was so honored in turn. The following organ works were dedicated to him:

César Franck: "Prélude, Fugue et Variation, Op. 18 (c. 1862)

Alexis Chauvet: *4 Offertoires (1867) expanded to 9 Offertoires de caractères gradués destiné au Temps de l'Avent et au Temps de Noël*, pour orgue ou harmonium (1869)

Alexandre Guilmant: *Scherzo Capriccioso*, Op. 36, for harmonium and piano duo (c. 1872)

Jules Grison: *Deux Offertoires pour la Fête de Paques*, Op. 30

Eugène Gigout: *Andante symphonique* (No. 5 of *Six Pièces*, c. 1880)

George Mac-Master: *Prélude*, Op. 42 (1891)

Otto Barblan: *Cinq Pièces*, Op. 5 (1893)

Samuel Rousseau: *Echo* (No. 3 of *Quinze Pièces*).

[2]It was composed April 1897. Bibliothèque Nationale Ms. 895.

double grand piano with a keyboard at each end. It was the latest but short-lived invention of Gustave Lyon and it was to him that the *Duos pour Deux Pianos*, Op. 8ᵇⁱˢ, were dedicated.

Saint-Saëns left to Alexandre Guilmant the task of arranging his music for the organ. Guilmant, in an article written while on a concert tour of the United States in 1898, defended his arrangements:

> It is true that I myself have arranged several works for the organ; but in each instance the composition had been previously played by the composer. Among these may be mentioned *Marche héroïque*, Prelude to *Le Déluge* (by Saint-Saëns). The *Berceuse*... was done at the special request of the composer. At the same time, M. Durand requested that I transcribe the finale from M. Saint-Saëns's *Suite Algérienne*. This I refused to do because the piece is not in the organ style.[3]

In all, Guilmant arranged seven pieces:

1883	Prélude du *Déluge*
1893	Marche héroïque, Op. 34
1893	Hymne à Victor Hugo, Op. 69
1896	Le Cygne
1897	Berceuse, Op. 105
1900	Rêverie du Soir (*Suite Algérienne*, Op. 60)
1907	Marche d'Hyménée (*Noces de Prométhée*)

Other noted organists transcribed excepts from his works: Gigout made an elaborate arrangement of the final chorus, "Tollite Hostias," of the *Oratorio de Noël*, Léon Boëllmann, the "Marche du Synode" from *Henry VIII*; and Henri Busser, the Andante from the *Cello Sonata*, Op. 32, and the Prelude to the second act of *Proserpine*.

As we have seen, Saint-Saëns did play transcriptions, but they were always arrangements of pieces which were successful on the organ. How could the composer of *The Nightingale and the Rose* have resisted the temptation to play Liszt's *Saint Francis of Assisi Preaching to the Birds*? Surely Liszt's great tempest portrayed in *Saint Francis of Paola Walking on the Waves* was a better storm than those improvised by the organists of Paris.

---

[3] Alexandre Guilmant, "Organ Music and Organplaying," *The Forum* (March 1898) 88.

Plate 38. Saint-Saëns in 1902

The only organ transcription of one of his works that Saint-Saëns published was the "O Salutaris" from his *Messe*, Op. 4. This he did in 1904, dedicated to Gaston Choisnel, and played for the first time at a benefit concert for the Association of Artists and Musicians at Salle Pleyel on 19 November 1904. The program, in which Saint-Saëns appeared as pianist, organist, and composer, was as follows:

Fantaisie pour piano, orgue et orchestre   Albert Périlhou
         Saint-Saëns, piano   Périlhou, organ

Sarabande (orchestrated by Saint-Saëns)   J. S. Bach
            Alfred Brun, violin

Two organ solos
            Saint-Saëns, organ

Third Symphony, Op. 78   Saint-Saëns
            Saint-Saëns, organ

Arthur Pougin wrote that the second of the two organ solos, the "O Salutaris," "was absolutely delightful and so enchanted the audience and so enthusiastic was the applause, that he should have repeated it."[4] The concert was the occasion for the inauguration of the new two-manual, eleven-rank Abbey organ. Jean Huré found "its sound charming and varied. In particular, I think I heard a very fine little Bourdon and an Hautbois whose tone was quite distinguished. The basses seemed a bit weak."[5]

[4]"Revue des Grands Concerts," *Le Ménestrel* (27 November 1904) 381.
The new Grande Salle Pleyel was opened in October 1931 and it was this organ, installed in the ceiling over the back of the stage and speaking downward through a grill that Alexandre Cellier described (in Cellier et Bachelin, *L'Orgue*, 195) as one of those *orgues invisibles*, with no facade and whose pipes are relegated to the attic."
[5]Jean Huré, "Inauguration d'un orgue à La Salle Pleyel," *Le Monde musical* (30 November 1904) 314, 319.

Coronation March for Edward VII

Sir Frederick Bridge, organist of Westminster Abbey, in charge of arranging the music for the coronation of Edward VII in 1902, recounted the circumstances under which Saint-Saëns's *Coronation March* was chosen and performed.

A number of composers sent in marches and all kinds of music, every item of which was handed to me, one or two foreign musicians also sending works. Among the most notable of these was Dr. Saint-Saëns, of whose well-known *Coronation March*, and his desire to have it performed at King Edward's Coronation, I first heard from Sir Francis Bertie. The Ambassador wrote to me as follows from the British Embassy at Paris:

"May 16th, 1902

Dear Sir Frederick Bridge,—Lord Lansdowne desires me to inform you that the French Ambassador told him on the 14th instant that Monsieur Saint-Saëns, the French composer, who has had the honour of playing on several occasions before the Queen, has composed a March in honour of the King's Coronation, and that he is very anxious that it should be played during the Coronation festivities.

Lord Lansdowne told Monsieur Cambon that he felt sure that the King would appreciate the compliment, and that he would endeavour to ascertain whether anything could be done to meet Monsieur Saint-Saëns's wishes.

It has been suggested to Lord Lansdowne that Monsieur Saint-Saëns should be placed in communication with you, and his Lordship suggested to the Ambassador that Monsieur Saint-Saëns should apply to you, and wishes me to ask you to receive him.

If Lord Lansdowne is mistaken in thinking that Monsieur Saint-Saëns should be referred to you, perhaps you will be kind enough to let me know to whom he should apply. Yours Truly,

Francis Bertie."

I at once replied that I should be honoured by being made the recipient of a work of Dr. Saint-Saëns, that he had specially composed for such an occasion. It was indeed a happy collocation of events that it should have been possible to include in the musical scheme a representative work by the doyen of French musicians. . . .

Sir Francis Bertie evidently lost no time in handing my reply to Dr. Saint-Saëns, for on the 27th of May I received the following autograph letter from the French composer himself:

27th May 1902

My dear Sir,—Very much obliged to you for your kindness towards my *Coronation March*.

Yours very truly,

And gratefully,

C. Saint-Saëns.

Dr. Saint-Saëns came over and himself rehearsed the performance of his *March*. Unfortunately, however, he could not come on the postponed date (9 August 1902) of the Coronation, and it fell to me to conduct his work.[6]

In recognition of this contribution to the music of his coronation, King Edward VII presented to Saint-Saëns the Cross of the Commander of the Order of Victoria, giving him the title of baronet and the right to be addressed as "Sir."

Saint-Saëns played the organ again on 26 March 1906 when at the Academy of Saint Cecilia in Rome, he played his *Fantaisie in E-flat*, a *Rhapsodie Bretonne*, and parts of his *Third Symphony*. He attended the Salzburg Mozart Festival held in honor of the 150th anniversary of the composer's birth and, according to Eloy de Stoecklin, "on 20 August he played on the organ the *Grand Fugue* and the *Fantaisie in C Major* of Mozart.[7]

Fantaisie pour Orgue-Aeolian

In 1906 Saint-Saëns was commissioned by the Aeolian Organ Company of New York to compose an original work for their mechanical self-playing pipe organs.[8] The result was the *Fantaisie pour*

---

[6]Sir Frederick Bridge, *A Westminster Pilgrim* (London: Novello, 1919) 188–89.

[7]Eloy de Stoecklin, *Le Ménestrel* (15 September 1906) 564.

[8]Composers before him had been induced to write for mechanical "organs"—K.P.E. Bach, Haydn, Handel, Mozart and Beethoven—but these instruments were either mechanical clocks which played a rank of stopped flute pipes or, as in Beethoven's case, Maezel's Panharmonicon. No one up to this time had composed a major work for a traditional automatic pipe organ of two manuals and pedal. Saint-Saëns was not the only distinguished musician of his day to be asked by the Aeolian Company to compose expressly for one of their instruments—though he was the only organist and *(continued)*

Orgue-Aeolian—his most ambitious organ work. To understand fully its importance, as well as the very interesting history surrounding its composition, it is necessary first to understand the phenomenon of the player organ at the end of the 19th century.

The origin of both the player piano and the player organ was in the player reed organ. The pneumatic player action common to both was first devised for the harmonium and later applied by Edwin S. Votey to the piano and the organ. A roll of paper, perforated with holes corresponding to the pitch and duration of the notes in the composition to be reproduced, passed over a tracker bar bored with small holes through which a stream of air was drawn whenever the passage was left free by the occurrence of one of the holes in the roll. The air, acting as substitute fingers, set the action in motion.

Player reed organs were manufactured as early as 1878 and the Aeolian Organ and Music Company was formed in New York in 1888 to manufacture automatic reed organs and perforated music rolls. In the late 1890s the player reed organ reached its apogee in the Aeolian Orchestrelle, one of which was set up in the Great Northern Hotel in Paris. From April 1899 to October 1901 *La Tribune de Saint-Gervais* carried advertisements for the Aeolian organ, "Le merveilleux instrument musical," which included enthusiastic testimonials from eminent Parisian organists. Charles-Marie Widor declared that:

> From now on, no more errors, no more misunderstandings. In the future, thanks to the AEolian, the composer can record his own works himself. This work will live *in aeternum*.

The professor of organ at the Conservatoire, Alexandre Guilmant, wrote, "I have heard the AEolian with the utmost pleasure. This instrument greatly interested me."[9]

---

consequently his work is more suited to the instrument than those by Engelbert Humperdinck, Moritz Moszkowski or Victor Herbert.

[9]Charles Bordes, director of the Chanteurs de Saint-Gervais and one of the founders of the Schola Cantorum, wrote: "I have been most interested in the AEolian invention and have already seen an original application to the repertoire of those modest parishes which, though they have a beautiful instrument, cannot afford both an organist and a maître-de-chapelle. The latter, while directing his choir, can accompany it and play fugues and offertoires. The precentor can do the same without leaving his podium. And as for the teaching of rhythmic flexibility—that can be left to the mechanical invention. Quelle leçon!"

When Mustel brought out its own player reed organ, the Concertal, Saint-Saëns in 1904 wrote an endorsement:

Thanks to this marvelous invention, everyone can interpret the most diverse things, not only the simplest but those, like symphonic works, which demand all the resources of the art.[10]

It was a logical step from the reed organ to the pipe organ, and the first modern reproducing pipe organ was built in 1893 for Oliver H.P. Belmont who, when he built his home, Belcourt, at Newport, Rhode Island, requested a player pipe organ. The Ferrand & Votey Organ Company of Detroit, Michigan, successor to Hilborne and Frank Roosevelt of New York, was engaged to build a two-manual, twenty-nine-rank organ to which the Aeolian Company fitted a player mechanism. In 1899 the Aeolian Company acquired control of the Votey Organ Company and for the next thirty years specialized in building organs which they proclaimed to be "The Home Orchestra of the Twentieth Century"[11] for "salons, music rooms, foyers, and reception halls in private residences."[12]

Saint-Saëns first became acquainted with the Aeolian Organ in England. The Orchestrelle Company, the British division of the Aeolian Organ Company, had taken over the Grosvenor Gallery on Bond Street, remodeled it (converting the former large west picture gallery into a 400-seat concert hall)[13] and opened it on 19 January 1904 as Aeolian Hall. A two-manual, forty-eight-stop organ had been built for the Aeolian Com-

---

[10]*Le Guide du Concert (Numéro Saint-Saëns)* iv. Saint-Saëns's association with the Aeolian Company predates this 1906 commission. A 1901 catalog of Orchestrelle rolls includes 19 rolls of music by him, including symphonic poems, the *Cello Concerto, Le Cygne*, &c., but not one original organ work. (*Music for the Aeolian Grand*, July 1901, 422–23).

[11]*The Duo-Art Monthly* (July 1924) 15.

[12]The Orchestrelle Company's letterhead.

[13]The Concert Hall, 40 feet by 100 feet, is described in *The Musical Times* (February 1904) 119: "The walls are panelled to the height of 8 feet 6 inches in fumed mahogany. Seats, upholstered in soft green, provide accommodation for an audience of 400, and from the back of the stage rises a large organ whose gilded pipes run up to the arched roof." See also "Aeolian Hall in London," *The Music Trades* (26 March 1904) 19–22.

Plate 39. Aeolian Hall, London

152

pany by the Hutchings-Votey Company of Boston[14] and shipped to London in September 1903. While he was in London in July 1906, Saint-Saëns no doubt visited Aeolian Hall in order to inspect the organ.[15] He would have wanted to experiment with those features the Aeolian Company felt to be most unique: the Echo Organ, Chimes and Harp—effects which he was obliged to incorporate into his commissioned piece.

The Aeolian Hall organ was eminently expressive, all stops except the Open Diapason of Manual I being enclosed. The ten-stop Echo division was installed in its own chamber in an adjoining room at the back of the hall. It contained a second Vox Humana.

Few Aeolian organs were not equipped with two stops new to the organ's palette and which were becoming prerequisites on the standard American organ: the Harp and Chimes. Almost unknown in Europe, the Harp (similar in construction to the marimba—metal bars suspended over tuned resonators and struck by hammers controlled electrically from the

[14]While the Aeolian Company took over the Votey Organ Company and established their own factory at Garwood, New Jersey, Edwin Votey's association with the newly merged company was short-lived. In 1901 he joined George Hutchings in Boston and for several years the Hutchings-Votey Organ Company built the actual instruments sold by and under the name of the Aeolian Organ Company.

The Aeolian Hall instrument was described in *Musical Opinion* (February 1904):

> There is now on view at the Orchestrelle Co.'s rooms a handsome large two-manual pipe organ (built by this firm at Garwood, New Jersey), playable by means of perforated paper rolls. Special "116 note" music—on which there are two separate rows of holes—is used, the topmost series of which causes the swell organ to play, whilst the bottom set of perforations acts on the great organ. An electric pneumatic action is used. On one keyboard a solo can be performed, an accompaniment being possible by the paper rolls acting on the other manual; or the positions concerning the melody and accompaniment may be reversed. In an adjoining room there is erected an echo organ, the music from which is obtained from the keyboard of the two-manual instrument. . . Of course, if an automatic rendition be not desired, the organ can be played in the ordinary manner. Certainly, all interested in the "king of instruments" should visit Aeolian Hall, New Bond Street.

[15]Surviving records of the earliest years of the Aeolian Company are incomplete but it is fairly certain that this was the first opportunity Saint-Saëns would have had to see, hear and play one of these new American instruments. A contract for a two-manual, thirty-one-stop Aeolian Organ in Salle Aeolian in Paris was not signed until 5 March 1906. It was inaugurated by Easthope Martin in December of that year. Few Aeolian Organs were ever delivered to Europe, in fact. In a geographical listing by country published in January 1930, covering nearly 2,000 instruments in the United States and its possessions, Great Britain had 92 Aeolian Organs, while France had only 14. Germany followed with 11, and Belgium and Spain each had 4 organs. (*Duo-Art Music*, January 1930.)

keyboard) was a relatively new addition to the Aeolian stoplist, their first one having been installed in 1904.[16] The Aeolian Hall organ did not have a Harp stop until 1909.

The Chimes must have delighted Saint-Saëns. They were tubular bells, exactly like orchestral bells, struck by electric-actioned hammers. Their compass was twenty notes: from ,A to "E, and they sounded an octave higher than the notes played on the keyboard—an effect Saint-Saëns realized in his notation.

The opportunity to include Chimes in an organ work would have been particularly irresistible to Saint-Saëns who had a positive mania for bells. At seventeen he had begun a "Grand Symphonie avec Choeurs" entitled *Les Cloches*.[17] He wrote two bell-inspired songs, *La Cloche* (1855) and *Les Cloches de la Mer* (1900), and three piano pieces: *Carillon*, Op. 72, No. 2 (1884), *Les Cloches du Soir*, Op. 85 (1889) and *Les Cloches de Las Palmas*, Op. 111, No. 4 (1899). He had even written an essay on bells as an acoustical phenomenon, "The Multiple Resonance of Bells."[18] He introduced the Chimes into the finale of his *Fantaisie* but, although he heard the somewhat "distant chime effect" of the enclosed organ chimes, he conceived their effect in his *Fantaisie* more along the lines of great clanging orchestral bells pealing in dialogue with the full organ.

The *Fantaisie pour Orgue-Aeolian* occupies a place in Saint-Saëns's oeuvre between the cantata *La Gloire de Corneille*, Op. 126 (written for the 300th anniversary of the birth of Pierre Corneille and performed at the Paris Opéra on 19 June 1906), and the *Fantaisie pour Violon et Harpe*, Op. 124. Saint-Saëns was in London for a concert on 12 July 1906 at Bechstein Hall where he accompanied Joseph Hollman in the premiere of his *Second Cello Sonata in F*, Op. 123. It was during this time that he composed "for a 'semi-automatic organ' a Fantaisie 'unplayable by the fingers and feet.'"[19] The first draft, entitled *Morceau écrit pour l'orgue-AEolian*[20] is written on Beale & Chapelle manuscript paper. Saint-Saëns brought the completed work with him to New York in October and gave it to Frank Taft, art director of the Aeolian Organ Company. He also inscribed a

---

[16]*The Diapason* (June 1930) 6.

[17]The 29 pages of fragments of this work are in the Bibliothèque Nationale, Ms. No. 872.

[18]Published originally in *Renaissance Musicale* (11 September 1881), it was reprinted in *Harmonie et Mélodie* in 1885, p. 241 ff.

[19]Bonnerot, 184.

[20]Bibliothèque Nationale Ms. No. 648.

Plate 40. Excerpt from the "chorale theme" of *Fantaisie pour Orgue-Aeolian*, inscribed to Frank Taft.

photograph to Mr. Taft with four measures of the "chorale theme" from the new work.

The Aeolian organ for which Saint-Saëns wrote did no more than reproduce the notes as punched on a paper roll—fifty-eight holes for the Great, fifty-eight holes for the Swell (or Echo division, if coupled to the Swell manual). (The same roll was also playable on the reed organ counterpart, the Solo Orchestrelle.) The rolls were perforated by hand by factory workers, euphemistically identified on the labels as the Aeolian Organ Guild. It was not until 1917 that a sophisticated player mechanism, the Aeolian Duo-Art, was developed which faithfully reproduced an individual artist's performance. By an ingenious, complicated apparatus the organist's playing was automatically recorded with not only the notes but the registration, stop changes, and swell-box movements controlled by the perforations on the roll.

All directions for interpretation were printed on the roll with rubber stamps. A color code aided registration: Swell stops were printed in blue or green, Great in red and Pedal in black. Names of the stops followed the Aeolian Company's not-to-be-misunderstood nomenclature: Flute F, String P, String Vibrato (Voix céleste), High Flute (4') and Deep Flute (16'). The swell pedals and the crescendo pedal were operated by the "organist." The latter pedal, designated "Tonal," was indicated in stages: 1/4, 1/2, 3/4 and TONAL ON FULL. The tempo (the speed at which the roll moved), accelerandi and ritardandi, were controlled by the TEMPO lever. While it was true, as Aeolian publicity asserted, that the rolls "render, without the slightest difficulty or uncertainty, complex musical compositions and transcriptions utterly impossible of rendition by the organist who has only his two hands to command the manuals,"[21] no little amount of rehearsal time was required of the "organist" to perfect his technique of manipulating all of the organ's controls as the roll wound from one spool to the other.

Twenty stops are indicated on the two rolls that comprise Saint-Saëns's *Fantaisie pour Orgue-Aeolian*:

GREAT	SWELL	ECHO (ON SWELL)
8 Flute P	8 Diapson	8 String PP
8 Flute F	8 Flute P	8 Vox Humana
8 String PP	8 String PP	Tremolo
8 String P	8 String P	
8 String F	8 String F	
4 High Flute F	8 Oboe	
Harp	8 Vox Humana	PEDAL
	Chimes	16 Deep Flute
	Tremolo	

A typical small residence organ, with a minimum number of stops but which included all of those required by the *Fantaisie pour Orgue-Aeolian* roll, was that built for the residence of John D. Rockefeller, Jr., 10 West 54th Street, in New York City.[22] It was installed in 1912 as Opus 1234. The thirteen stops of Manual I were duplexed on Manual II. Not unlike most other residence installations the Echo Organ was "located in a mezzanine closet between the second and third floors and provided with a tone exit into the main hall."[23]

The specification of this organ follows; the twenty stops called for in the *Fantaisie* are printed in italics. Opposite each stop is its equivalent in standard organ terminology.

---

[21]Quoted in Q. David Bowers's *Encyclopedia of Automatic Musical Instruments* (Vestal, New York: Vestal Press, 1972) 788.

[22]See Rollin Smith's "A Pair of Rockefeller Organs," *The Tracker* (Summer 1976) 13.

[23]Ibid.

MANUAL I AND II

1. Diapason F	Open Diapason
2. *Diapason MF*	tapered
3. *String F*	Viole d'Orchestre
4. *String P*	Gemshorn
5. String Vibrato P	Vox Celeste
6. *String PP*	Aeoline
7. *Flute F*	Gross Flute
8. *Flute P*	Flauto Dolce
9. *High Flute*	Harmonic Flute 4'
10. Trumpet	
11. *Oboe*	
12.Clarinet	
13. *Vox Humana*	On its own chest in a separate swell box

Tremolo

ECHO

14. Flute P	Stopped Diapason 8
15. *String PP*	Aeoline
16. *Vox Humana*	

Tremolo

PEDAL

17. Deep Flute F	Bourdon 16'
18. *Deep Flute P*	Bourdon 16'

PERCUSSION

19. *Harp*	49 notes
20. *Chimes*	20 notes

Couplers

II-I   8' 4'   I - Pedal

II-II 16' 8' 4' II - Pedal

I-I 16'   Echo - I

Echo - II

Plate 41. A facsimile of the first page of the autograph manuscript, *Fantaisie pour Orgue-Aeolian*

The Aeolian catalog provided the following descriptive program note for Saint-Saëns's *Fantaisie pour Orgue-Aeolian*:

This *Fantaisie* was composed especially for the Aeolian Pipe-Organ and in it Saint-Saëns has availed himself of the privileges afforded by the technical facilities of this instrument. . . Saint-Saëns here has disregarded the limitations of the human performer and has embraced the opportunities of the enormous technique of the Aeolian Pipe-Organ. The introduction to the work is very brilliant and rhapsodic. Then there is voiced a graceful theme, with which the composer toys liberally and interestingly. After this there follows a set of variations. The first one is florid, with runs and trills, the second one is interesting with imitations. A complete change of mood occurs in the next variation, which is dramatic and exceedingly brilliant. This last variation is repeated. In this composition the writer has made effective use of the harp of the Aeolian Pipe-Organ.

With the opening of this, the concluding section of the *Fantaisie*, the mood becomes subdued and a plaintive melancholy pervades the music. Then, over a broadly sustained chord the theme is martially trumpeted forth. Again the mood veers, and harp arpeggi surround the tender theme. Now the main melody appears in the guise of a chorale, its appealing qualities enhanced by its manner of presentation. Then the tempo grows faster, and the bells clang forth the melody, interrupted by comments from the other voices. The mood becomes dramatic and the very close is brilliant.[24]

The Aeolian Company lost no time getting the new work into circulation and by the next year the *Fantaisie pour Orgue-Aeolian* was on the market. An item in their monthly newsletter stated that:

A most interesting concert was given at Vassar College recently. The pipe organ, played by means of the Aeolian attachment and perforated rolls, was the instrument used. The program consisted of a *Fantaisie* by Camille Saint-Saëns, written expressly for the Aeolian Pipe-Organ, and Tschaikowsky's Symphony No. 6 ("Pathetique") in four parts, arranged by Wallace Goodrich, organist of Trinity Church, Boston.[25]

[24]Gustav Kobbé, *The Aeolian Pipe-Organ and Its Music* (New York: The Aeolian Company, 1919) 245.
[25]*AEolian Notes* (September 1907) 3.

159

CHAPTER VI

The Final Years

Saint-Saëns sailed aboard the *Provence* for the United States on 20 October 1906. This was his first trip to North America—he had played several concerts in South America in 1904. There had, in fact, been discussion of his participating in the Universal Exposition of 1893 in Chicago and some magazines even published the programs, but the project was abandoned. Nevertheless, there had been rumors of a previous visit and in the summer of 1906 the *New York Sun* ran a paragraph stating:

> . . . according to testimony of very positive witnesses Saint-Saëns had slipped into the city incognito several years ago on a steamer from the south and remained concealed in a French hotel until the departure of one of the liners for Paris. Saint-Saëns for some years past has had the disappearing habit. . . While returning from one of his trips. . . he landed in New York, preserved a strict incognito and rarely went out of the hotel on University Place, where he was recognized and addressed by name by some French musicians who happened to be there at the time and explained to the landlord what a distinguished stranger he was sheltering.[1]

[1]*The Musician* (September 1906) 458.

The Musician, which had reprinted the news item, soon received the following letter:

> Rue de Longchamp 17
> Paris, 22 September '06
>
> Cher Monsieur:
>
> I do not understand why the rumor is spread that I previously went to New York *incognito*. I have never gone to the United States.
>
> It is also false that I have the disappearing habit. For reasons of health, I went to the Canaries *incognito* fifteen years ago; since then my close friends have always known where I was. *The disappearing habit* is a myth.
>
> C. Saint-Saëns[2]

Four days out of port Saint-Saëns fell ill with diphtheria and still had a fever when he arrived in New York. In spite of this, he appeared with the Boston Symphony on 30 October 1906 and with Walter Damrosch and the New York Symphony Orchestra at Carnegie Hall on 4 November. Richard Aldrich wrote:

> His playing is full of charm and of wonderful facility when his years are considered, and it is necessary to consider them. There are sparkling clearness, grace and elegance in his rippling passages and runs; he phrases and sings a melody with distinction and point, and all is done with perfect repose, though on a somewhat miniature scope and within restricted limits of dynamic contrast and tonal color. Nothing that he played (*Africa, Wedding Cake, Allegro appassionato*) called for eloquence or for feeling that even scratched the surface; and he gave no sign of either.[3]

On 15 November he played again with Walter Damrosch and included his *Concerto in G Minor* ("I was compelled to find again my former fingers to play the *Concerto* which everybody wanted to hear interpreted by the composer. That hardly pleased me as nowadays young people play it better than I."[4]), his *Fantaisie on themes from Gluck's "Alceste,"* and the organ part in his *Third Symphony* and *Sérénade*, Op. 15.

---

[2]Ibid.

[3]Richard Aldrich, "New York Symphony Orchestra, Walter Damrosch, Camille Saint-Saëns, 4 November 1906," *Concert Life in New York* (New York: Putnam, 1941) 148.

[4]Saint-Saëns, "Impressions of America," *Outspoken Essays on Music* (Boston: Small, Maynard, 1922) 144.

Dr. Saint-Saëns, at 72, has no longer the power to produce a tone to cope with that of the orchestra. Under the circumstances, it was a remarkable performance, in the clearness and cogency with which he propounded the themes of the first movement even though he did not reveal fully the grandeur of the opening measures breathing the spirit of Bach. There was much clearness, sparkle and vivacity in his playing of the brilliant passage work of the last two movements; delightfully rhythmical in the second, he was sometimes a trifle carried away by the impetuosity of the last.[5]

On 27 November at Carnegie Hall Saint-Saëns gave his only piano recital. The program was made up of Bach's *Italian Concerto*, two movements from a *Suite*, pieces by Rameau, Beethoven's *Sonata in A-flat*, Op. 26, Chopin's *Barcarolle*, some transcriptions and four waltzes by himself. "The Bach and Beethoven pieces were charmingly played, with repose, clarity and distinction; the Chopin was rather dry."[6]

William C. Carl gave a recital of Saint-Saëns's organ works (which the composer attended), and a farewell banquet in his honor was given at the Lotos Club on 23 December. It was attended by many notable musicians and Sigismund Stojowski played piano works of the honoree.

Saint-Saëns attended as well as participated in innumerable concerts in many cities. He heard Gabriel Pierné's *Children's Crusade* in New York, his own *Samson et Dalila* in Philadelphia, visited Cincinnati and Detroit, played his *G minor Concerto* in Washington, D.C., at a concert attended by President Theodore Roosevelt, visited important museums and art galleries, and even ate in New York City's Chinatown. Upon his return to Paris (where he spent forty-eight hours before going on to Egypt)[7] he contributed a long article to *Le Figaro* giving his impressions of America.[8] He said that he had been warned that everything would shock his artistic taste and that he would find only hustling, nervous crowds—a hysterical England. But instead, he found the people rather quiet as compared with Frenchmen; courteous, hospitable and sympathetic—and he especially admired the ladies. He was delighted to find so many modern French paintings and to find them so well understood and appreciated. At

[5]*The New York Times* (16 November 1906) 9.
[6]*The New Music Review* (January 1907) 93.
[7]*Le Monde musical* (15 January 1907) 15.
[8]Reprinted as "Impressions of America," in *Outspoken Essays on Music*, pp. 137–51.

his concerts he never had a more attentive, more silent, nor more enthusiastic audience. He delighted in the clean cities, skyscrapers with electric elevators in which one could reach the top in but a few seconds, large hotel rooms, pleasant railway journeys, and the fact that everyone had his own telephone. In short, he looked forward with delight to his next visit.

On his two-month visit to the United States Saint-Saëns's only connection with the organ was delivering his recently completed *Fantaisie pour Orgue-Aeolian* to Frank Taft at Aeolian Hall in New York, and playing the Roosevelt organ in Carnegie Hall in his *Third Symphony* and the *Sérénade*.

Saint-Saëns's organ music was as well known as that of Franck and Widor, though none was quite as popular as that of Guilmant. Pirated editions of Saint-Saëns's organ music were published by several American music firms and, in the days before reciprocal copyright agreements, these channeled-off royalties were viewed by him with the same indignation as that expressed by Alexandre Guilmant. As early as 1876, G. Schirmer had published the *Three Breton Rhapsodies*, the *Bénédiction nuptiale*, and *Élévation ou Communion*, "edited, revised, and registration indicated with reference to the nomenclature of English and American organs" by Samuel P. Warren, organist of Grace Church, New York City. Clarence Eddy had included Saint-Saëns's works in his series *The Church and Concert Organist*: *Élévation ou Communion* in 1882 and *Bénédiction nuptiale* in Volume II in 1885. Even Horatio Parker had published a transcription of *The Swan*.[9] Clarence Dickinson "edited" Saint-Saëns's arrangement of Liszt's *Saint Francis of Assisi Preaching to the Birds*[10] and, as was his custom with most works he played or edited, "cut" the sermon—he deeming it not of sufficient interest to hold the attention of his American organ recital audiences. When Edwin H. Lemare published his transcription of *Danse macabre* in 1919,[11] Dickinson promptly used it as the basis for his organ duet version.[12]

---

[9]G. Schirmer, 1895.

[10]H.W. Gray

[11]G. Schirmer, 1919.

[12]H.W. Gray. Shortly after Saint-Saëns left the country, William Churchill Hammond gave a Bach and Saint-Saëns organ recital in Mary Lyon Chapel, of Mount Holyoke College, South Hadley, Massachusetts, 23 January 1907. (*The New Music Review*, March 1907, p. 279). *(continued)*

During the last twenty years of his life Saint-Saëns still played the organ in public but never in solo recitals—only during church services or during a concert in which he was performing. On 9 October 1910, to celebrate his seventy-fifth birthday, he played the organ of the Cathedral of Lucerne with the blind organist Albert Harnisch. A festival of his works was held at Vévey between 18 and 23 May 1913. At the Church of Saint-Martin he played the organ part of his *Third Symphony*, an *Ave Maria*, and his *Coronation March* for Edward VII. In September 1913 he conducted his oratorio *The Promised Land* at Gloucester Cathedral for the Three Choirs Festival. It is unlikely that he did not try out the cathedral organ while attending rehearsals.

Then, shortly after his seventy-eighth birthday, he gave a concert publicized as his farewell recital, at Salle Gaveau for the benefit of the work of the Cercle National pour le Soldat de Paris. He appeared as composer, pianist and organist. The program, 6 November 1913, consisted of:[13]

Marche religieuse	Saint-Saëns
Quintette	
Deux Fantaisies for lute, transcribed for harp	
Introduction et Rondo Capriccioso	
O Salutaris	
Duo pour Violon et Harpe	
Concerto in B-flat	Mozart
Fantaisie sur le Choral du *Prophète*	Liszt

Prelude and Fugue in A Minor	J. S. Bach
Rhapsodie in E Minor	Saint-Saëns
Élévation in E Major	
Bénédiction nuptiale	
Fantaisie in E-flat Major	
Prelude to *The Deluge*	
Adagio from the *Third Symphony*	
Prelude to *Proserpine*	
Marche du Synode from *Henry VIII*	

[13]Bonnerot, 199.

Plate 42. Saint-Saëns at the organ of Salle Gaveau, 6 November 1913

Saint-Saëns had originally planned to begin the program with one of his *Rhapsodies Bretonnes* "to give the latecomers time to arrive,"[14] but eventually settled on his *Marche religieuse*. No aspect of the program escaped his attention and he wrote, "On the programs it will be necessary to list the movements of the *Fantaisie*: Introduction, Adagio, Fugue and Final."[15] When he read in the press a reference to the "*Ad nos*" *Fantaisie* for organ and orchestra he wrote to Arthur Dandelot (who was organizing the concert: "Where in the devil did you get that the Liszt *Fantaisie* was with orchestra? It is for organ solo. I hope you will correct this mistake."[16]

The review in *Le Ménestrel* described the concert:

> On a stage decorated with flowers, the Maître, younger and more carefree than ever, came forward and was greeted with tumultuous applause. The organ and piano resounded one after the other under his always-agile and exceedingly eloquent fingers.[17]

Marcel Dupré and his Prix de Rome

As France's preeminent musician, as well as a member of the Académie, Saint-Saëns was a power behind the Prix de Rome awards. Henri Busser secured his participation in 1914 when Marcel Dupré competed for the Prix de Rome. Saint-Saëns had gone out to Saint-Cloud, where Busser was organist, to attend a Mass during which all the music performed was his own. Afterwards:

> He was delighted and said, "My dear Busser, ask me what you would like and I will give it to you." I answered him tit for tat: "My dear maître, come to the Prix de Rome competition the third of July." He hesitated a little because he no longer went to the Institute since the election of Gustave Charpentier, but I insisted and he finally acquiesced.
>
> ... At the concours de Rome I persuaded Saint-Saëns to come to vote for Marcel Dupré, who had all the makings of a composer. With the help of the votes of the painters and sculptors he won the Grand

---

[14]Letter from Saint-Saëns to Arthur Dandelot, Berlin, 11 October 1913, in Dandelot, *Petits Mémoires Musicaux* (Paris: La Nouvelle Revue, 1936) 106.

[15]Ibid., 107, letter from Saint-Saëns to Arthur Dandelot written between 20 and 26 October 1913.

[16]Letter from Saint-Saëns to Arthur Dandelot, Paris, 27 October 1913.

[17]René Brancour, "Revue des grands concerts," *Le Ménestrel* (15 November 1913) 365.

Prix. That same evening the young laureate came to thank me for my intervention in securing Saint-Saëns's vote which had assured me his victory.[18]

Marcel Dupré supplied a different account in his memoirs. He wrote that Saint-Saëns was not present when the voting began and it was only after Dupré and Marc Delmas were tied on the first ballot that Widor sent a hurried message[19] to Saint-Saëns urging him to come and break the tie. Saint-Saëns agreed, and on the second ballot Dupré won the Premier Grand Prix de Rome. Widor urged him to call on Saint-Saëns "to thank him for your prize. He wants to know you better."[20]

Having prepared and memorized a fine greeting, I arrived at the Maître's very nervous, knowing that the great musician was not always agreeable.

He opened the door. "What do you want?"

"Maître, I have come to thank you for your kindness. . ."

No time for my fine greeting!

"Kindness, nothing. I voted for you because you deserved it. You don't have to thank me. I read your biography in this morning's paper. Is it true you were a child prodigy?"

I remained still.

"But, why not admit it. I, too, was a child prodigy."

From then on he was charming and interesting. Then, as I stood to leave:

"No, stay." He kept me a long time, talking about Dieppe, Rouen, the great organ at Saint-Ouen, Cavaillé-Coll, for whom he had a profound admiration, and then about technique and orchestration. I was in ecstasy when I left.[21]

Panama-Pacific Exposition in San Francisco

Saint-Saëns returned to the United States in May 1915 as France's official representative to the Panama-Pacific International Exposition held in San Francisco, California—a cultural fair celebrating the opening

[18]Henri Busser, *De Pelléas aux Indes Galantes* (Paris: Fayard, 1955) 194.

[19]A message not among the 50 letters from Widor to Saint-Saëns preserved in the archives at the Chateau-Musée de Dieppe.

[20]Marcel Dupré, *Marcel Dupré raconte. . .* (Paris: Bornemann, 1972) 75–76.

[21]Ibid., 77–78

of the Panama Canal. His official title was "First Delegate to the Franco-American Commission for the Development of Political, Economic, Literary and Artistic Relations."

The day of his arrival in San Francisco (21 May) Saint-Saëns "declined in a most polite manner to discuss the works of any contemporaneous composers and avoided the subject of the war" (then raging in Europe). However, the next day the newspapermen were able to bring up American music, and the Sunday paper reported an interview with him quoting one of those unbelievably undiplomatic statements which had become so characteristic of France's most illustrious musician.

> I asked Camille Saint-Saëns. . . if he had made a study of the works of American composers and he said hesitatingly that he had not. I asked him timidly what he thought of them and he said he had never heard of any.[22]

The quote had little impact on his popularity, for that very evening during a performance of his *Third Symphony* by Karl Muck and the Boston Symphony Orchestra, word spread throughout the house that the composer was in attendance and at the conclusion of the *Symphony* calls for "Saint-Saëns! Saint-Saëns!" arose

> . . .first from one quarter and then another and then from all over the large auditorium, and continued until the white-haired Master, eighty years old, arose and bowed to his nearly 4,000 admirers gathered there. The applause and enthusiasm, led by Dr. Muck and his orchestra, mounted in tremendous crescendo until it became one of the thrilling, inspiring episodes of the Exposition year.[23]

The Exposition concerts were given in the 3,782-seat Festival Hall—the acoustics of which were described by Karl Muck as so bad that

[22]Walter Anthony, "Saint-Saëns Talks Music," *The San Francisco Chronicle* (23 May 1915) 24.
The day before, Redfern Mason, in his customary display of good taste and diplomacy, printed his version of the interview:
Saint-Saëns: "As for American music, I should be chary of expressing an opinion, for I am entirely unfamiliar with it."
Mason: "And its future?"
Saint-Saëns: "I am no prophet."
Redfern Mason, "Saint-Saëns Brings Muse to This City," *San Francisco Examiner* (22 May 1915) 5.
[23]Frank Morton Todd, *The Story of the Exposition* (New York: Putnam, 1921) 406.

all orchestras sounded alike. The stage contained the case of the four-manual, 117-rank Austin organ, the seventh largest organ in the world, and the publicity stated that in the largest of its chambers "a banquet for seventy-five persons sitting at tables could be served."

During the third week of June three all-Saint-Saëns concerts were presented. The *Third Symphony*, four symphonic poems, two concerti, and numerous miscellaneous works were performed, and at each concert Saint-Saëns's specially commissioned work, *Hail! California*, was heard.[24] This gigantic twenty-minute fantasia, "Saint-Saëns' tribute to the spirit of the West and his musical celebration of the completion of the Panama Canal,"[25] incorporated *The Star-Spangled Banner*, the *Marseillaise* and Spanish themes, and was performed by the combined forces of the Boston Symphony Orchestra (augmented by four saxophones), Sousa's Band, chorus and organ. The conducting responsibilities were divided between Saint-Saëns and Richard Hageman of New York City's Metropolitan Opera. The official exposition organist, Wallace A. Sabin, played the organ at all of the concerts and prepared the chorus.

---

[24]*Hail! California* was but one of a number of commissions from unlikely sources—all of which demonstrated that Saint-Saëns's 18th- and 19th-century formal and harmonic aesthetic ably served 20th-century purposes. He, in fact, ushered in the present century with a cantata written in honor of electricity—*Le Feu céleste*—performed at the opening of the 1900 Paris Exposition. (Electricity was still a novelty for, although the Eiffel Tower had depended on electric elevators since it was erected in 1889, and many public buildings were illuminated with electricity, most Parisian homes still depended on gas for lighting.) Saint-Saëns's 1906 *Fantaisie* for the Aeolian player organ was followed two years later by the first score written expressly for a film: *L'Assassinat du duc de Guise*, Op. 128. (It opened at the Salle Charras on 16 November 1908.) Scored for strings, piano and harmonium its introduction and five tableaux are musically cued to each scene of the twelve-minute film recalled by D.W. Griffith as his "best memory of the cinema." (Georges Sadoul, *Dictionary of Films*, Berkeley and Los Angeles: University of California Press, 1972, p. 16.) A series of proletarian choral works later appeared: *Aux Aviateurs*, Op. 134 (1912), *Aux Mineurs*, Op. 137 (1912), *Hymne au travail*, Op. 142 (1914), and *Les Conquérants de l'air*, Op. 164.

[25]Redfern Mason, "Saint-Saëns Wins Hearts of Musicians," *The San Francisco Examiner* (16 June 1915) 8.

Saint-Saëns was paid $9,675.25 for *Hail! California* and the three concerts. By comparison, Paderewski, for one benefit concert, received $5,666.75 and Fritz Kreisler received $2,018.90 for one concert. (Excerpts from the *Report of the Department of Music to the President of the Pan-Pacific International Exposition*. Manuscript in the San Francisco Archives, San Francisco Public Library.)

In the company of John Philip Sousa and other noted musicians, Redfern Mason, music critic for the *San Francisco Examiner*, attended Saint-Saëns's first rehearsal with the orchestra and noted the pleasure which his companions took in watching him conduct.

The men of the orchestra were just as full of enthusiasm. They knew that this patriarch of composers was one of the leaders of the republic of music and his directing part of the true gospel of tone, and they played *con amore*.

Many of these men are Germans, but that made no difference. Here was a master of the craft and his mastery was evident, palpable; it "leaped to the eyes," as the French say. That was enough to insure their faithful cooperation. Nay, they cared not even though their instruments had to sing the *Marseillaise*, and God knows they would have preferred the *Wacht am Rhein*. Artistic loyalty is a subtle and wonderful thing.

Rehearsing is fraught with many practical difficulties. When Wallace Sabin began to play the organ part in Saint-Saëns's *C-Minor Symphony* he had to forget the interpretation he had learned from Dr. Muck. The score was scrawled all over with directions. But Saint-Saëns has his own notions about the interpretation of his own work. So there was much discussion till eventually the organ part sounded as the composer intended it should sound.

Then, when Sousa's tuba players grappled with the part for military band which Saint-Saëns adds to the orchestral and organ parts in the final glories of *Hail! California*, it came out that the French copyists had written the music, not in the American fashion but for a transposing instrument, as is the French custom. So the tuba players had to read one note and play another. . . .

There was none of the humdrum of an ordinary rehearsal in the air. The musicians were participating in a sort of tonal feast day, and Saint-Saëns was the god of their idolatry. Sometimes he would sing, not in the raucous Kapellmeister voice of tradition, but with a good tone. Often there were errors in the parts, and then he would segregate an instrumental choir and make them play till he could determine just what the fault was and remedy it.

For two hours this young man of four score rehearsed, and every minute was put to good hard work. Master and men were pleased; the orchestral fabric unfolded smooth and gracious, Saint-Saëns was all bonhomie and the players all enthusiasm.[26]

[26]Ibid.

171

The first two concerts of the week were well received but the last was described in the *San Francisco Chronicle* under a bold headline, "Mishap Mars Melody at Concert!" Before the Sunday afternoon concert began, the organ developed a cipher of such magnitude that the critic, Walter Anthony, wrote that "After yesterday's unprogrammed prelude the music of Schoenberg, Stravinsky and Ornstein has no terrors for me. All three may play at once and they shall not confound my ears!"[27]

Throughout the weeks of the Exposition the organ console was constantly being moved back and forth across the rough boards of the stage (the Festival Hall was a temporary building) and the main cable which connected the console to the organ was so inflexible that wires were constantly being broken. This time a "run" occurred which caused every pipe in the organ to sound simultaneously! Louis Schoenstein, who with his father had installed the organ, described the scene:

> Festival Hall was packed with people. The chorus was seated. Wallace Sabin at the console was all in readiness, albeit in a nervous tension waiting for the distinguished composer and organist to begin. Behind the stage at this time the organ motors had just been turned on, and an unearthly roar from the organ bellowed forth. Evidently stops were in an "on" position by either the stop knobs being drawn, crescendo or the sforzando pedal being on. . . . Mr. Sabin, in his faltering and hesitant speech, tried to explain to the audience that the trouble was being corrected. He likewise tried to reassure Saint-Saëns, but his limited knowledge of the French language and Saint-Saëns's inability to converse in English only increased the tenseness of the situation. It was then decided to abandon use of the organ and to move the console from the stage. As some stage hands began to move the console from its place, the organ immediately became silent and docile, as it should have been from the start. With quiet restored and Sabin at the console, it did not take long for the concert to begin.[28]

After the organ "ceased its extemporaneous groanings and shriekings and wailings," the concert got under way. But nerves were frayed and the final disaster occurred in Saint-Saëns's oratorio, *The Promised Land*.

[27]Walter Anthony, "Mishap Mars Melody at Concert, Final Affair of Saint-Saëns's Series Develops Two Bad Disasters—Organ Plays Uninvited—Choir Needing More Rehearsals, Loses Its Way In *The Promised Land*," *San Francisco Chronicle* (Monday, 28 June 1915) 7.

[28]Louis J. Schoenstein, *Memoirs of a San Francisco Organ Builder* (San Francisco: Cue Publications, 1977) 352.

172

The chorus, greatly in need of more rehearsal (a mistake in filling the order for scores had delayed the beginning of the rehearsal season), "floundered helplessly in the face of a new director. . . whose beat is not characterized by definiteness."[29] In the final chorus the basses missed an entrance "and, after a snarl of voices had reminded us of the organ's unannounced prelude, Saint-Saëns stopped the agony and the number was begun all over again—a somewhat necessary evil since it was the finale of the work."[30]

There was little that was not professionally required of Saint-Saëns during the weeks he spent in San Francisco. He began his activities with a lecture, *On the Execution of Music, and Principally of Ancient Music*, at the Salon de Pensée Française. In addition to composing and conducting, attending countless concerts and receptions, eating endless luncheons and dinners, he played two piano recitals. He even endured a lawsuit as the following item, which appeared at the bottom of the front page of a daily paper, attests:

> Camille Saint-Saëns, famous French musician and composer, was sued for $800 by Rudolph Aronson yesterday in the Superior court. Aronson claims that he made arrangements with the directors of the Panama-Pacific Exposition for the musician to give three concerts on a commission of $1,000. He says Saint-Saëns has paid only $200.[31]

Saint-Saëns returned to New York by train and after a few days sailed for France aboard the *Rochambeau* on 17 July. His article, "Music in the Church," a recycling of his previously published articles on organ and sacred music, appeared in *The Musical Quarterly*, January 1916.

Sept Improvisations

In December 1916, while confined to his bed with bronchitis, Saint-Saëns began composing his *Sept Improvisations*—his first organ music in ten years and his first to be published in eighteen. He worked on them

---

[29]Walter Anthony, loc. cit.
Mason of the *Examiner* (28 June) mentioned only that "the work sounded a trifle incoherent at times" and referred, in passing, to "the instrumental relapses which necessitated a re-start of one of the numbers."
[30]Ibid.
[31]"Camille Saint-Saëns Is Sued for $800," *San Francisco Examiner* (30 June 1915) 1.

slowly for two months, between 9 December 1916, and 12 February 1917.[32] Here, for the first time in sixty years—not since the *Choral* of the *Six Duos for Harmonium and Piano*—Saint-Saëns employed Gregorian chant in his organ music. Three of the seven improvisations are based on plainchant: No. 2, *Feria pentecostes*, is based on the first hymn sung at Lauds on Pentecost, "Beata nobis gaudi"; No. 5, *Pro Martyribus*, uses three phrases from the Offertory for the *Commune unius Martyris non Pontificus*: Mass of a Martyr not a Bishop, "Gloria et honore coronasti eum"; and No. 6, *Pro Defunctis*, is based on the first phrase of the Offertory of the Requiem, "Domine Jesu Christe."

The set is notable for a more expanded harmonic vocabulary (the first *Improvisation* is Saint-Saëns's only work based on the whole-tone scale) and its further exploration of church modes than is encountered in any other of the composer's organ music, even though, as Daniel Fallon observed, "For Saint-Saëns, 'modality' often meant little more than avoiding leading tones and introducing plagal cadences. His modal excursions never strayed far from the conventions of major/minor tonality."[33]

Although the fourth *Improvisation* closes with a quasi-Mixolydian cadence, modality is most prominent in the three pieces based on plainchant. The second and fifth pieces are in the Aeolian mode (the plainchant of the second being in the Dorian mode but with an altered sixth, and the fifth concluding with a plagal cadence on G major), and the second section of the sixth, quoting the "Domine Jesu Christe," begins in F Mixolydian.

When the *Sept Improvisations* were completed and before he played them in public, Saint-Saëns went with Albert Périlhou to the Temple de l'Étoile to try them on the organ.

> On the appointed day Saint-Saëns arrived punctually, climbed to the tribune without trouble. . . He said that he found the keyboards quite comfortable but the Récit to Positif coupler was a little stiff and he criticized the irrational disposition of the expression pedals: that of the Récit at the left and that of the Positif at the right. In the course of this tryout and in spite of the Maître's treating himself like an "old fool" whenever something was hard to read, he was quite pleased to find that

---

[32]Bonnerot, 114–15.

[33]Fallon, *The Symphonies and Symphonic Poems of Camille Saint-Saëns*, 3

there was no comparison between the pieces played on the piano and their effect on the organ.[34]

At one point he turned to the church's organist, Alexandre Cellier, and said enthusiastically, "Don't you think it's really fun to play the organ?"[35]

Saint-Saëns premiered the *Sept Improvisations* at the Théâtre des Nations in Marseille on 25 March 1917. He repeated the program in Nice, 28 March, and again in Lyon, 1 April. The set was dedicated to Eugène Gigout, who upon Alexandre Guilmant's death in 1911 succeeded him as professor of organ at the Paris Conservatoire. At the time of his appointment Saint-Saëns wrote:

... I regard him as the greatest organist I have ever known. He has the finest technique but, moreover, he is a marvelous improviser and, with him, the fine art of improvisation, so French and, in my opinion, so necessary, will not be jeopardized.[36]

Last Organ Music

The year 1919 brought forth three interesting works in three genres: *Cyprès et Lauriers*, Op. 156, for organ and orchestra (and later arranged for two pianos), was composed at the end of February; his last solo organ work, the *Troisième Fantaisie*, Op. 157; and in November the *Prière*, Op. 158, for cello and organ. Dedicated to André Hekking, the *Prière* was arranged for violin and organ the next year and published as Opus 158bis.

Cyprès et Lauriers was given its premiere at Ostende on 18 April 1919. Its first performance in Paris was at the Trocadéro on 24 October 1920. Saint-Saëns conducted the orchestra of the Société des Concerts du Conservatoire and Eugène Gigout played the organ.

Death of Saint-Saëns

In 1921 Saint-Saëns sailed for Algiers later than usual. He had a rough trip and it proved to be his last for, at the Hôtel de l'Oasis, at 10:30 Friday evening, 16 December 1921, he died. His last words: "This time I think it's really the end."

[34]Alexandre Cellier, "Une heure avec Camille Saint-Saëns," *L'Orgue*, No. 73 (October–December 1954) 122–24.
[35]Ibid.
[36]Letter from Saint-Saëns to Gabriel Fauré, 1 May 1911. In *Correspondance*, 91.

Plate 43. The last photograph of Saint-Saëns

176

Two funerals were held. His body lay in state in his apartment over the weekend and on Monday morning, 19 December, it was carried to the cathedral at six o'clock and an imposing ceremony was presided over by the Archbishop of Algiers and the Governor-general. The music, performed by the singers and orchestra from the Opéra d'Algier, included Saint-Saëns's *Marche héroïque, Le Cygne* and *Ave verum*. As his body was carried from the church, the "Funeral March" from Beethoven's *Third Symphony* was played.[37]

His body was then taken to Marseille and thence by train to Paris where, arriving at the Gare de Lyon, it was taken to the Madeleine late in the afternoon of 22 December. Saint-Saëns lay in state all the next day.

The state had provided 40,000 francs for the funeral expenses. The facade of the Madeleine was hung with black silver-edged draperies with Saint-Saëns's initials emblazoned on the cartouche. Above the catafalque in the center aisle rose a kind of funerary dome surrounded by torchères with lighted candles.

The requiem was set for ten o'clock Saturday morning—the day before Christmas. Well before the hour crowds stormed the gates of the Madeleine and tight security measures allowed only those with official invitations to enter. The great church quickly filled to overflowing with people standing in the smallest nooks and galleries. The Entrée was shared by Henri Dallier, the organist of the Madeleine, and Eugène Gigout. The music of the Mass consisted of:

Ego sum (from *Mors et Vita*)	Charles Gounod
De Profundis (in faux bourdon)	Gregorian
Kyrie	
Rex tremendae (from *Requiem*)	Saint-Saëns
Oro supplex	
Pie Jesu	Saint-Saëns
Adagio (*Third Symphony*)	Saint-Saëns
Libera	Samuel Rousseau
In Paradisum (from *Requiem*)	Gabriel Fauré
Sortie, Marche héroïque	Saint-Saëns

[37]The details of Saint-Saëns's funeral are taken from Arthur Dandelot's *La Vie et l'Oeuvre de Saint-Saëns* (Paris: Editions Dandelot, 1930) 255–58.

Plate 44. Widor delivering his eulogy at Saint-Saëns's tomb, Montparnasse cemetery 24 December 1921

From the church the great funeral cortège wended its way to the cemetery of Montparnasse. There, before the Saint-Saëns family mausoleum, seven official eulogies were pronounced. Among the representatives were Eugène Gigout who spoke briefly in the name of Saint-Saëns's friends and former students at the École Niedermeyer and Charles-Marie Widor who, as perpetual secretary of the Académie des Beaux-Arts, spoke in the name of the Institut de France. The speakers paid homage to one of the longest and most illustrious of musical careers. By the time of his death, at the age of eighty-six, he had passed three-quarters of a century before the public. Camille Saint-Saëns was no more, but, Widor reminded his listeners, "his spirit, alive and glorious, hovers over the world and will continue to hover so long as there are orchestras and instruments."[38]

---

[38]Charles-Marie Widor, "Discours," *Discours prononcés aux funérailles de C. Saint-Saëns le samedi 24 décembre 1921 au cimetière du Montparnasse.*

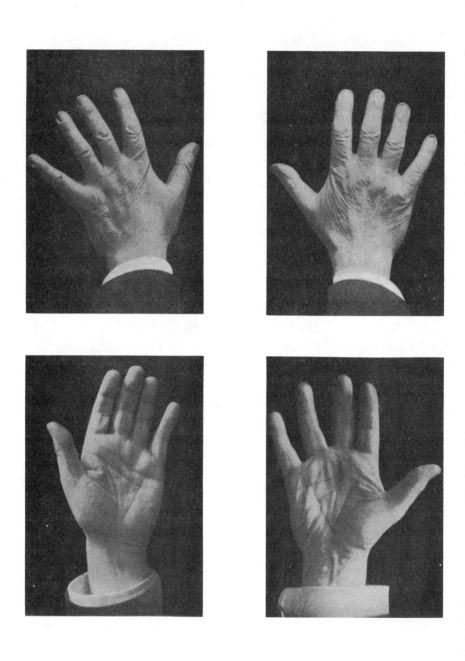

Plate 45. Saint-Saëns's hands

CHAPTER VII

Saint-Saëns, The Organist

Manual Technique

Saint-Saëns was the outstanding example of his own definition of "The Perfect Organist": "A virtuoso hardened to every difficulty and an ingenious improviser."[1] His was an astounding keyboard facility which combined speed with an infallible precision—he played rapidly with no wrong notes! Fifteen sides of phonograph recordings testify to his virtuosic prowess. His playing as a pianist was praised for its exquisite beauty of tone, complete evenness of touch and extreme delicacy. He was the "master of exquisite finesse"[2] whose

> . . . playing is full of charm and a wonderful facility. . . There are sparkling clearness, grace and elegance in his rippling passages and runs; he phrases and sings a melody with distinction and point, and all done with perfect repose. . .[3]

---

[1]Saint-Saëns, "Music in the Church," 5.

[2]Redfern Mason, "Saint-Saëns Honor Guest at Reception," *The San Francisco Examiner* (Friday, 2 July 1915) 6.

[3]Richard Aldrich, review of his concert at Carnegie Hall, New York, 4 November 1906, "New York Symphony Orchestra, Walter Damrosch, Camille Saint-Saëns," *Concert Life in New York* (New York: Putnam, 1941) 148.

Arthur Hervey noted that "his lightness of touch was quite unique. He is, perhaps, heard at his best when interpreting Bach, with those works he is as intimately acquainted as any living musician."[4]

Saint-Saëns's style adapted equally to the piano or the organ. He played Bach's *Italian Concerto* with repose, clarity and distinction[5] on the piano and that same composer's *Fugue in D Major*, BWV 532, with "cleanliness, ease and precision"[6] on the organ. Louis Kelterborn described his playing in Basel in the 1880s:

> His technique was extremely brilliant, clear in the finest details, rich in colors, wonderfully refreshing in rhythmic life, elegant and graceful, yet always virile, absolutely free from sentimentality and excess of the rubato, which so many modern virtuosi seem to hold indispensable for an exhibition of "taste or feeling"; and so was his interpretation always that of a superior artist who was intimately acquainted with the individual style of every master. Thus his readings of Bach were marvels of lucidity, refinement, combined with strength and grandeur.[7]

His manual technique was flawless. His fingers stayed close to the keys and their touch was fluent, deft and immaculate. As arpeggios rippled up and down the keyboards, often in contrary motion, a younger generation of organists would say that his "performance at the organ remained more pianistic, less scientific than that of Guilmant and Widor."[8]

Even in his mid-seventies Saint-Saëns was still a great player but not unaware of the hazards of old age. He referred frequently in his letters to things not being as they used to be. Having practiced all day for an evening concert, he wrote, "The agility has come back completely, but that evenness of which I was so proud is no longer as beautiful as in the past and I have to pay more attention to it." He then added, philosophically, "How lucky are those who never play well in public for, as the years go by, they only play less well and no one notices!"[9]

[4]Arthur Hervey, *Masters of French Music* (London: Osgood, McIlvaine & Co., 1894) 116.

[5]*The New Music Review* (January 1907) 93. Review of Saint-Saëns's piano recital at Carnegie Hall, 27 November 1906.

[6]Joseph d'Ortigue, "Inauguration des Orgues de Saint-Merry à Paris," *La Maîtrise* (15 December 1857) 142.

[7]Louis Kelterborn, "A Few Reminiscences of Camille Saint-Saëns," *The Musician* (May 1906) 250.

[8]Joseph Bonnet, "Preface," *Historical Organ Recitals*, Volume V (New York: G. Schirmer, 1929) viii.

[9]Letter from Saint-Saëns to Caroline de Serres, London, 27 May 1913.

Though he had a perfectly natural technique, Saint-Saëns worked to keep it impeccable—more so as he grew older. He practiced two hours every day up to and including the last day of his life. At his Paris apartment he practiced on an upright piano in his study; his Erard grand was too large to fit into the room. While traveling he had a two-octave silent clavier, the touch of which was adjustable by a screw at one side. His valet would sit opposite him holding the keyboard on his knees while Saint-Saëns did exercises to limber up his fingers and arms.[10]

His powers of execution never diminished. When the Scottish organist, A. M. Henderson, was in Paris in the summer of 1908, he mentioned to Saint-Saëns that his *Fantaisie in E-flat Major* had long been in his repertoire, and the composer

> . . . responded by saying that he had composed it. . . at Saint-Merry and that he wished to have me hear it there. On the appointed Sunday, after the service, he played the *Fantaisie* for me with evident enjoyment. The opening movement with the alternating chords on contrasted manuals was especially effective on this old organ, and in the concluding allegro— where some of the pedal passages are far from easy—he showed that his feet as well as his hands had lost none of their cunning.[11]

Henderson also wrote of hearing the seventy-seven-year-old Saint-Saëns in a concert of his own compositions at Salle Gaveau in 1912. He played the piano part in the *Septet* for piano, trumpet and strings, and on the organ the *Prélude et Fugue in E Major*, Op. 99, No. 1. "When I remarked that the evening was a wonderful tour de force for one of his years, he replied instantly: 'Not at all, my friend. You see, I am much too busy to get old. There is simply no end to my interminable career!'"[12]

---

[10]Letter of Paul Sabatie, La Chapelle Saint-Remy (Sarthe), 20 October 1955. Quoted in Seth Bingham, "Glimpses Over the French Horizon, Part 3," *The American Organist* (June 1959) 202–03.

[11]A.M. Henderson, "Visits to Saint-Saëns Recalled: Memories of a Famous Organist," *The Diapason* (February 1951) 24.

The author mentions further that the Cromorne on the Positif delighted Saint-Saëns. "To display its quality he improvised with great charm and readiness."

[12]Ibid.

Saint-Saëns was justifiably proud of his long career. Marcel Dupré recounted a conversation he overheard while walking behind Saint-Saëns: A few months before his death Saint-Saëns and a fellow member (his own age) of the Académie des Sciences were walking to the Institut where Saint-Saëns was to play the piano part of his *Septet*, for piano, trumpet and strings. As they walked together slowly, one said to the *(continued)*

Plate 46. Boëly at his organ at Saint-Germain-l'Auxerrois

Pedal Technique

Saint-Saëns's pedal technique was as formidable as his manual technique. The first published reference to his performance (on a pédalier) of an organ work, Bach's *Fugue in D Major*, BWV 532, noted that he played "almost as agily and as intelligently with his feet as with his fingers."[13] This observation is all the more remarkable because Saint-Saëns employed only his toes in pedal playing—never his heels. An all-toes pedal technique might well have been established by the short pedals on the first organs he played. A. P. F. Boëly, Saint-Saëns's first organ teacher, had a "German" pedalboard on his organ at Saint-Germain-l'Auxerrois but, although the compass was extended enough to play the pedal parts in Bach's organ music, the length of the natural keys, while longer than those customarily found on French organs of the time, were, if we can judge by a contemporary drawing of Boëly at his organ (opposite), hardly long enough for the organist to use his heels comfortably. But by the time Saint-Saëns was acquiring his pedal technique, the pédaliers and all new organs (as well as the recently rebuilt ones) had a compass of at least two octaves and longer natural keys.

Organ methods were available (J. P. E. Martini's *École d'Orgue* appeared in Paris about 1805, and Miné's *Manuel Simplifié de l'Organiste*, which reprinted Kegel's *Leçons d'Orgue*, to name but two) which introduced the student to pedal playing with exercises for both alternate toes and alternate heel and toe with the same foot. That modern heel-and-toe pedaling was in common usage is further evidenced in the pedaling indications in the music of Charles-Valentin Alkan and César Franck's arrangements for organ of Alkan's harmonium music. Use of the heel was frequent; pedal glissandi, toe-heel substitution and double pedaling were all part of the organist's technique. Although in the absence of a national school of organ playing and a uniform system of pedaling everyone

---

other, "Well, M. Saint-Saëns, our old legs don't go like they used to." To which the other replied, furiously, "Yes, our legs, but you will soon see how my fingers work!" (*Marcel Dupré raconte. . .* 80.)

[13]Henri Blachard, "Concerts et Auditions musicales," *Revue et Gazette musicale* (15 March 1857) 83.

developed an individual pedal technique—the limitation of the alterna-tives (a heel and toe of two feet) imposed a similarity of choices.

Certainly, by playing only with the toes Saint-Saëns achieved that clarity and articulate precision which so distinguished his playing, but also achieved a flawless legato when he so desired.[14] Of course, by excluding the use of the heel, Saint-Saëns was obliged to devise some original pedal-ing solutions. The following is the only example of his pedaling indica-tions:

Saint-Saëns, *Rhapsodie Bretonne*, Op. 7, No. 2, m. 51.

Characteristics of His Style

What Saint-Saëns knew about the organ and how he played it is our most important guide to the interpretation of his music. Three charac-teristics set him apart from other turn-of-the-century French organ com-posers and in large measure they serve as a guide to those investigating his playing style.

First, his technique and style developed out of what remained of the French Classic tradition that survived into the 19th century. His play-ing style never changed, so that, in his later years, Saint-Saëns appeared as a historical curiosity to the younger generation of Conservatoire-trained organists. There is no question that "His organ playing owed more to his natural virtuosity and to his superior intelligence than to fun-damental principles instilled from an organ method by a teacher passing

---

[14]J. Ermand Bonnal, "Saint-Saëns à Saint-Séverin," *Bulletin Trimestriel des Amis de l'Orgue*, No. 24 (December 1935) 7. Charles Tournemire, in his *Précis d'éxécution, de registration et d'improvisation à l'orgue* (Paris: Éditions Max Eschig, 1936, p. 33), decries the heaviness and inelegance in pedal playing which relies too heavily on a preponderance of the use of the heel, and writes that "Camille Saint-Saëns qui n'était peut-être pas un très grand tech-nicien de l'orgue, ne se servait que des 'pointes'—il y mettait même beaucoup de coquet-terie, tout en se réclamant du grand Cantor."

on a 'tradition.' "[15] Unlike the works of Widor, Vierne and Dupré—the interpretation of which is directly influenced by the teaching of the Belgian pedagogue Jacques Lemmens and refined and codified by Marcel Dupré—Saint-Saëns's music is a reflection of his very personal manner of playing: a 20th-century link to the 18th century.

Second, unlike organ music of other French composers who were associated with particular instruments (Franck: Sainte-Clotilde; Widor: Saint-Sulpice; Vierne: Notre-Dame Cathedral; and Messiaen: La Trinité), no particular organ influenced his compositions.

Third, Saint-Saëns indicated little registration. With a few early exceptions, his pieces carry no directions for drawing the stops or for the quality of tone desired, i.e., Fonds, Anches or solo stops. More often pitches are indicated 16' 8' 4'. Whereas César Franck was precise, Saint-Saëns was, at best, vague.

Objectivity

Saint-Saëns's playing exhibited none of those "Romantic" traits so typical of his 19th- and early 20th-century contemporaries. When Reynaldo Hahn referred to him as "musical art's last great classicist,"[16] he was describing his playing style as much as his writing style. Jacques Durand's memory of his "impeccable playing, flawless, pearly touch and amazing virtuosity, but an interpretation devoid of romanticism"[17] is echoed by Claudio Arrau: "The most even scales you can imagine, and great power in the fingers. Ice cold, but amazing."[18] But a style felt by another to be "full of taste and moderation, controlled emotion and magisterial simplicity."[19] His improvisations were marked by that same objectivity which "appealed more to the mind than to the senses and that is why, undoubtedly, all emotion was voluntarily excluded."[20]

[15]Bonnal, "Saint-Saëns à Saint-Séverin," 7.

[16]Reynaldo Hahn, *Excelsior*.

[17]Jacques Durand, *Quelques souvenirs d'un éditeur de musique* (Paris: A. Durand & Cie., 1924) 75–76.

[18]Claudio Arrau, in Joseph Horowitz, *Conversations with Arrau* (New York: Knopf, 1982).

[19]Eloy de Stoecklin, Salzburg, reviewed in *Le Ménestrel* (15 September 1906) 564.

[20]Bonnal, "Saint-Saëns à Saint-Séverin," 7.

Articulation

The most obvious feature of Saint-Saëns's playing was his non-legato style—an articulation which could be likened to that spoken of by the clavecinists of the 18th century. His clean, precise playing was particularly apparent at a time when Widor and Guilmant, the eminent organ professors at the Paris Conservatoire, were indoctrinating their students with the "true Bach tradition" as handed down to them through their teacher, Jacques Lemmens. This tradition was founded on an absolute legato. We can appreciate today the abhorrence of a player such as Saint-Saëns, whose favorite composers were Bach, Rameau, and Mozart, for that *absolute legato* which has become the hallmark of the French school.

Saint-Saëns described the evolution of legato playing as a reaction to a detached keyboard style which had become exaggerated by the beginning of the 19th century. He recalled that in his youth,

... in the middle of the last century, aged persons were still to be heard whose piano playing was singularly détaché. The old non-legato, through exaggeration, had become a staccato, and this exaggeration brought about a reaction that has been carried too far. The tyrannical reign of the perpetual legato succeeded. It was decided that in piano playing, unless indicated to the contrary and even at times in spite of such indications, everything everywhere should be tied together.[21]

Saint-Saëns deplored this style of playing, and his numerous piano recordings testify to his preference for a detached, clean, dry touch. He criticized Friedrich Kalkbrenner's school of playing:

... which invented continuous legato, so false and so monotonous, the abuse of little nuances, and the mania for a continual *expressivo* applied without discernment. All that revolted my natural instinct; I could not conform to it, and I was reproached for it.[22]

---

[21]Saint-Saëns, *On the Execution of Music, and Principally of Ancient Music*. A lecture delivered at the Salon de la Pensée Française, Panama-Pacific International Exposition, San Francisco, 1 June 1915. Done in English with explanatory notes by Henry P. Bowie (San Francisco: The Blair-Murdock Co., 1915) 7–8. See also Saint-Saëns's "Preface" to Mozart's *Oeuvres complètes pour piano seul*, Vol. I, *Sonates* (Paris: Durand & Cie., 1915) iv.

[22]Saint-Saëns, *École Buissonnière*, 7.

Precision

All notes of a chord (which is not to be arpeggiated) must reach the ear at exactly the same time. The two hands should function together—not one after the other as too often happens, sometimes through simple negligence but sometimes because it is believed that this gives the playing grace and charm. This is a great error: pretentious and mannered playing results.[23]

One of the most easily acquired habits of keyboard players and a habit which became an interpretative trait of 19th-century players, was that of arpeggiating chords and a slovenly, inexact precision of attack between the hands. Saint-Saëns's playing was free of this characteristic, and he counseled students against it.

Interpretation

The music should unfold as exactly as possible, omitting none of the composer's written indications. Rests should be scrupulously observed.[24]

Much in Saint-Saëns's playing that was often considered studied or unemotional was merely a very literal interpretation of the score. Part of his objective approach was his musicological curiosity and his search for historical authenticity. He was one of the very few composers of his time—and instrumental virtuosi—who not only was familiar with early music, but who was concerned enough to investigate performance practices of the past. His own music is as devoid of interpretative suggestions as are the scores of his favorite composers (Rameau, Bach and Mozart), and he knew the confusion and misrepresentation of a composer's intentions that over-editing could create.

He likewise took exception to modern editions which constantly indicate legato, molto legato and sempre legato. In the preface to his edition of Mozart's complete piano *Sonatas* he wrote:

Nothing of this kind exists in the manuscripts and the old editions of Mozart's music. On the contrary, everything points toward the belief that this music should be performed lightly... When Mozart desired a legato effect he indicated it.[25]

[23]Saint-Saëns, "Conseils pour l'Étude du Piano," *Le Monde Musical* (15 February 1899) 53.
[24]Ibid.
[25]Saint-Saëns, "Preface," Mozart's *Complete Piano Works*.

Tempo

We know from detailed accounts of his playing, as well as from his phonograph recordings, that Saint-Saëns played very quickly. Eugène Gigout used to tell of Saint-Saëns's improvising five- and six-voice fugues at breakneck speed and saying, "If you don't hear, watch my fingers and feet. I have brought in the subject a number of times."[26] Such a comment would hardly be made by an organist concerned with every voice being heard distinctly in a reverberant nave. But Saint-Saëns's was a paradoxical personality, even contrary, more often than not. If asked his opinion of a chosen tempo, he might answer as he once did Sir Thomas Beecham, who had asked if he were satisfied with his performance of the *Third Symphony*. The seventy-eight-year-old Maître replied: ". . . I have lived a long while, and I have known all the conductors. There are two kinds: one takes the music too fast, and the other too slow. There is no third!"[27] He criticized rubato playing: "It is better to play naturally and steadily as tempo rubato is in the realm of transcendental execution."[28]

Registration

Saint-Saëns was a master of the art of registration—a fact little supported by the few stop indications in his music. Neither is there any evidence of his appreciation of French Classic registration, but Joseph Bonnet recalled that his "use of stops was colorful, distinctive, and thoroughly in conformity with the traditions of the old French masters."[29] He delighted in the timbres of classic registrations and would ask those about the console to draw "gaies sonorités," "bien carillonnantes," "an old Cromorne" or a "delectable Cornet."[30] He was well versed in French Classic registration formulae, was familiar with old Dutch organs, and "understood the charm of a Nasard combined with a Gambe or Bourdon, a Cornet solo, a Grosse quinte or a Carillon in the Pédale and a Récit de Tierce en taille or en dessus." One had to see the connoisseur's delight

[26]Un organiste [Jean Huré], "Un Cours d'Improvisation par Marcel Dupré," *L'Orgue et les organistes* (15 October 1925) 8.

[27]James Harding, *Saint-Saëns and his Circle* (London: Chapman & Hall, 1965) 209.

[28]Saint-Saëns, "Conseils pour l'Étude du Piano."

[29]Bonnet, "Preface," *Historical Organ Recitals*, viii.

[30]Jean Huré, *L'Ésthétique de l'orgue* (Paris: Sénart, 1923) 167.

with which he would ask one of his friends to "Play me a trio with a Cornet in the soprano, a Cromorne in the tenor and a Grosse flûte in the bass."[31] He avoided "thick" sonorities when improvising, as he often did so in two or three voices.[32]

Once in a particularly memorable improvisation at the Offertoire on All Saints' Day, he used for bell effects the Grand-Orgue Cornet, the smaller Positif Cornet and the Récit mixture. "With these colors Saint-Saëns worked up a wonderful symphony—truly a feast reserved for the angels' delight."[33] But at Vespers, when the mood of the day changed from one of celebration to one of rendering homage to the dead, he changed his registration, the colors darkened and the rhythms grew heavy. "The laws of aesthetics submitted to the imperatives of faith."[34]

His art was succinctly described by an old organblower at the Madeleine: "We have had the very best organists here—M. Dubois and M Fauré—but only M. Saint-Saëns could make such beautiful effects with very little wind." An opinion from the blower room which confirms that of the masters.[35]

The Improviser

Saint-Saëns's keyboard virtuosity, his facility with counterpoint and his genius as a composer combined to create one of the most original improvisers. "No one who had the pleasure of hearing him will ever forget his extraordinary improvisations, so authentically classic in style and so dazzling in their virtuosity," wrote Joseph Bonnet.[36]

> Saint-Saëns's genius as an improviser has often been praised, but these eulogies have always seemed insufficient to me. His genius was of an indescribable splendor. It was even more extraordinary then the description which Forkel gives of Bach's genius.[37]

[31]Jean Huré, "Saint-Saëns: Organiste honoraire de Saint-Séverin," *Le Guide du Concert (Numéro Saint-Saëns*, 1914/1922) 9–10.
[32]Jean Huré, "Eugène Gigout," *L'Orgue et les organistes* (December 1925) 506.
[33]Ibid.
[34]Ibid.
[35]Alexandre Cellier in *L'Orgue et les organistes* (October 1924) 30.
[36]Bonnet, "Preface," viii.
[37]Huré, "Gigout," 5–6.

He frequently improvised in the style of his *Third Symphony* and, without the slightest hesitation, played incredibly difficult fugal allegros.[38]

Following a marvelously ordered plan, he improvised counterpoint in two, three or four voices with such a purity and logic in the progression of parts that the most erudite musician with the most experienced ear believed he was hearing a thoughtfully carefully written down composition. So difficult were certain of these impromptus that it would have taken a year of assiduous work for our most skilled organists to play them.

For example, for the Sortie of the High Mass Saint-Saëns would improvise a strict fugue in three real voices on the manuals. The clean, clear, incisive subject, the surprisingly ingenious countersubject, the exquisitely imaginative and inventive episodes would continue imperturbably in a vertiginous movement when, all of a sudden, in the stretto the last motet sung by the choir was heard in the pedal and continued, as the entrances came closer and closer together, until a dazzling conclusion. This he called a "little joke."

Lastly, I heard him improvise an Offertoire in which the right hand moved in legato fifths and sixths, the left hand arpeggiated wide chords from one keyboard to another while the pedal sang the melody in the tenor. And the rhythm did not falter for an instant.[39]

Because of his remarkable facility for recalling and repeating note for note an improvisation which pleased him, "One did not know if he had improvised or played a work already written. I had to hear a certain chorale on the 'O Salutaris' several times before I realized that it was not the result of an improvisation."[40] The foregoing reminiscences date from Saint-Saëns's later years, but one of his friends said that "Whoever didn't hear Saint-Saëns in his early days doesn't know how far the communicative power of the spontaneous melody can go."[41]

His Knowledge and Use of the Organ

Camille Saint-Saëns was probably the only eclectic French organ composer—particularly of the 19th century. The very reason that he did

---

[38]Huré, *L'Ésthétique de l'orgue*, 172.
[39]Huré, *Guide du Concert*, 9–10.
[40]Bonnal, "Saint-Saëns à Saint-Séverin, 7.
[41]Bonnerot, 36.

not compose for a specific organ partly explains why his music sounds well on a variety of instruments. In a survey of some sixty organs he is known to have played, we find instruments built by Silbermann, Richard and Clicquot; Pechard-Barker, Puget, Cavaillé-Coll, Merklin-Schütze and Abbey; Walcker, Kuhn, Voit and Goll; Gray & Davison, Bryceson and Willis; Roosevelt and Austin. His eighty-six years spanned the most varied period in the organ's history, both as regards new developments in mechanical and tonal concepts and new compositional techniques which took advantage of these innovations.

Saint-Saëns's career began at the time when the French Classic organs of the 17th- and 18th-centuries were still in use, bridged the entire career of Aristide Cavaillé-Coll, and continued well into the 20th century. Along the way he heard his *Third Symphony* played on such diverse instruments as the eleven-stop Abbey organ in Salle Pleyel in Paris and the 111-stop Austin in the Festival Hall of San Francisco's Panama-Pacific Exposition. He played organs from Notre-Dame Cathedral to Carnegie Hall. In London he played the organ in George Ashdown Audsley's home. The two-manual, nineteen-stop organ had been built by the noted organ architect according to his system of "compound expression," i.e., the entire organ was enclosed (except for three pedal stops and the Great Diapason) and divided between two swell boxes. Saint-Saëns played this organ for nearly two hours,[42] pronounced it unique, said it was the "most expressive organ he had ever played"[43] and remarked that he wished he had such an instrument at his disposal in Paris.

In 1883, while on tour in England, Saint-Saëns had occasion to discuss many organ matters with Pierre Veerkamp, one of Cavaillé-Coll's employees. Saint-Saëns spoke at length of his experiences with the many different types of organs with which he was familiar and, fortunately, Veerkamp noted down their conversation for posterity.[44]

---

[42]George Ashdown Audsley, "The Small Two-Manual Organ," *The Organ*, 15 (January 1925) 138–49.

[43]George Ashdown Audsley, *The Organ of the Twentieth Century* (New York: Dodd, Mead and Co., 1919) 229.

[44]François Sabatier, "Remarques à propos d'un manuscrit inédit de Pierre Veerkamp," *L'Orgue*, No. 195 (July–September 1985) 10–11.

Moving from his native Holland to Paris, Veerkamp (1849–1923) worked for Cavaillé-Coll from 1873 and was technical director of his shop from 1884 until he joined Mutin in Caen for whom he worked from 1892 until 1913. After the First World War he occupied himself, until his death, in writing a 300-page study of the organ. This work is to be published by the Association Cavaillé-Coll.

Saint-Saëns felt mechanical action to be very sympathetic but objected to its oversensitivity in which "the slightest touch of the key causes it to sound" and to the unevenness of touch between the bass and the upper octaves. "An evenness of touch from one end of the keyboard to the other is not an illogical request. Among the benefits of the pneumatic lever is that of having overcome both of these problems. This last type of action is, therefore, the most sympathetic. As for the slight delay which results due to the little relief pallet (*soufflet*), it is not disturbing and only noticeable in instruments which have both a mechanical-action keyboard and another provided with a pneumatic lever."

He found the touch of tubular-pneumatic organs "all right, but the attack is not felt under the fingers as in mechanical action. It is too spongy, as well. There is not an absolute evenness in the speed of the action or, I might even say, for certain instruments, in the slowness."

A single experience with electric action made the same impression on him:

> One has the very distinct impression of the intervention of an intermediary agent in the transmission of the musical thought. You feel as though you are directing instead of playing because you don't feel the precise attack of the sound. Nevertheless, I have no reason to disqualify these types of actions to which I have no trouble adapting.

Saint-Saëns was most comfortable with the Cavaillé-Coll console—the epitome of contemporary design—and preferred the pédales de combinaison operated by the feet which activated all couplers and added or subtracted the reeds and mixtures from the foundation stops of each division. When asked his opinion of Hilborne Roosevelt's adjustable combination pistons, he said they were interesting but for the few times he used combinations he would just as soon use the "English type which always bring on the same stops (and often those not wanted) or the French type which, though adjustable, only operate certain stops."[45] He shared all organists' fears of unfamiliar consoles and novelties: "In certain organs the combinations, far from being an accessory, seem to have been their builders' principal preoccupation. The result: the organist, seated before such a Chinese puzzle, refuses to use the combinations then and there for fear of an inevitable gaff."[46] In foreign countries he made no concessions

---

[45]Veerkamp, Unpublished manuscript, excerpt from Chapter XI.
[46]Ibid.

for different types of organs or console controls. Thus, when he played in Karlsruhe around 1910, his playing, "though excellent in itself, was entirely marred by the lengthy pauses he made whilst altering his registration... [because] he refuses to use pistons to aid his registration, preferring to set all stops by hand."[47]

With personal opinions strongly held with, perhaps, a bit of national chauvinism, Saint-Saëns's preferences were born of years of practical experience and his criterion for a good organ was that of every organist: "It is very simple: I measure the excellence of an organ by the satisfaction and pleasure I derive from playing it."[48]

[47]James Wedgewood, *Some Continental Organs and Their Makers* (London: Wm. Reeves, 1910) 31.

[48]Veerkamp, op. cit.

APPENDIX A

Five Essays by
Camille Saint-Saëns

I. The Works of Boëly

An impeccable composer and a theorist of the first rank, Boëly had that unique trait of drawing his inspiration from the past. He took great pains to write in the style of Scarlatti and Bach, the object of his greatest admiration.

An artist steeped in such a tradition need not depend on the approval of his contemporaries; he only attracts attention later, when the current issues no longer exist. Thus the time has come to appreciate the works of this very talented and conscientious musician.

He applied, often successfully, the same compositional devices to Gregorian melodies that Sebastian Bach employed with the German chorales. The result was a great many pieces perfectly adapted to the Catholic liturgy. In these one is pleased to find not one error of taste, compositional fault or hint of popular style which would be out of place within the austerity of the Church.

His best pieces are written in a classical style. Some of them, like the Toccata in B Minor, Op. 43, No. 13, of the posthumous works, are pure masterpieces. But his most original work, and the one which places him in the ranks of the greatest musicians, is the small collection of sixteenth century *Noëls*, Op. 15, harmonized for organ. It is to his credit that he discovered these admirable hymns and brought them to light in a consummate (and much appreciated) style. The student of J.S. Bach equals his model.

This book of *Noëls* should be in every organist's repertoire. To the naïveté indispensable to hymns of the nativity is added an elevation and stylistic perfection which reminds one of the illuminations in missals or of the statuettes in cathedrals. It is a pure masterpiece.

Camille Saint-Saëns
Member of the Institut

Camille Saint-Saëns, "Preface," *Recueil de Noëls*, Op. 15. Fourteen Preludes or Pieces for organ composed by A. P. F. Boëly on the Cantiques of N. Denizot. (Paris: Costallat, 1902) 1.

II. Sacred Music

The concept of reform seems to hold a kind of fascination for mankind. From the "transfer of ownership" in small businesses to constitutional revisions and changes of government, it seems as though all reforms were intended to bring back a golden age to earth. My generation still remembers the 1848 revolution carried out to deafening cries of "Vive la réforme!" advanced by a crowd which did not even know the meaning of the word "reform." It was enough to ask any of the rabble at random to be convinced. Alas! Very often, the reform brought about, the "transfer of ownership" effected, men found themselves as before, with their passions, their virtues and their faults; everyone just went back to bed....

These melancholy thoughts came to mind, in spite of myself, while reading the account of the Holy Father's plans for musical reform. At the same time I became anxious for the future—a state suggested sometimes by the preciseness of the pontifical instructions and sometimes, perhaps even more uneasy, by their vagueness. I would like to point some of them out, but the subject is broad and it is hard to organize the many questions raised and to treat them in a few words.

Camille Saint-Saëns, "Musique religieuse," *École Buissonnière* (Paris: Lafitte, 1913) 159–67.

    This essay is the development of Saint-Saëns's opinions expressed in a letter written in response to the publication of Pope Pius X's Instructions on the Reform of Sacred Music (*Motu proprio*). Saint-Saëns's "Letter to the editor" was published in *Le Monde Musical* (15 February 1904) 34.

    The Pope's music reforms seem very nice in theory but, most of the time, impossible to put into practice.

    A return to the *primitive purity* of Gregorian chant seems the most difficult— and who would define the essential difference between the sacred style and the secular? Palestrina's madrigals and Handel's operas impress today's audiences as extremely religious music. It is impossible to draw the line.

    How can cymbals and drums (among other things) be forbidden when angels in primitive paintings are portrayed with them? Everything depends on the way in which the instruments are used. Who will judge the length of the interludes and decide whether they are allowed or forbidden. Who will identify the *universal* melodies?

    In all of this I see words and sentences of a very noble effort—and nothing else. The world will go on as before.

First, it is only proper to express our gratitude to His Holiness Pope Pius X for his interest in church music demonstrated in such a visible way. He is very concerned with the bad music in churches. What a valuable advantage, if the present state of things could really be remedied. Such is certainly the Pope's intention. It remains to be seen if His Holiness's confidence in the wisdom of his advisers is justified; if, in wanting to get rid of the chaff, he has not exposed part of the wheat to destruction. This we are going to examine.

A return to the primitive purity of Gregorian chant was discussed. I must admit to a certain skepticism in this regard. The old Gregorian manuscripts are sealed books, accessible only to the initiated. Not long ago some of these "initiates," struck by the textual differences in various modern editions, tried to go back to the sources and made an edition in which *primitive purity* would be restored. The result was astonishing! The fastidious repetition of interminable series of notes put off the most skilled performers. Imagine a passage like this: la do la do la do—la do la do—la do la do la do la do, etc., for entire pages! With our slow performance of plainchant, this is intolerable. It must be assumed that these passages were performed rapidly, rather like trills—an assumption which upsets all of our present ideas concerning the performance of this kind of music. In reality, after so many centuries, we have lost the key to this ancient art. It is a dead language and, as such, is imbued with an arcane character which nothing could replace. Surrendering to the chimera of primitive purity, the Pope has designated the Solesmes edition as the authentic version. He could not have done better and its adoption will undoubtedly be a very great benefit.

But one cannot be confined to sixteenth century music. By what right can the musical expression and devotion of succeeding centuries be ignored? The Pope goes no further. He even extols the use of sixteenth century polyphonic music of which Palestrina is the most illustrious representative. Only the human voice, alone and in chorus, and the organ, should be heard beneath the sacred vaults. The Pope denounces violins and other secular instruments and absolutely forbids the use of loud instruments: cymbals, trombones, etc.

On the surface all this appears very judicious and readily yields to a deeper examination.

Instruments are nothing in themselves. They only exist for the use that can be made of them. That is why trumpets, trombones and cymbals can be used so effectively in church. Everything depends upon their role. But, what am I saying? Did not trombones sound in the Temple of Solomon? In the paintings of Fra Angelico and other old masters, do we not see angels in heaven playing all the instruments then in use: viols, citharas, sackbuts, drums, tambourines, oboes? They also hold small picturesque portative organs in their heavenly hands. But at that time those instruments were just as secular as the others. A well-known Italian painting, [Titian's *Venus Diverted By Music*, in the Prado Museum] portrays a gentleman playing the organ before a lady. She is not sumptuously dressed—as a matter of fact, she has nothing on at all!

And when you think of it, who says that all those instruments in the hands of the Evangelists did not appear on earth to be used in ancient religious ceremonies? Palestrina's music was written for voices alone, but there is no proof that sometimes the voices were not supported by instruments. In the instrumental music of the same period the various parts are written in a vague way with no indication of which instruments would play them. If, in the vocal works, nothing indicates the presence of an accompaniment, there are no indications to the contrary. Nor are tempo and expression, so important in modern music, indicated. This lack of precise details gives rise to all the conjecture.

The more the question is studied the more obvious it becomes that there is no reason for excluding from the divine service so-called secular instruments with the exception of the organ. If that were to happen, then the psalm in which we are exhorted to praise the Lord on stringed instruments, trumpets and even clanging cymbals would have to be suppressed from the liturgy!

The music of the sixteenth century is not a dead language but a dying language, the traditions of which are lost. Everyone interprets it as he likes and claims to know the only true manner of performing it. That is not the point. But what is particularly religious about this polyphony in which melody is almost entirely absent? Palestrina's madrigals—the famous pavane "Belle qui tient ma vie"—differ very little from the religious music of their time. Sung to Latin words they would seem to modern ears like the purest examples of sacred music. It would be the same with many of the arias from Handel's operas, nearer our own time, but already distant. It is the distance which creates the mystery, and the mysteriousness passes for holiness. So, too, the pointed arch took on a mysterious air as soon as it disappeared from contemporary architecture.

Those are illusions. How will one go about obeying the Pope's orders that the melodies sung in church be of an essentially religious character? How will this character be recognized? A feeling of anxiety cannot be helped when, in reading in the report of the director [Vincent d'Indy] of the Schola Cantorum in audience with the Pope, and their lamentations over the performance of *masses in all keys, with tenor solos,* one sees Mozart's *Requiem* among the forbidden works!

If that famous *Requiem* is banned, should we conclude that all the masses of that period are banned—those of Mozart, Haydn and Beethoven? Does the same fate befall the works of Jomelli, Porpora, Marcello? Mention has been made of composers working behind the scenes to replace the forbidden works. In plain language, that would mean that the Schola would dictate to the Catholic world which ancient and modern works were appropriate and which were not. That, it will be agreed, is a grave responsibility. I see it as going to war, one defending the side of the Pope, the other, as in the historiograph of the Blessed Claudine, brandishing the flaming sword of the archangels in an august hand. It is a fine sight. But will the whole Catholic world submit to this tyranny? Does it not risk running into that immovable stone wall which Leo XIII ran up against when he wanted to lead the French Catholics into the field of politics? It is difficult to change time-honored habits overnight. Do you want an example?

One fine day the order came from Rome to replace the Parisian Rite with the Roman Rite. This disposition suppressed the "Dies irae" from the requiem mass. It was mortifying. The dead could not believe themselves really dead if the "Dies irae" were not sung at their funerals. What was done? The words of the "Pie Jesu" began to be set to the melody of the "Dies irae" and it was introduced surreptitiously as a motet. Then a verse of the forbidden poem was slipped in—then two—then three. Finally, the "Dies irae," reestablished little by little in its entirety, was sung as before.

Each age, each country perceives devotion and consequently, sacred music, in its own way. In Andalusia, piety is expressed gaily. Processions in the streets are accompanied by firecrackers and sky rockets and when the cortège goes back into the church the faithful before the doors, dance madly in a circle to the sounds of wild music. At Christmas it is even better: inside the church itself masses are sung in the style of sequidillas, accompanied by castinettes. To us all this seems the height of ridiculousness.

203

If it were suppressed those faithful would understand nothing of an austerity which is neither in their character nor in their customs. It might even not be improbable that in wanting to remedy what seemed to be a scandal, a more serious scandal would be created.

In France, similar customs are not being fought, only routine and wretched mediocrity. Do you know what I would do if I had the power and authority? I would begin by imposing in the seminaries the study—superficial, but serious in its brevity—not only of music but of all branches of the arts. The complaint is often made of what little artistic taste is evidenced by the clergy. How could it be otherwise? Artistic sentiment is rarely inbred in us; ordinarily it is developed by education. And when a priest, supreme authority in his church, lacks such an education, how could the most disastrous consequences not result?

Then I would ruthlessly forbid all music, even that of the great masters, which was not composed to sacred words but to which, on the contrary, words were more or less successfully adapted. Such pieces are artistic crimes; nothing justifies them given the prodigious amount of music specifically written for the Church between the sixteenth century and now.

Also forbidden would be motets written by composers unfamiliar with Latin texts, such as the "O salutaris," in which the words "da robur, fer—da robur, fer" are repeated in a way that makes no sense; and those in a vulgar style, like the motets of the Reverend Father Lambillotte who was probably a holy man but whose dreadful music is completely out of place beneath sacred vaults!. . . Because, in art, holiness is not sufficient. Talent is necessary. Style is necessary. And where will great style find refuge if not in church where the applause, success and miseries of Art do not exist?

It will surprise many people that I would ban almost all the works of Sebastian Bach from the Catholic Church. His marvellous chorale preludes are the very essence of Protestantism and, with few exceptions, his preludes and fugues, fantaisies and toccatas are primarily virtuoso pieces. They are music for the concert hall, not the church.

And then I would allow everyone complete freedom to sing God's praises as they please. To try to dictate the least detail—to regulate, for example, the length of the organ interludes—one risks, in being too exact, nothing happening.

Am I being pessimistic? It will not be amusing if our churches must be limited to plainchant and Palestrina. But, on the whole, one does not go to mass to be amused and this diet would be a hundred times preferable to that drivel inflicted on us daily to the detriment of Art and to the benefit of no one.

III. The Organ

When the cloven-hooved god Pan joined reeds of different lengths and so invented the flute which bears his name, he, in reality, created the organ. Only a keyboard and a bellows needed to be added to the flute to make one of those lovely instruments depicted by early painters in the hands of angels. As it developed and gradually became the most grandiose of instruments, its tone modified and increased tenfold by the reverberation of the great cathedrals, the organ assumed a religious character.

But the organ is more than a single instrument. It is an orchestra—a collection of Pan's pipes of every size, from those as small as a child's plaything to those as gigantic as temple columns. Each one corresponds to what is termed a "stop." The number is unlimited.

The Romans made organs which must have been simple from a musical standpoint, though they were complicated in their mechanical construction. They were called hydraulic organs. The employment of water in a wind instrument greatly perplexed historians but Cavaillé-Coll solved the problem by demonstrating that water compressed the air. This system was ingenious but imperfect since it was applicable only to the most primitive instruments. The keys, it seems, were very large and were struck by blows of the fist.

But let us leave erudition for art and primitive instruments for perfected new ones. By the time of Sebastian Bach and Rameau, the organ had taken on its grandiose character. The stops had multiplied and the organist selected them by means of registers which he drew out or pushed in at will. In order to put more resources at his disposal, the builder increased the number of keyboards. To the claviers for the hands was added

Camille Saint-Saëns, "L'Orgue," *École Buissonnière* (Paris: Lafitte, 1913) 169–76. This essay originally appeared in *L'Echo de Paris* 1 (January 1911). The manuscript is in the possession of Yves Gérard, Paris.

a pedal clavier. At that time Germany alone had pedals worthy of the name able to play an interesting bass part. In France and elsewhere the rudimentary pedals were only used for the most important bass notes or for holding very long notes. No one outside of Germany was capable of playing Sebastian Bach's compositions.

Playing the old instruments was tiring and uncomfortable. The touch was heavy and when the manuals were coupled a real display of strength was necessary. A similar effort was necessary to draw or push in the stops, some of which were beyond the player's reach. In short, an assistant was necessary—in fact, several assistants when playing large organs like those at Haarlem or Arnheim in Holland. It was almost impossible to change registration. All nuances, except for an abrupt change from loud to soft and vice-versa were impossible.

It remained for Cavaillé-Coll to change all this and open up new vistas for the organ. In France he introduced pedalboards worthy of the name and, by his invention of harmonic stops, gave to the upper octaves a brilliance they lacked. He invented wonderful combination pedals which allow the organist to change his combinations and, to vary the tone without the aid of an assistant or without leaving the keyboard. Even before his day a scheme had been devised of enclosing certain stops in a box protected by shutters which a pedal opened and closed at will; this permitted the finest shadings. By a different system the touch of the organ was made as light as that of the piano.

For some years Swiss organbuilders have been inventing new devices which make the organist a sort of magician. The manifold resources of the marvellous instrument are at his command, obedient to his slightest wish.

These resources are prodigious. The compass of the organ far surpasses that of all the instruments of the orchestra—only the violin's harmonics reach the same height but with little carrying power and limited effect. As for the lower range, what can compete with the thirty-two foot pipes which go two octaves below the violoncello's low C. Between the *pianissimo* which almost reaches the edge of silence down to a range of formidable and terrifying power, every degree of intensity can be obtained from this magical instrument. The variety of its timbre is immense: Flute stops of different kinds, Gambe stops that approximate the timbre of stringed instruments, Mutation stops in which each note, sounding several pitches simultaneously, plays its fundamental and its harmonics—a special kind of sonority which only the organ possesses; imitative orchestral stops, such as the Trumpet, Clarinet and the Cromorne (an obsolete instrument with a timbre peculiar to itself) and the Bassoon. There are several kinds of Voix célestes, created by combinations of two similar ranks of pipes which are not tuned in perfect unison; the famous Voix humaine, a favorite with the general public, which is seductive even though it is tremulous and nasal; and innumerable combinations of all these different stops, with the gradations that may be obtained through infinite combination of the tones of this marvellous palette.

Add to all this the deep breathing of the monster's cavernous lungs which give its sounds that incomparable and inimitable steadiness recognized by everyone. For a long time the only power known for filling these lungs was manpower—that of organblowers pumping with hands and feet. We do much better now. The reservoir of the organ in the Royal Albert Hall, London, is supplied with air by a steam engine which assures the organist of an inexhaustible supply and far from all possibility of an unexpected performance. Other instruments use gas engines which are incomparably more manageable. Finally, there is the hydraulic system which is very powerful and easily used, for one has only to open a valve to set the bellows in motion.

These mechanical systems, however, are not entirely free from accidents. I discovered that fact when I was concluding the first phrase of the *Adagio* of Liszt's great *Fantaisie on the Choral from Le Prophète* (in the beautiful Victoria Hall in Geneva). The pipe which brought in the water burst and the organ fell silent. I have always thought, perhaps wrongly, that malice had something to do with the accident.

Liszt's *Fantaisie* is the most extraordinary organ piece in existence. It lasts forty minutes and the interest doesn't lag for a moment. Just as Mozart in his *Fantaisie* and *Sonata in C Minor*, foresaw the modern piano, so Liszt, writing his *Fantaisie* more than half a century ago, seems to have foreseen today's instrument of a thousand resources.

Are these resources really taken advantage of as they can and should be? Let us have the courage to admit that too often they remain ignored or only partly utilized. To draw from a large instrument all of its possibilities one must first be thoroughly familiar with it—and that understanding cannot be gained overnight because, as we have seen, the organ is a collection of an indefinite number of instruments. It places before the organist an extraordinary means of expressing himself. There are not two instruments in the world alike. The organ is only a theme with innumerable variations, determined by the place in which it is to be installed, by the amount of money at the builder's disposal, by his inventiveness and by his personal whims. Only with time can an organist come to know his instrument like the "back of his hand," to move automatically, like a fish in water, having nothing more to concern himself with than the music. Then to play freely with the colors on his vast palette, there is but one way—to throw himself headlong into improvisation.

Now, improvisation, the glory of the French School, has been attacked lately by the influence of the German School. Under the pretext that an improvisation is not as good as one of Sebastian Bach's or Mendelssohn's masterpieces, young organists have been discouraged from improvising.

That point of view is harmful because it is false; it is simply the negation of eloquence. Consider what the senate, the pulpit and the courtroom would be like if nothing were heard but speeches learned by heart. We all know the orator and lawyer who is brilliant when he speaks but who loses his spark when he takes pen in hand. The same phenomenon occurs in music. Lefébure-Wély, who was a wonderful improviser (I can say this—I heard him) left only a few insignificant organ pieces. I could mention, among our contemporaries, those who only express themselves completely through their improvisations. The organ is thought-provoking. Upon touching it the imagination is awakened, and the unforeseen rises from the depths of the unconscious. It is a world of its own, always new, which will never be seen again, which comes out of the darkness, as an enchanted island rises from the sea.

Instead of this fairyland, what do we see too often? Some of Sebastian Bach's or Mendelssohn's pieces repeated continuously; very beautiful pieces, to be sure, but concert pieces out of place in, and not in accord with, the Catholic service; pieces written for old instruments which employ either badly or not at all, the resources of the modern organ. There are those who believe this is progress.

I know very well what can be said against improvisation. There are bad improvisers whose playing is devoid of interest. But there are preachers, and even politicians who speak badly. That has nothing to do with the real issue. A mediocre improvisation is always endurable if the organist has grasped the idea that church music should harmonize with the service and aid meditation and prayer. If organ music is played in this spirit and results in a harmonious noise rather than in precise music which is not worth writing down, it is comparable with the old stained-glass windows in which the individual figures can hardly be distinguished but which are more charming than the finest modern windows. Such an improvisation will be worth more than a fugue by a great master on the principle that nothing in art is good unless it is in its proper place.

During the twenty years I played the organ at the Madeleine, I almost always improvised, giving my imagination the widest range. That was one of the joys of my life.

But there was a legend that I was a severe, austere musician. The congregation was led to believe that I continually played fugues; so much so that a young lady about to be married begged me not to play one at her wedding mass.

It is true that another young girl asked me to play funeral marches. She wanted to cry at her wedding and, as she had no natural inclination to do so, she counted on the organ to bring tears to her eyes.

But this case was unique. Ordinarily, they were afraid of my severity—although this severity could be well-tempered.

One day one of the parish vicars undertook to instruct me on this point. The congregation of La Madeleine, he said, was composed, in large part, of wealthy persons who frequently attended the Opéra Comique. There they formed musical tastes which ought to be respected.

"Monsieur l'abbé," I replied, "when I hear the dialogue of the Opéra Comique spoken from the pulpit, I will play appropriate music, but not before."

At that time gaiety reigned at the Salle Favart.

IV. Pronunciation of Latin in the French Church

The desire for reforms, or if I dared to say frankly what I thought, the mania for reforms, is one of the characteristics of our time. Suddenly, customs in use for centuries demand urgently to be changed—like the rabbit in the kitchen of old who asked to be skinned alive. Just so, the combination of dialogue and song, a practice going back to the ancient Greeks, was declared abominable and inartistic. It also resulted in prizes being given to youths who neither knew how to play comedy nor speak dialogue in prose or verse, so that the performance of comic operas of the old repertoire became impossible. Consequently, what is now thought to be great progress in setting prose to music will seem quite ridiculous when the fad has passed.

Such is the wish expressed by our Holy Father, the Pope, of seeing the Roman pronunciation of Latin propagated in France.

Some priests, bishops and cardinals see this as beneficial to the Church. Their authority is not to be disputed, but is it very enlightened? Do they not see things subjectively rather than objectively? In other words, do they not see from inside out rather than from outside in?

Without wanting to settle so specialized a question, may we not be permitted to consider and anticipate the effects of such a reform if it were carried out? There will be a complete revolution in the choral world—from both men and boys, none of whom know the Italian language nor its pronunciation. What do you expect? We are French, not Italian. If it were only a question of substituting the diphthong *ou* for the vowel *u*, it would not be difficult. But, can you see these honest, poorly-educated men leaving the forge or workbench to come to sing plainchant, forced to say *Yésouce* for Jésus, *ekçaoudi* for exaudi, *ekché* for ecce, *laouda* for lauda, *éoudgé* for euge, *miki* for mihi? They will ruin their Latin—you may well say so.

And should those of the faithful who like to join in the singing of hymns and responses learn Italian also?

Liturgical unity—we are told—has always been the desire of the Church. It is very possible. However, I have read a Mozarabic breviary

Camille Saint-Saëns, "La Prononciation du latin dans l'Église de France," *École Buissonnière* (Paris: Lafitte, 1913) 177–86.

from an old rite, very different from the Roman breviary, in which there were many fine things. Unity and uniformity are not the same as was seen when Pope Pius IX imposed the Roman rite on the Church of France.[1] I can still see the pastor of the Madeleine, the illustrious and much-lamented Deguerry, going up to the pulpit and proclaiming in his beautiful thundering voice that the Roman rite would be adopted from then on, *en principe*. In reality, nothing changed and after two years the Pope's orders were issued anew in order to exact obedience—but only reluctantly and incompletely.

If uniformity is so difficult to achieve, it is because it is apparently contrary to human nature. People's temperaments vary and, on the whole, require different customs.

* * *

This reform is to be avoided as much as that of the famous *Motu proprio* which dates from 22 November 1903. The authors of the petition allude to it. "We have endeavored," they said, "in joyful submission to promote it, in so far as its strict observance depends on us." It would have been more valuable, perhaps, not to reawaken that memory, because the zealous promoters were unsuccessful and their joy was turned to sadness. Ah! If the Holy Father had limited himself to asking for the suppression of all music not expressly composed for the Church, perhaps he would have been obeyed and the result would have been beneficial. A whole library of interesting works, many of which are admirable and lie unjustly forgotten, would once again see the light of day and take the place usurped by operatic pieces or others, uselessly adapted to the Church, which has already occurred.

But this is the music of Beethoven, we are told, of Mozart and of Sebastian Bach. That is not the issue. That would only be excusable if there had been a dearth of choral music written for the church. But the opposite is the case. The famous saying, "The right man at the right place," is the pure truth in art. The most beautiful thing in the world loses its value if it is not in its place.

---

[1] This was directed by the Archbishop of Paris, 1 May 1856. Saint-Saëns was still organist of Saint-Merry.

But the *Motu proprio* asked too much: forbidding the use in church of instruments other than the organ (which was reduced to short interludes); suppression of soloists in the choir; and, except for plainchant, the exclusive employment of sixteenth-century music; what else do I know? It was a complete overthrow of time-honored practices. What happened? Except in rare instances, nothing.

What should be banned from the church are hymns set to secular melodies which contain any number of faults of prosody which are contrary to musical taste, literary taste and religious sentiment all at the same time. Such are the ridiculous compositions of Father Lambillotte, happily almost forgotten, whose *Regina Coeli*, in which the Latin prosody is outrageously violated, remains legendary. Such horrors are best left unmentioned.

After what transpired in the wake of the *Motu proprio* it is easy to predict what will happen with the subject of the imposition of Roman pronunciation in France. No attention will be paid to it and the only result will be the distress felt by His Holiness at seeing, for a second time, his wishes ignored.

Let me add that some musician-priests with whom I discussed this delicate affair, found themselves of the same opinion as myself.

Several very interesting letters have been addressed to me on this subject. Some agreed with me, others disagreed; it would be quite extraordinary if everyone agreed on the same subject. Abbé Meunier, the director of a small seminary, discussed it in *L'Univers*. He agrees with me and received a letter of approbation from M. Léon Bourdeux, who sent me a copy, accompanied by reflections in which he deplores "this senseless infatuation with Italian pronunciation."

If I believed a long anonymous letter which I received and another, also anonymous, published in *L'Univers*, women are not in favor of the reform. Fearing to compromise themselves, they put up a pretense and their arguments are bizarre. My correspondent asks why I do not ask "great artists" for their opinions. But it is not the great artists that it disturbs. The lady correspondent in *L'Univers* wants Latin to be a living language. "What!" she says. "You Catholics who have spoken the same language to express the same faith for 2,000 years, who will speak it until the end of time and who speak it from one end of the earth to the other, do you really dare to say that this language is dead?"

As is well known, it is difficult to reason with women.

And yet, she, herself, says from afar: "Reason!"

I will spare you their reasons. It is better to cite the words of M. Léon Bourdeux:

"I am a Catholic: a respectful son of the Pope in all that which pertains to faith and dogma. Latin pronunciation is not dogma; therefore, I can discuss it and think as M. l'Abbé Meunier and M. Saint-Saëns."

Abbé Meunier, who is a knowledgeable philologist, seems to have touched upon the heart of the matter when he said: "The Italians, and even the Romans of today, do not pronounce Latin better than the French. . . There is a shocking anachronism in uttering sixth century Gregorian melodies with twentieth century Italian sounds. Italian pronunciation is not Latin pronunciation, but an evolved pronunciation."

Like myself, Abbé Meunier is afraid of the Pope encountering troublesome opposition were he to impose Roman pronunciation everywhere. He dreads national irascibility and the protests of academies and universities in the name of knowledge and historic truth.

Another subject also needs to be discussed. I have learned that in certain spheres I have been accused of distorting our Holy Father the Pope's intentions as expressed in his famous *Motu proprio*. I have only one way to answer those accusations: to present my readers with some excerpts from the very text of the *Motu proprio*.

Classic Polyphony—by which is meant the music of Palestrina and of his school—agrees admirably with Gregorian Chant, the supreme model of all sacred music. (II. 4.)[2]

And the *Motu proprio* concludes that it should be preferred to all others in the more solemn rituals of the Church.

Except for tonal ambiguity, "classical polyphony" really has nothing in common with Gregorian Chant—in which there is no polyphony. They are similar only in that, like Latin, both are dead or almost dead, languages—a fact which renders them eminently suited to the Church by reason that they are intangible and immutable. Just as the majority of the faithful understand that neither Latin (which either they have not learned or have forgotten) nor plainchant (the key to which is lost and the performance of which is arbitrary) so they would not understand Palestrinian

---

[2]The paragraphs in italics are quotations from "Instructions on Sacred Music" from the "Motu Proprio of Pope Pius X on Sacred Music" found in *Papal Documents on Sacred Music* (Glen Rock, N. J.: J. Fischer, 1947) 7–11.

music, foreign to our ears and which has no indications to guide us in its interpretation. Of this unintelligibility is born the mystery. That which discounts modern music, whatever its value, has nothing to put in its place.

In the middle of the last century a school was founded in Munich, whose objectives were to revive the art of Palestrina, and many compositions were written in that style. They were about as worthwhile as a schoolboy's Latin exercises. The project was given up.

The *Motu proprio*, in spite of its preference for the art of the sixteenth century, does not forbid modern music in the Church. It says:

Still, since modern music has risen mainly to serve secular uses, greater care must be taken with regard to it, in order that the musical compositions of modern style which are admitted to the Church may contain nothing secular, be free from reminiscences of motifs adopted in the theaters, and not be fashioned, even in their external forms, after the manner of secular pieces. (II.5.)

Nothing is easier than excluding motifs heard in the theater. Nevertheless, would the beautiful prelude to the Church Scene of *Faust* be out of place in Church? But let us move on.

How—I call upon all musicians—can it be discerned if *something secular* exists or not in a composition? By what sign will it be recognized? The difference between the motets and madrigals of Palestrina is so slight that from our distance we are no longer aware of it.

It is said that the *Motu proprio* does not prohibit solos. See how:

Solo singing should never predominate to such an extent as to have the greater part of the liturgical chant executed in that manner; the solo phrase should have the character or hint of a melodic projection (spunto), and be strictly bound up with the rest of the choral composition. (V. 12.)

So, the exquisite "Pie Jesu" from the Fauré *Requiem*, and many other pieces that I could mention which are gems of scared art, would be forbidden.

The use of the piano is forbidden in church, as is also that of noisy or frivolous instruments such as drums, cymbals, bells and the like. (VI. 18.)

The pianissimo rolls of the bass drum and cymbals, such a mystical effect in Gounod's *Saint Cecilia Mass*, and the terrifying clashes of the gong which underline in such a marvelous way the words "vivos et mortuos" in the Credo of Liszt's *Mass*, remain forbidden.

As for the piano, of course it would be ridiculous if it were used in church the same way as in a concert hall or a salon. But it would be valuable for replacing the harp when that delightful instrument is not available.

It is permitted, after the Offertory prescribed for the Mass has been sung, to perform, during the time remaining, a short motet composed on words approved by the Church. (III. 8.)

The *Motu proprio* does not say that it is permitted to substitute an organ piece for this motet, but it is to be noted that it does not forbid it. It only says:

The sound of the organ in the accompaniment of chant, in preludes, interludes and other similar pieces, must be not only governed by the special nature of the instrument, but must participate in all the qualities proper to sacred music. (VI. 18.)

Although it would not be very easy to define "the qualities *proper* to sacred music," the *Motu proprio* here speaks gold and it is unfortunate that its voice is not better heard.

In my chapter on the organ I spoke against the established custom, under the pretext of *great art*, of playing during services toccatas and preludes and fugues of Sebastian Bach and others, which are concert pieces and not at all suited to the ritual of the Catholic Church. When I was an organist I very often used to take the theme of "the offertory chant prescribed for the mass" and develop it appropriately. That is why, outside, I was accused of playing only fugues when, at the Offertory, I never played a single one.

The *Motu proprio* strictly forbids playing what are called (VI. 20) *fanfares* in church; and, in spite of this prohibition, you will hear, in the middle of ceremonies on the Feast of the Blessed Sacrament, bugles blare loudly and military trumpetings which produce the most shocking and scandalous effects.[3]

---

[3]"Fanfares or military music were rather frequent and even obligatory on certain days, such as national holidays, political Te Deums, etc., or when a prefect, the imperial court or when all others of constitutional authority made their official entrance. (*Revue de musique sacrée*, 15 November 1862, p. 38–39.)

If the clergy pays so little attention to pontifical instructions in cases in which it would be so easy, do you think it will be more submissive when it is a matter of overcoming the difficulties of changing Latin pronunciation?

It would be foolish to believe so; one can only hope.

V. Music in the Church

Concerning this subject, floods of ink have flowed; and yet more shall flow. Vast, immense, is the field, innumerable are the points of view; everyone regards it in his own way, according to his artistic education, his belief, his temperament—according to the time and place in which he has lived. Hence it is impossible, in a few lines, to do justice to such a subject, a labyrinthine forest into which we shall take only some cautious steps, without venturing into its formidable depths.

What music is most suitable for the church? Shall it be that which is executed by voices alone, as in the Greek Church? Or chorales, accompanied by instruments and the organ, as in the Lutheran Church? Or the florid counterpoint of the Catholic Church in the sixteenth century? Or pure Gregorian plainchant? Should we admit or exclude the light and ornate music of the eighteenth century, and our contemporary music?

All this is very difficult to decide; or, rather, impossible to decide—and for the very simple reason that in reality there is no religious art, properly so called, absolutely to be distinguished from secular art. There is good music, and there is bad music; for the rest, it is a matter of fashion, of convention, and nothing else.

In England they would not build a chapel otherwise than in the Pointed Style considered to be the essentially religious style. That is merely illusion; the Pointed Style of the thirteenth to the fifteenth century was employed for all buildings, sacred and profane.

The same applies to the "religious" character of the organ—a notion so prevalent at present that the anti-clerical authorities of a small town in Belgium once refused to permit the installation of an organ-class in a certain Conservatory. They would doubtless have exercised greater tolerance if they had been acquainted with the Italian picture which

Camille Saint-Saëns, "Music in the Church," *The Musical Quarterly* (January 1916) 1–8.

portrays a young nobleman, magnificently apparelled, playing on an organ before a lady clad solely in her loveliness. The organ, by its breadth of tone and its incomparable calm, lends itself admirably to religious music, but it was not invented for the latter, and everybody knows that the earliest instruments of this kind were used at Rome to accompany the circus-plays; Nero did not disdain to try his imperial hands upon them.

* * *

As I was brought up in France, as a Catholic, the music of our French Catholic churches is naturally that most familiar to me; and it is of that music which I may be permitted to write with a certain authority.

For a great many people, plain-chant is the true religious music. But what does this term mean to them? Probably the sequences and some few hymns. For the rest, they are not fitted for a comprehension of the incomprehensible; possibly it is this quality of incomprehensibility that charms them by its mystery, like the use of the Latin language. The music of the proses, with its well-marked tripartite rhythm, is easily understood; with the hymns, bereft of rhythm, the enigma commences, for there is nothing to prove that these hymns, in ancient times, were not rhythmical, and that their rhythm was not determined by prosody, which would have rendered its musical indication superfluous. As for the Introits and the Graduals, nowadays executed heavily in equal notes, it is not merely probable, but indubitable, that what we now hear does not resemble that which was sung of old.

St. Isidore, after having passed in review the various qualities of voice, says that there are some perfect ones, high, sweet and clear, to which should be confided the execution of the plain-chant.

A man's voice which is high, sweet and clear, is what we at present call a lyric tenor (*tenore leggero*).

Consequently, we are permitted to conjecture that the interminable "neumes" (of which our modern editions give only a considerably abridged version) were nothing but light vocalises, derived from those which issued so easily from Oriental throats. These resemble what we are accustomed to hear from our *bassi profundi* very much as a butterfly's flight resembles the walk of an elephant.

But our predecessors were not satisfied with detaching each of these light notes and setting them down ponderously one beside the other; they made an accompaniment, a solid chord for each note, and, as a climax of illogicalness, they transported, by means of said useless accompaniment, this music composed in the ancient modes into modern tonalities. A remedy for these evils was sought by Niedermeyer, who, despairing of extirpating the error involved in an accompaniment to plain-chant, attempted to render it at least rational by conserving its "modal" character by means of an ingenious system. And for the propagation of his system he founded the School which bears his name, and still exists despite the mortal blow dealt it by the Decree of Separation. But the task is accomplished; his system has made its way throughout France, and has even surpassed its aim by showing the possibility of introducing the ancient modes into modern harmony, thus enriching it in an unexpected manner.

During my childhood I often heard the Introits performed on feast-days in the following fashion: The tenor or the bass executed the chant in the time of one note to a measure, and around this chant the three other parts embroidered a florid counterpoint. The result was a music divested of sense, but whose hieratic character had a peculiar charm. Moreover, it was in this way that Masses were written in the sixteenth century on the themes of (in some cases) indecent songs. Palestrina, by abolishing this plan, laid the cornerstone whereon his fame was built. Still, the inconsistency of the procedure is wholly theoretical; a theme, whatever be its nature, becomes unrecognizable when treated in this manner. Take whatever popular air you will, turn every note into a semibreve to the total neglect of all rhythm, entwine about the theme concertante parts in crotchets and quavers, and then see what is left of the melody!

But enough of plain-chant; let us come down to the sixteenth century, and the school to which Palestrina gave his name. It is occidental Europe. Vague in tonality, this music pleases more especially by its mystery; for no one knows precisely what it signifies, indications concerning the manner of its execution being totally lacking. And so everyone interprets it in his own way. I have heard it sung brutally, vociferously; I have heard it in a murmur, extremely slowly; certain modern editions mark some passages "molto expressivo," whereas all expression is banished from certain performances. In spite of these serious uncertainties and obscurities, this style has its fanatic devotees, who proclaim that it alone has produced real religious music; and some forty years ago there was formed in Germany a school of performers writing solely in this style, never considering that as the entire sixteenth century had produced mountains of such music, one needed only to delve in this gold mine instead of seeking to create useless imitations.

What illusions, alas! were cherished by these admirable blind men! The madrigals of Palestrina differ so little from his sacred music, that if we were to take one of them and fit Latin words to it, and have it sung in church, the faithful melomaniacs would doubtless discover therein that true religious style which they refuse to recognize in modern music. Certain dance-tunes of the same period, sedate in aspect, and strictly set in four parts, would produce the same effect; they would, in any event, be less out of place within the sacred precincts than some hymns by the R.P. Lambillotte.

In my humble opinion this music, with its consonant harmonies and its disdain for melody, should take but little thought for what we call expression. There are some melodic and expressive designs in Palestrina, notably at the inception of his *Stabat Mater*, yet these are, all in all, simple hints rather than melody and expression as we understand them; at all events, these designs, perhaps strongly marked—one dare neither affirm nor deny it—are extremely rare; they are novelties, audacities presaging the future.

In the seventeenth century, melody, until then relegated to songs and dance-tunes, entered into the Church altogether with modern harmony; in the eighteenth, its sway was complete, and religious music reached the point where all gravity was lost; at that time the gay and frisky character of certain Masses appeared perfectly natural and scandalized nobody. "The Church likes to laugh," so the clergy said. Such is still the case in some countries where the sun expands the soul. In Andalusia one may hear Masses constructed on popular rhythms and accompanied by castanets and tambours de basque; there the Church is not satisfied with laughing—it dances.

Here at home we are more reserved. But what bad taste frequently prevails in our churches in France! and how can it be otherwise so long as the clergy receive no musical education whatever in their seminaries! Neither choirmasters nor organists always possess the courage to enforce their taste; furthermore, there are some among them who themselves require to be led. But, though taste be in abeyance, one ought at least to be sensible of the proprieties. Does it not argue a want of this, to choose pieces written for the theater or the drawing-room and adapt Latin words to them, when we possess such a prodigious quantity of pieces written expressly for the Church? or to sing motets that should express pure sentiments elevated beyond terrestrial passions, with extravagant expression and exaggerated inflections which the excessive sonority of the church still further exaggerates? When a High Mass is performed, what necessity can there be for taking the Kyrie from one work and the Gloria from another, the Sanctus from a third and the Agnus from a fourth, instead of executing one Mass in its entirety and thus presenting an ensemble of uniform style? What shall one say of these odious canticles which are imposed on the children and the more or less mature maidens of the religious societies, some being models of platitude and insignificance, while others are parodies on operatic airs—leaving the prosody quite out of consideration—thus forming deplorable habits in those who sing them!

Attempts have been made to combat this bad taste, and praiseworthy efforts have been put forth; unhappily, the good work has been overdone.

The Schola Cantorum joined the fray with excellent intentions; but instead of using persuasion, it sought to succeed through violence; without sufficient reason it strove to prescribe works by certain composers and to proscribe those of others; it brought about the dismissal of poor choirmasters who died in misery and disgrace; it has made itself detested, and has achieved no results.

The Pope then followed; in a celebrated Motu Proprio he raised his mighty voice. Ah! if His Holiness had confined himself to demanding some indispensable reforms, such as the exclusion of all secular music "adapted" for the Church, he would have been obeyed, and the benefit would have been great. But he in no wise cared to take into account inveterate secular habits, or the attraction with which music endows the ceremonies of the Church. We should have had to limit ourselves to Gregorian chant, banish the solos, interdict every instrument except the organ, and reduce the latter to accompaniments and a few short interludes. That was asking too much of human frailty, and the mighty voice was lost in space.

What music, then, ought there to be in the Church? Music of a grand style, in accord with the elevated sentiments expressed in the liturgy. But the grand style is rare. Where unattainable, one may be content with correctness in the writing and gravity in the expression—a gravity which does not exclude sentiment, but prevents it from turning into sentimentality. There being no intention, in the Church, of exciting applause, one should not strive after effect; consequently, one should not hesitate to perform fine works of ancient date which might, in some other place, have no success. But to my mind it is a great mistake to exclude modern works; every epoch has the right to express the religious sentiment in its own way, and our time has produced very beautiful compositions of this kind. Gounod and César Franck have left us superb models in this genre; certain purists affect to condemn the former and exalt the latter; I confess that I can perceive no essential difference between their sacred works; but, if I had a preference, it would be for Gounod, whose *St. Cecilia Mass*, with his oratorio *The Redemption*, and above all the oratorio *Mors et Vita*, seem to me perfectly to characterize modern religious music.

Shall I speak of the fugal style, so frequently employed? Berlioz thought it out of place in the Church; in his *Damnation de Faust* he presents a caricature of it which misses its aim, as it is always applauded—which did not hinder him from employing the same style in his famous *Requiem*, a distraught, sublime work that one must hesitate to classify among sacred compositions, so violently does it shock the nerves of the auditors. His *Te Deum*, less familiar and too seldom performed, of a marvellous breadth of style, is far better adapted for the sacred edifice.

These grandiose, overgrown works lead me to mention two colossal compositions, the *B-minor Mass* by Sebastian Bach, and the *Mass in D* by Beethoven. These marvels, which disarm criticism by their magnificence, surpass the frame for which they were fashioned. The Bach mass is too highly developed for the exigences of the Catholic cult; besides, (and this is a bizarre phenomenon,) the author's style adapts itself ill to the Latin words; the finest portions of the work are borrowed from his cantatas, and lose through transplantation.

The *Mass in D* has not these defects—it has others. Ambroise Thomas has been laughed at for remarking apropos of this gigantic work: "Very fine, but dangerous for young people!"—The words are those of a sage. Beethoven, through some inexplicable caprice, left out of calculation the *tessitura* of the voices, risking them without scruple at inhuman heights from where they dash themselves to destruction. And when he evokes the image of war in the Agnus Dei, to motivate the Dona nobis pacem, when the trumpets and drums give out the inception of a march, when the contralto cries out in anguish ("ängstlich"), "Agnus Dei, qui tollis peccata mundi," one is no longer in the church—one does not know where one is.

These grand works are better adapted for sacred concerts than for the Church; the latter has need of greater calm and serenity.

* * *

I have mentioned the deficient taste sometimes shown by members of the clergy; I now take the liberty of citing a rather amusing instance of it.

I was young, and had been organist at the church of the Madeleine for a short time. I had been greatly impressed by the talent of my predecessor, Lefébure-Wély—by his skill in exploiting the various registers, by the clearness of his execution, by his graceful harmonies. These fine qualities, of which the music he has published gives no idea whatever, were too frequently marred by a frivolous and secular style. I exerted myself to copy them as far as lay in my power while applying them to a different style; and so it often happened that I selected the plain-chant of the offertory as the subject of an improvisation, for I almost always improvised. But with such methods I could not be diverting, like my predecessor, which many listeners regretted.

One of the vicars of the parish sent a request that I should visit him. I called upon him, as desired, and after a lengthy discourse, which was quite unintelligible to me, he finally came to the point:

"Do not misunderstand me. The parishioners of the Madeleine are for the most part persons of wealth, who frequently go to the theater or the Opéra-Comique, where they have become accustomed to a style of music to which you are expected to conform."

"Monsieur l'abbé," I replied, "whenever I shall hear the dialogue of the Opéra-Comique spoken in the pulpit, I will play music appropriate to it; until then I shall continue as hitherto."

Another time, after I had played, at a wedding, the delightful "St. Francis Preaching to the Birds," by Liszt, the officiating priest called me into the sacristy to tell me that "it sounded as if I were tuning the organ, and that if I went on that way they would engage another organist."

"I will go whenever it may be desired," was my answer.

But I did not go until I myself desired.

These recollections lead me to speak of the part which the organ plays in our French churches. Formerly, improvisation was the basis of the organist's talent; his virtuosity was slight—music written for organ with independent pedal was beyond his powers. Little by little our organists have bent themselves to acquire the virtuosity which they lacked, and the fugue with obbligato pedal has become familiar to them; but at the same time, under the influence of the German School, improvisation has fallen into disrepute. It is impossible for me not to deplore this needless decadence. Without speaking of the monotony which results from it—for all organists have very nearly the same repertoire—it is improvisation alone which permits one to employ all the resources of a large instrument, and to adapt one's self to the infinite variety of organs; only improvisation can follow the service perfectly, the pieces written for this purpose being almost always too short or too slow. Finally, the practice of improvisation frequently develops faculties of invention which, without it, would have remained latent. I have just spoken of Lefébure-Wély, whose published works for organ possess such scant interest, and who was a marvelous improviser; I might mention others whose improvisations were superior to their written compositions. Necessity, and the inspiring character of the instrument, sometimes accomplish what meditation is unable to achieve. It may excite surprise to learn that the Andante of my first Sonata for piano and violoncello, and the conclusion of my Symphony in C minor, were created on the manuals of the organ.

The most beautiful things are beautiful only in their place. And so, how can a fugue or a toccata by Johann Sebastian Bach make its way into an offertory? They are concert pieces which bear no relation whatsoever to a Mass, and which inspire neither a meditative nor a prayerful mood; beyond the comprehension of the audience to which they address themselves, they can interest but a few rare auditors familiar with them.

A virtuoso hardened to every difficulty, an ingenious improviser—such should the perfect organist be. It is to form such organists that they are laboring in the organ-class at the Conservatory of Paris, where execution and improvisation receive an equal meed of honor.

Plate 47. Louis Vierne at 27 in 1897

APPENDIX B

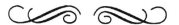

Saint-Saëns's Sacred Music
by Louis Vierne

In order to assign Saint-Saëns his place in sacred art, it is necessary to know the state of that art at the time the master began writing.

With the exception of Gounod, who was a cultivated man, church musicians knew nothing of their art. To them Latin was a formless gibberish which they set in any way to any kind of music which, most of the time, was contrary to common sense and to the most elementary taste. It can be said that the period between 1830 and 1860 presents the most lamentable spectacle for sacred music. Disregarding the meaning of the texts which they set to music, the composers wantonly distorted them, enlivening certain prayers with tunes of drinking songs, embellishing hymns of serene joy with tra-la-las worthy of a roadside inn, and multiplying common absurdities, awkward faults of prosody and nonsense. It was the happy time of insipid repetition of words which, by themselves, have no significance: strings of Kyries, rosaries of Quoniams, endless Amens and the coarsest effects. A sad, decadent period of which only a wretched output remains.

Louis Vierne, "Le musique religieuse de Saint-Saëns," *Le Guide du Concert* (Numéro Saint-Saëns 1914/1922) 37–39.

With so strong a classical background, literary as well as musical, Saint-Saëns immediately understood the problem and, since he entered the arena, strove to combat it. He reacted strongly against the bad taste of the times by writing music strictly appropriate to the character of the liturgical words of the given text. He banished from his works all useless decoration and theatrical effects, in a word, all those trappings which so delighted his contemporaries, to return to formal purity, true prosody and sound, solid writing.

Deeply imbued with classical music, he set out on the course on which the masters had pledged the art of church music but which had been abandoned: a course of wisdom and truth. In this way he produced a body of works as considerable by its quantity as by its quality. It is perhaps in this genre that his personality is the most marked. If we are sometimes conscious of the influences of J. S. Bach, Handel, Carissimi, Mozart, Haydn and Mendelssohn, it is only by comparison to their methods: the idea remains autonomous and the esthetic original. In these works the masterful qualities of all great artists are united: purity and elegance of form, the right amount of expression, impeccable writing and an irreproachable style. Here and there are even found, with all due respect to those who disagree, curiously modern harmonic discoveries. These "discoveries" in no way prevent the understanding of the works because, faithful to his principles, Saint-Saëns does not sacrifice the thought to the procedure: they only have more flavor (relish).

Saint-Saëns's vocal writing style and his solo and ensemble treatment must be pointed out. With a technical ease and variety of coloration worthy of the greatest old master he draws from his admirable means of expression all the effects of which it is capable. His love for the voice is felt and he works hard to place it under the best possible conditions to make it clear and expressive.

A volume would be needed to analyze completely Saint-Saëns's sacred music but that would extend beyond the scope of a short article such as this, so I shall confine myself to discussing at random some of his most characteristic works.

The first is the *Mass* for solo, choir, two organs and orchestra. This very early youthful work is surprising in the economy of means and the surety of its writing. The *Kyrie* seems a little over-developed, which also seems to be the opinion of the composer; cuts are made when it is performed during the mass. The *Gloria* is a marvel of composition and style, amazing when we know that the maître was but 21 when he wrote it. The *Credo*, like that of Dumont's *Messe Royale*, is harmonized curiously. The magisterial *Sanctus* is elaborate and noble; the following organ solo, which replaces the *Benedictus*, is charmingly effective. Against the old *O Salutaris* of Duguet the composer has woven a counterpoint between the harps and bassoons worthy of old Bach. Its *Amen* is incomparably elegant. Finally, the *Agnus Dei*, so reminiscent of Bach, ends in B major with an utterly seraphic dialogue between the two organs.

In the *Requiem* Saint-Saëns evidenced his deep penetration of the special meaning of that admirable text which accompanies the liturgy of the dead. Thrilling in effect, it should be sung, like Fauré's marvellous *Requiem*, at important funerals.

Among the miscellaneous motets I will mention the *Ave Marias*, of which that in two voices is a pearl. The *Ave verums* in B minor and E-flat, the latter in a style similar to that by Mozart, and, appropriately, sometimes sung at the Société des Concerts du Conservatoire. The *Sub tuum* for two voices is truly a little masterpiece of expression and realization. The superb *Inviolata*, written for Pauline Viardot, requires a beautiful contralto to interpret it and that voice being so rare is undoubtedly the reason it is so seldom sung. The *Tantum ergo* for three treble voices and unison treble choir, in which the repeat is supported by a sustained organ note is very effective. The list is long and to be fair it would be necessary to mention everything.

Can *Le Déluge*, *l'Oratorio de Noël* and the psalm, *Coeli enarrant*, be included with Saint-Saëns's sacred music? If these works do not fit into the liturgy, as such, at least they were written on biblical subjects or gospels, which classifies them as such and quite naturally determines their execution in artistic religious performances such as sacred music concerts, recitals, low masses, etc.

I have always regretted the smallness of the Conservatoire's concert hall since hearing the second part of *Le Déluge* there. The enormous orchestra required by this piece was suffocated. How much more powerful would have been the effect in a great building. All of the sonorous fullness and dramatic majesty would otherwise be brought out. Likewise, I should think the *Oratorio de Noël* would be perfectly appropriate in church, at midnight mass.

Apropos of that work, I will say that I much prefer the original version of the trio to that adopted by maîtres-de-chapelle who make it a three-part choral piece and reinforce the vocal parts with instruments. Besides the major drawback of approximate accuracy and the difficulty for children's voices to reach the high B-flats and B-naturals, this way of arranging the piece takes away all its freshness and grace, and makes it considerably duller and thicker.

The organ music of Saint-Saëns remains to be discussed. It is to be expected that the famous organist of the Madeleine, so widely renowned as an improviser, should have produced for the colossal instrument a body of works of the greatest interest. Nothing is lacking. There, as elsewhere, Saint-Saëns evidences a refined sense of insight in bringing to light under the most artistic conditions, the organ's special character. He is partial to the picturesque element but he also delights, if such should be the case, in the severe and grave style which more nearly approaches that of the old masters.

The art of registration was no secret to him. He brought to it, as to the orchestra, an astonishing precision and an unquestionable invention. To pick some examples at random, it is enough to mention the bells at the beginning of *Bénédiciton nuptiale* (that little masterpiece of written-out improvisation), the passage in the second *Rhapsodie* in which he indicates the Voix humaine without tremulant (an effect unknown until then and which has never been duplicated), the effect of the Cromorne in the third *Rhapsodie* (so pastoral and so perfectly suited to the essence of the music which it colors), and the delightful ending of the Fantaisie in D-flat for 8' Bourdon and 4' Flûte.

A few organ works were written during each period of Saint-Saëns's formidable career from the *Bénédiction nuptiale*, Op. 9 and the *Élévation ou Communion*, Op. 13 to the six *Préludes et Fugues*, Op. 99 and 109. Each piece of this group merits a special descriptive analysis as much for its form as for its color. The *Trois Rhapsodies sur des cantiques bretons* and the *Bénédiction nuptiale* are the most familiar and the most frequently played. It seems to me that the six *Préludes et Fugues* deserve to be in the repertoire of all organists truly worthy of the name, as much for their superb style as for their virtuosic demands. The *Fantaisie in D-flat*, dedicated to Queen Elisabeth of Romania, is a splendid concert piece which would make a great impression on an organ recital. In church the *Marche religieuse* in F major is very effective. In short, Saint-Saëns's contribution to organ literature is very important and greatly honors the French school.

The maître also wrote *Six Duos* for harmonium and piano but these cannot be included with his sacred music; rather, they find their place in the concert hall or the salon.

In summary, the size of the stone brought by Saint-Saëns for the reconstruction of the temple of sacred music is of utmost consequence. It happened at just the time when church music was in a state of distressing disorder and of incoherent unintelligibility. He brought his share of good will together with his craft to the rebuilding of the crumbling edifice. Artists who truly love their art and who are free from the prejudices of academe and of fashion should acknowledge it and be thankful to him.

Prizewinners at the
École Niedermeyer 1859–65

The following list of students was compiled from *Le Ménestrel* and *La Revue et gazette musicale de Paris*. It is not a complete list of students enrolled, but only of those who were awarded a prize at the end of each school term. It is, however, the only list we have of those who made up the piano class during Saint-Saëns's tenure as professor of piano at the École Niedermeyer and documents the musical education of his two most famous students: Gabriel Fauré and Eugène Gigout.

The list begins in 1859 rather than 1861 (the first year Saint-Saëns was associated with the school) to place his advanced students in perspective. Note that Gabriel Fauré had already won a first prize in piano before Saint-Saëns joined the faculty.

1859

COMPOSITION		
(Second Division)	Eugène Gigout	Prix unique
ORGAN	Eugène Gigout	First prize
ACCOMPANIMENT		
OF PLAINCHANT	Eugène Gigout	Prix unique
PIANO	Gabriel Fauré	First accesit

1860

COMPOSITION	Eugène Gigout	First accesit
HARMONY	Gabriel Fauré	Prix *ex aequo*
ORGAN	Eugène Gigout	First prize, repeat
ACCOMPANIMENT OF PLAINCHANT	Eugène Gigout	First prize, repeat of first prize of 1859
PIANO	Gabriel Fauré	First prize
	Adam Laussel	Second first prize
	Eugène Gigout	Second prize
	Adolphe Dietrich	First accessit
	Émile Lehmann	Second accessit

1861 (22 July)

COMPOSITION	Eugène Gigout	First prize
	Gabriel Fauré	First accessit
HARMONY	Émile Lehmann	First prize
	Ernest Legrand	First accessit
ORGAN	Eugène Gigout	First prize, repeat
	Émile Lehmann	Second prize
	Edmond Audran	Accessit
ACCOMPANIMENT OF PLAINCHANT	Eugène Gigout	First prize, repeat
PIANO (First Division)	Gabriel Fauré	First prize, repeat
	Adam Laussel	Second first prize
	Eugène Gigout	First prize
	Adolphe Dietrich	Second prize
	Albert Périlhou	Second second prize
	Emile Lehmann	First accessit
	Ernest Legrand	Second accessit
(Second Division)	Édouard Marlois	Prix
	Eugène Wintzweiller	First accessit
	Fidèle Koenig	Second accessit
	Donat Schuler	Honorable mention
SOLFÈGE	Eugène Gigout	Prix
	Adolphe Dietrich	Accessit
ORGAN	Émile Lehmann	Prix
	Laurent Giroux	First accessit
	Adam Laussel	Second accessit
ACCOMPANIMENT OF PLAINCHANT	Émile Lehmann	First prize, repeat
	Adolphe Dietrich	First prize
	Gabriel Fauré	Accessit

PIANO	Eugène Gigout	First prize, repeat
(First Division)	Gabriel Fauré	Prix d'excellence, *ex aequo*
	Adolphe Dietrich	First prize, *ex aequo*
	Albert Périlhou	First prize
	Émile Lehmann	Second prize
	Laurent Giroux	Accessit
(Second Division)	Fidèle Koenig	First prize
	Eugène de Wintzweiller	Second first prize

1863

COMPOSITION	Gabriel Fauré	Very honorable mention
ORGAN	Laurent Giroux	First prize
(First Division)	Adam Laussel	Second prize
	Gabriel Fauré	Accessit
(Second Division)	Théodore Laurent	First prize
	Édouard Marlois	Second prize
	Donat Schuler	Accessit
	Aloys Durrwaechter	Honorable mention
	Ludovic Fremont	Honorable mention
PIANO	Albert Périlhou	First prize, repeat
(First Division)		No first prize awarded
	Adam Laussel	Prix d'excellence
	Julien Koszul	Second prize
	Édouard Marlois	Accessit
(Second Division)	Victor Bellemant	Second prize
	Aloys Durrwaechter	First accessit
	Jules Stoltz	Second accessit
	Louis Lecloître	Honorable mention
	Paul Rakowski	Honorable mention

1864

COMPOSITION	Adam Laussel	First prize
	Gabriel Fauré	Second prize
	Laurent Giroux	Accessit
ACCOMPANIMENT	Laurent Giroux	First prize, repeat
OF PLAINCHANT	Albert Périlhou	First prize
	Gabriel Fauré	Second prize, *ex aequo*
	Ludovic Frémont	Second prize
ORGAN	Laurant Giroux	First prize, repeat
(First Division)	Adam Laussel	First prize
	Julien Koszul	Second prize, *ex aequo*
	Albert Périlhou	Second prize
ORGAN	Victor Bellemant	Second prize
(Second Division)	Ludovic Frémont	First accessit
	Jules Brayer	Second accessit

233

1864 (continued)

PIANO	Albert Périlhou	Prix d'excellence
(First Division)	Julien Koszul	First prize
	Édouard Marlois	Second prize
(Second Division)	Édouard Delarroqua	First prize
	Jules Brayer	Second prize
	Alexandre Georges	Accessit

1865 (28 July)

COMPOSITION	Gabriel Fauré	First prize
	Albert Périhou	Second prize
COUNTERPOINT		
& FUGUE	Gabriel Fauré	Prix
	Antoine Hellé	Honorable mention
HARMONY	Édouard Marlois	Prix
	François Limonet	First prize
ACCOMPANIMENT	Georges Langlone	Second First prize
OF PLAINCHANT	Jules Stoltz	Accessit
ORGAN	Albert Périlhou	First prize
(First Division)	Édouard Marlois	Second prize
(Second Division)	François Limonet	First prize
	Jules Stoltz	Second prize
	Édouard Delarroque	Accessit
	Georges Langlone	Accessit
PIANO	Édouard Marlois	First prize
(First Division)	Joseph Roger	Second prize
	Édouard Delarroqua	First accessit
(Second Division)	Charles Rauwel	First prize
	Alexandre Georges	Second prize

Organs Played by Saint-Saëns

The following list includes pertinent facts about those instruments for which there is definite corroboration that Saint-Saëns inaugurated, tried out, played in recital or as part of a concert, or on which he played the organ part of his Third Symphony. Perusal of the list gives a composite picture of the type of organ with which he was familiar and for which he composed: from the French Classic instruments of Clicquot and Richard to the 20th-century organs of Austin and Roosevelt.

Given Saint Saëns's intellectual curiosity and enthusiastic interest in the organ, it is doubtful if he did not ask to try out any instrument he came upon. Thus, he certainly would have played Gigout's, Gounod's and Widor's orgues de salon, the organ of Gloucester Cathedral during the Three Choirs Festival, and the organs of Boston Symphony Hall and San Francisco's Panama-Pacific Exposition. Undocumented reference has also been made to his having played, between 1875 and 1900, the Cavaillé-Coll organ in Ketton Hall, the home of John Turner Hopwood, the London music publisher.

Because so many of the organs listed were rebuilds of earlier instruments, only the name of the builder connected with the organ at the time Saint-Saëns played it is given.

A stop followed by an asterisk (*) denotes a jeux de combinaison activated by one of the ventil pedals.

(IN) denotes an organ inaugurated by Saint-Saëns. The pédales de combinaison are printed vertically as they appear on the console.

ORGANS PLAYED BY SAINT-SAËNS

Date Played	Location	Builder	Manuals	Stops
1847	Paris, Saint-Germain-l'Auxerois	Clicquot 1771; Dallery 1838	3	33
1848-1851	Paris, Conservatoire de Musique	Unknown	2	c.11
1853-1857	Paris, Saint-Merry	Clicquot 1781; Dallery 1804–18	4	37
1856	Paris, Cavaillé-Coll atelier; Organ for Cathedral of Saint-Michel, Carcassonne	Cavaillé-Coll, 1856	4	51
10 Oct. 1857	L'Isle-Adam, Saint-Martin (In)	Cavaillé-Coll, 1857	1	8
3 Dec. 1857	Paris, Saint-Merry (In)	Cavaillé-Coll, 1857	3	39
1858-1877	Paris, La Madeleine	Cavaillé-Coll, 1846	4	48
1855-	Paris, Orgue de Salon, Pauline Viardot	Cavaillé-Coll, 1851	2	14
29 Apr. 1862	Paris, Saint-Sulpice (In)	Cavaillé-Coll, 1862	5	100
15 May 1862	Paris, Saint-Thomas-D'Aquin (In)	Cavaillé-Coll, 1862	3	34
22 Oct. 1862	Saint-Dizier, Notre-Dame (In)	Cavaillé-Coll, 1862	3	34
28 Oct. 1862	Paris, Merklin-Schütze atelier: Organ for Cathedral of Arras	Merklin-Schütze, 1862	4	52
26 July 1866	Rouen, Saint-Maclou (In)	Merklin-Schütze, 1866	2	23
Aug. 1866	Rennes, Saint-Sauveur	Merklin, 1865	2	c.23
6 Mar. 1868	Paris, Notre-Dame Cathedral (In)	Cavaillé-Coll, 1868	5	86

APPENDIX D

Date Played	Location	Builder	Manuals	Stops
14 Aug. 1868	Dreux, Saint-Pierre (In)	Cavaillé-Coll, 1868	2	22
16 March 1869	Paris, La Trinité (In)	Cavaillé-Coll, 1869	3	45
27 March 1869	Paris, Cirque de l'Impératrice	Merklin-Schütze, 1868		
27 Jan. 1869	Paris, Saint-Augustin	Peschard-Barker, 1868	3	44
April, 1871	London, Crystal Palace	Gray & Davison, 1857	4	65
Oct. 1871	London, Royal Albert Hall	Willis, 1871	4	111
Dec. 1871	Bordeaux, Cercle Philharmonic	Merklin	3	
21 Feb. 1873	Versailles, Chapelle (In)	Cavaillé-Coll, 1873	2	23
7 May 1873	Paris, Cavaillé-Coll atelier: Organ for Albert Hall, Sheffield, England	Cavaillé-Coll, 1873	4	64
8 July 1874	Neuilly, Saint-Jean-Baptiste (In)	Abbey, 1874	2	22
28 Sept. 1878	Paris, Palais du Trocadéro	Cavaillé-Coll, 1878	4	66
2 July 1879	London, Saint James's Hall	Gray & Davison, 1858	2(?)	35
8 July 1879	Sens, Cathedral	Richard, 1774	2	31
8 July 1880	Windsor, Saint George's Chapel	Gray & Davison, 1853	3	35
March, 1882	Strassbourg, Cathedral	J. A. Silbermann, 1714–16	3	42
July 1882	Zurich, Cathedral			
1882	Mulhouse, Saint-Étienne	Cavaillé-Coll, 1863	3	40

Date	Location	Builder		
19 May 1886	London, Saint James's Hall	Bryceson Bros. & Ellis, 1882	2	19
21 June 1898	London, George Ashdown Audsley, Chamber Organ	Audsley, 1865-72	2	19
Sept. 1889	Paris, Universal Exposition	Merklin, 1889	4	35
1890	Paris, Saint-Séverin	Abbey, 1889	3	40
13 June 1893	Cambridge, Trinity College Chapel	Smith, 1708		
1896	Béziers, Cathedral of St. Nazaire	Puget, 1869	3	45
1896	Tour of Switzerland: 27 Sept. to 3 October			
	Winterthur, Stadtkirche	Walcker, 1888	3	52
	Zurich			
	Berne			
	La Chaux-de-Fonds			
	Neuveville			
	Vévey			
	Neuchatel			
	Lausanne, Cathedral	Kuhn	4	72
	Geneva, Victoria Hall	Kuhn, 1894	3	46
1896	Ghent, Swiss Exposition			
3 Oct. 1897	Paris, Saint-Vincent-de-Paul	Cavaillé-Coll, 1852	3	47
13 Oct. 1897	Bruxelles, Royal Conservatoire	Cavaillé-Coll, 1880	3	44

APPENDIX D

Date Played	Location	Builder	Manuals	Stops
14 Oct. 1897	Bruxelles Exposition, Grand Salle de Fêtes	Merklin, 1897		
Nov. 1897	Madrid, San Francisco	Cavaillé-Coll, 1884	2	26
19 Nov. 1904	Paris, Salle Pleyel (In)	Abbey, 1904	2	11
26 March 1906	Rome, Academy of Saint Cecilia	Walcker		
July 1906	London, Aeolian Hall	Hutchings-Votey, 1903	2	48
15 Nov. 1906	New York City, Carnegie Hall	Frank Roosevelt, 1891	2	27
c. 1910	Karlsruhe	Voit		
9 Oct. 1910	Lucerne, Cathedral	Geisler 1651; Haas 1862; Goll, 1899	3	79
18-23 May 1913	Vévey, Saint-Martin	Goll	3	35
6 Nov. 1913	Paris, Salle Gaveau	Mutin-CavailléColl	3	36
28 June 1914	Saint-Cloud, Parish Church	Cavaillé-Coll, 1876	2	19
June 1915	San Francisco, Festival Hall, Panama-Pacific International Expo.	Austin, 1915	4	117
1917	Paris, Temple de l'Étoile	Mutin, 1914	3	32
25 March 1917	Marseille, Théâtre des Nations (Premiered *Sept Improvisations*)			
28 March 1917	Nice (Le Casino Municipal?)	Mutin-Cavaillé-Coll, 1913	3	42
1 April 1917	Lyon (Salle Rameau?)	Mutin-Cavaillé-Coll, 1908	3	33

APPENDIX E

Specifications of Important Organs Played by Saint-Saëns

I. LA CONSERVATOIRE NATIONAL DE MUSIQUE

Builder unknown. Compass: Manuals, 54 notes; „C – ‴F
In use from c. 1810. Pedal, 20 notes: „C–,G

GRAND-ORGUE

8 Montre
8 Bourdon
8 Flûte (?)
4 Prestant

RÉCIT

5 "expressive" free-reed stops.

PÉDALE

16 Bourdon
8 Flûte
and some "expressive" free-reed stops.

SOURCE

Norbert Dufourcq, "L'enseignement de l'orgue au Conservatoire National avant la nomination de César Franck (1872)," *L'Orgue*, No. 144 (Oct.-Dec. 1972) p. 123.

Plate 48. Saint-Merry, the organ

II. THE ORGAN OF SAINT-MERRY AS PLAYED BY SAINT-SAËNS

Clicquot, 1791
Dallery, 1802, 1818
Callinet, 1828
Daublaine et Callinet, 1841   Cavaillé-Coll, 1857

Compass:
Positif   ⎫
Grand-Orgue ⎬ 50 notes: ,C–'''D
Récit   ⎫
Écho   ⎬ 30 notes: ,A–'''D
Pedal   21 notes: ,,,A–,F

Compass:
Manuals, 54 notes: „C–'''F
Pedal, 27 notes: „C–'D

PÉDALE		PÉDALE
8 Flûte	⟶	16 Flûte
4 Flûte	⟶	8 Flûte
16 Bombarde		16 Bombarde
8 Trompette		8 Trompette
4 Clairon		4 Clairon

I. POSITIF   I. POSITIF

8	Montre 44 notes: ,G–'''D	8	Montre
8	Bourdon	8	Bourdon
8	Dessus de flûte 27 notes: 'C–'''D	8	Dessus de flûte
4	Prestant	4	Prestant
$2\frac{2}{3}$	Nasard	$2\frac{2}{3}$	Nasard
2	Doublette	2	Doublette
$1\frac{3}{5}$	Tierce	$1\frac{3}{5}$	Tierce
V	Plein jeu	V	Plein jeu
8	Trompette	8	Trompette
8	Cromorne	8	Cromorne
8/4	Hautbois-Clairon	8/4	Hautbois-Clairon

II. GRAND-ORGUE   II. GRAND-ORGUE

16	Montre	16	Montre
16	Bourdon 44 notes: ,G -'''D	16	Bourdon
8	Montre	8	Montre
8	Bourdon	8	Bourdon
8	Dessus de flûte 44 notes: ,G - '''D	8	Dessus de flûte
4	Prestant	8	Dessus de gambe
$2\frac{2}{3}$	Nasard	4	Prestant
2	Quarte de nasard	4	Dulciane
$1\frac{3}{5}$	Tierce	2	Doublette

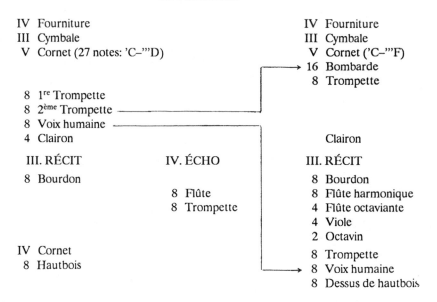

IV Fourniture
III Cymbale
V Cornet (27 notes: 'C–'''D)

8 1ᵉ Trompette
8 2ᵉᵐᵉ Trompette
8 Voix humaine
4 Clairon

IV Fourniture
III Cymbale
V Cornet ('C–'''F)
16 Bombarde
8 Trompette

Clairon

III. RÉCIT
8 Bourdon

IV. ÉCHO
8 Flûte
8 Trompette

III. RÉCIT
8 Bourdon
8 Flûte harmonique
4 Flûte octaviante
4 Viole
2 Octavin
8 Trompette
8 Voix humaine
8 Dessus de hautbois

IV Cornet
8 Hautbois

PÉDALES DE COMBINAISON

Orage
Tirasse Grand-Orgue
Anches
Pédale
Grand-Orgue
Récit
Octaves graves
Grand-Orgue sur machine
Positif au Grand-Orgue
Récit au Grand-Orgue
Tremblant
Expression Récit

SOURCE

Norbert Dufourcq, *Les Grandes Orgues de Saint-Merry de Paris à travers l'histoire*, L'Orgue, Dossier II (Paris: L'Association des Amis de l'Orgue, 1983, p. 62).

SPECIFICATIONS OF IMPORTANT ORGANS

AN ORGAN OF UNKNOWN ORIGIN

8 Flûte
8 Flûte bouchée
8 Bourdon
4 Prestant
2 Doublette
8 Hautbois
8 Trompette

This organ of one manual of 54 notes and a 13-note pedalboard seems to be of 18th-century origin. It may have been the orgue-de-choeur during Saint-Saëns's tenure at Saint-Merry as Merklin did not install an orgue-de-choeur until December 1880. Although this organ was in good condition it was no longer used after 1914. A photograph of the back of the instrument showing a view of the case is in Helbig's *La Grande Pitié des Orgues de France*, (Bibliothèque Nationale Rés. Vmc. ms. 15, Vol. 4, p. 87).

SOURCE

Gustave Helbig, *Monographie des Orgues de France*, Bibliothèque Nationale Rés. Vmc. ms. 13, Vol. II, p. 373.

III. CATHÉDRALE DE LUÇON
(Originally intended for Saint-Michel de Carcassonne)

Cavaillé-Coll Organ, 1857

Compass: Manuals, 54 notes; „C–'"F
Pedal, 27 notes: „C–'D

I. POSITIF	II. GRAND-ORGUE	III. GRAND-RÉCIT EXPRESSIF
8 Montre	16 Montre	16 Quintaton
8 Bourdon	16 Bourdon	8 Bourdon
8 Salicional	8 Montre	8 Flûte harmonique
4 Prestant	8 Bourdon	8 Salicional
4 Flûte douce	8 Flûte harmonique	8 Gambe
3 Quinte	8 Viole de gambe	4 Dulciane
2 Doublette	4 Prestant	16 Bombarde*
8 Trompette	4 Viole d'amour	8 Trompette*
8 Cromorne	4 Flûte octaviante*	8 Hautbois*
4 Clairon	3 Quinte*	8 Voix humaine*
	2 Doublette*	4 Clairon*
	IV Fourniture*	
	III Cymbale*	
	16 Bombarde*	
	8 Trompette*	
	4 Clairon*	

IV. PETITE-RÉCIT EXPRESSIF

8 Flûte douce
8 Flûte harmonique
8 Viole d'amour
4 Flûte octaviante
2 Octavin
8 Trompette harmonique*
8 Basson-hautbois*
8 Voix humaine*

PÉDALE

16 Contrebasse
8 Basse
4 Octave
16 Bombarde*
8 Trompette*
4 Clairon*

PÉDALES DE COMBINAISON

Orage	Tirasse G.O.	Anches Pédale	Octaves graves G.O.	Grand-Orgue	Grand-Récit	Petit-Récit	Petit-Récit	Grand-Récit	Positif	G.O. sur machine	Tremblant Petit-Récit	Tremblant Petit-Récit	Expression Petit-Récit	Expression Grand-Récit
				Anches			Accouplements au Grand-Orgue							

In 1861 this organ was installed in the Cathédrale de Luçon.[1] At that time the third clavier, Grand-Récit expressif, was returned to its original, pre-1856 state—a single freee reed manual, called *Euphone*. The present specification has been reconstructed from two sources. The first is "contracts in the archives of Aude, giving details of the instrument before the addition of the Grand-Récit."[2] The second source is César Franck's manuscript of the first version of the *Fantaisie in C* in which the composer identified most of the Pédales de Combinaison by number and listed most of the stops of the Grand-Récit in the registration at the beginning of the piece.

[1]Delhommeau, *Orgues et Organistes de la Cathédrale de Luçon*, 16–18.
[2]Eschbach, "Preface."

SOURCES

Jesse Eschbach and Robert Bates, "Preface," *César Franck; Fantaisie für die Orgel in Drei Versionen* (Bonn-Bad Godesberg: Forberg, 1980).

Abbé Delhommeau, *Orgues et Organistes de la Cathédrale de Luçon* (Luçon, 1966) 16–18.

IV. ÉGLISE DE LA MADELEINE

Cavaillé-Coll Organ
Inaugurated: 29 October 1846

Compass: Manuals, 54 notes: „C–'"F
Pedal, 25 notes: „C–'C

I. POSITIF

8 Montre
8 Viola di gamba
8 Flûte douce
8 Voix céleste
4 Prestant
4 Dulciana*
2 Octavin*
8 Trompette*
8 Bassoon et Hautbois*
4 Clairon*

II. GRAND ORGUE

16 Montre
16 Violon-basse
8 Montre
8 Salicional
8 Flüte harmonique
8 Bourdon
4 Prestant
3 Quinte*
2 Doublette*
X Plein jeu*
8 Trompette
8 Cor anglais*

III. BOMBARDES

16 Sous-basse
8 Basse
8 Flûte harmonique
8 Flûte traversière
4 Flûte octaviante
2 Octavin*
16 Bombarde*
8 Trompette harmonique*
8 Deuxième Trompette*
4 Clarion*

IV. RÉCIT EXPRESSIF

8 Flûte harmonique
8 Bourdon
4 Flûte octaviante*
2 Octavin*
8 Trompette harmonique*
8 Musette
8 Voix humaine
4 Clairon*

PÉDALE

32 Quintaton
16 Contre-basse
8 Violoncelle
8 Grosse flûte
16 Bombarde*
16 Basson*
8 Trompette*
4 Clairon*

PÉDALES DE COMBINAISON

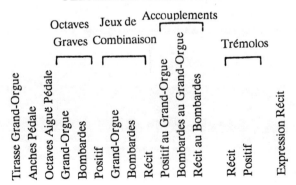

SOURCE

"L'Orgue de la Madeleine," *L'Illustration, Journal Universel* (7 November 1846) 147–48.

Plate 49. The Madeleine, the organ

250

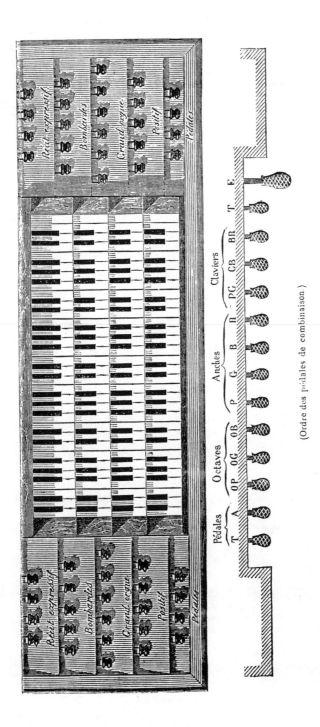

(Ordre des pédales de combinaison)

Plate 50. The Madeleine, the console

V. ÉGLISE DE SAINT-SULPICE

Cavaillé-Coll Organ
Inaugurated: 29 April 1862

Compass: Manuals, 56 notes: „C–"'G
Pedal, 30 notes: „C–'F

I. GRAND CHOEUR

8 Salicional
4 Octave
IV Grosse fourniture
VI Grosse cymbale
IV Plain jeu
V Cornet
16 Bombarde
16 Basson
8 Ire Trompette
8 2e Trompette
8 Basson
4 Clairon
2 Clairon-doublette

IV. POSITIF

16 Violon-basse
16 Quintaton
8 Flûte traversière
8 Quintaton
8 Salicional
8 Viole de gambe
8 Unda maris
4 Flûte octaviante
4 Flûte douce
4 Dulciana
2 $\frac{2}{3}$ Quinte*
2 Doublette*
1 $\frac{3}{5}$ Tierce*
1 $\frac{1}{3}$ Larigot*
1 Piccolo*
III-VI Plein jeu harmonique*
16 Euphone*
8 Trompette*
8 Clarinette*
4 Clairon*

II. GRAND-ORGUE

16 Principal harmonique
16 Montre
16 Bourdon
16 Flûte conique
8 Montre
8 Diapason
8 Bourdon
8 Flûte harmonique
8 Flûte traversière
8 Flûte à pavillon
5 $\frac{1}{3}$ Grosse quinte
4 Prestant
2 Doublette

V. RÉCIT

16 Quintaton
8 Flûte harmoniqu
8 Bourdon
8 Violoncelle
8 Voix céleste
4 Prestant
4 Flûte octaviante
4 Dulciana*
2 $\frac{2}{3}$ Nasard*
2 Doublette*
2 Octavin*
IV Fourniture*
V Cymbale*
V Cornet*
16 Bombarde*
16 Cor anglais*
8 Trompette harm.*
8 Trompette*
8 Basson-hautbois
8 Cromorne
8 Voix humaine
4 Clairon*

III. BOMBARDE

16 Soubasse
16 Flûte conique
8 Principal
8 Bourdon
8 Flûte harmonique
8 Gambe
8 Violoncelle
8 Kéraulophone
5 $\frac{1}{3}$ Grosse quinte*
4 Prestant
4 Flûte octaviante
4 Octave*
3 $\frac{1}{5}$ Grosse tierce*
2 $\frac{2}{3}$ Quinte*
2 Octavin*
V Cornet*
16 Bobmarde*
8 Trompette*
8 Baryton*
4 Clairon*

PÉDALE

32 Principal-basse
16 Contre-basse
16 Soubasse
8 Flûte
8 Violoncelle
4 Flûte
32 Contre-bombarde
16 Bombarde*
8 Trompette*
8 Ophicléide*
4 Clairon*

SPECIFICATIONS OF IMPORTANT ORGANS

PÉDALES DE COMBINAISON

	Tirasses		Anches Pédale	Octaves Graves					Jeux de Combinaison				Accouplements au Grand-Choeur						
Orage	Grand-Choeur	Grand-Orgue	Anches Pédale	Grand-Choeur	Grand-Orgue	Bombarde	Positif	Récit	Grand-Orgue	Bombarde	Positif	Récit	Grand-Choeur	Grand-Orgue	Bombarde	Positif	Récit	Tremblant du Récit	Expression du Récit

SOURCE

Abbé Pierre-Henri Lamazou, *Étude sur l'orgue monumental de Saint-Sulpice et la facture d'orgue moderne* (Paris: Repos, [1863]) 23–26.

VI. ÉGLISE DE SAINT-THOMAS-D'AQUIN

Cavaillé-Coll Organ, 1862   Compass: Manuals, 54 notes: „C - '"F
Rebuild of François-Henri Clicquot Organ   Pedal 30 notes: „C - 'F
of 1769.
Inaugurated by Saint-Saëns: 15 May 1862.

I. GRAND-ORGUE		II. POSITIF EXPRESSIF	
16	Bourdon	8	Bourdon
8	Montre	8	Flûte traversière
8	Bourdon	8	Gambe
8	Flûte harmonique	8	Voix céleste
8	Salicional	4	Flûte octaviante
4	Prestant	2	Octavin
4	Gambe	8	Trompette
V	Fourniture	8	Clarinette
V	Cornet	4	Clairon
16	Bombarde		
8	Trompette		
4	Clairon		

III. RÉCIT EXPRESSIF

8	Principal
8	Cor de nuit
8	Viole de gambe
4	Flûte douce
8	Trompette harmonique
8	Basson-hautbois
8	Voix humaine

PÉDALE

16	Flûte
16	Sous-basse
8	Flûte
16	Bombarde
8	Trompette
4	Clairon

PÉDALES DE COMBINAISON

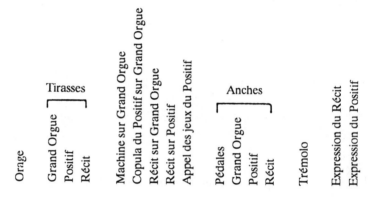

SOURCE

Félix Raugel, *Les Grandes Orgues de Paris*, 136–37.

VII. ÉGLISE DE NOTRE-DAME-DE-SAINT-DIZIER

Cavaillé-Coll Organ Compass: **Manuals, 54 notes „C–'"F**
Rebuild of Richard Organ of 1792 Pedal, 27 notes „C - 'D
Inaugurated by Saint-Saëns: 22 October 1862.

I. GRAND-ORGUE		II. POSITIF	
16	Bourdon	8	Principal
8	Montre	8	Bourdon
8	Flûte harmonique	4	Prestant
8	Bourdon	2	Doublette*
8	Gambe	8	Trompette*
4	Prestant	8	Cromorne*
4	Octave		
3	Quinte*		
2	Doublette*		
III- VI	Plein jeu*		
V	Cornet*		
8/16	Bombarde*		
8	Trompette*		
4	Clairon*		

III. RÉCIT EXPRESSIF		PÉDALE	
8	Flûte traversière	16	Contrebasse
8	Viole de gambe	8	Basse
8	Voix céleste	4	Flûte
4	Flûte octaviante	16	Bombarde*
2	Octavin*	8	Trompette*
8	Trompette*	4	Clairon*
8	Basson-hautbois*		
8	Voix humaine*		

PÉDALES DE COMBINAISON

Orage — Tirasse Grand-Orgue — Appel Anches Pédale — Octaves graves Grand-Orgue — Récit au Positif — Tirasses [Grand-Orgue — Positif — Récit] — Copula Grand-Orgue [Annulation — Positif — Récit] — Trémolo Récit — Expression Récit

SOURCE

(Chanoine) A. Bourdon, *Notice sur le grand orgue de Notre-Dame-de-Saint-Dizier construit par M. Cavaillé-Coll.* (Bar-le-Duc: Numa Rolin, 1863).

255

VIII. ÉGLISE DE SAINT-MACLOU-DE-ROUEN

Merklin Organ
Inaugurated: 26 July 1866

GRAND-ORGUE		RÉCIT		PÉDALE	
16	Bourdon	8	Bourdon	16	Bourdon
8	Montre	8	Flûte	8	Flûte
8	Bourdon	8	Violoncelle	16	Bombarde
8	Flûte	8	Voix céleste		
8	Salicional	4	Flûte d'écho		
8	Gambe	2	Flageolet		
4	Prestant	8	Basson-hautbois		
V	Fourniture	8	Voix humaine		
16	Bombarde	8	Clarinette		
8	Trompette				
4	Clairon				

PÉDALES DE COMBINAISON

Tirasses

Grand-Orgue
Récit
Copula
Fonds Grand-Orgue

Anches

Grand-Orgue
Récit
Pédale
Trémolo
Expression

SOURCES

Gustave Helbig, *Monographie des Orgues de France*, Bibliothèque Nationale Rés. Vmc. ms. 13 (Vol. 2) 553.

Marcel Dupré, *Disposition des jeux aux consoles des orgues jouées par Marcel Dupré*, Bibliothèque Nationale, Rés. Vmc. ms. 923 (Vol. I) 59. Dupré lists the Récit 4' as Flûte octaviante and the Pédale 16' Trombone.

IX. CATHÉDRALE DE NOTRE-DAME-DE-PARIS

Cavaillé-Coll Organ   Compass: Manuals, 56 notes: „C–"'G
Inaugurated: 6 March 1868   Pedal, 30 notes: „C–'F

I. GRAND CHOEUR	II. GRAND-ORGUE	III. BOMBARDE
8 Principal	16 Violonbasse	16 Principal-basse
8 Bourdon	16 Bourdon	16 Sousbasse
4 Prestant	8 Montre	8 Principal
$2\frac{2}{3}$ Quinte	8 Flûte harmonique	8 Flûte harmonique
2 Doublette	8 Viole de gambe	$5\frac{1}{3}$ Grosse quinte
$1\frac{3}{5}$ Tierce	8 Bourdon	4 Octave
$1\frac{1}{3}$ Larigot	4 Prestant	$3\frac{1}{5}$ Grosse tierce
$1\frac{1}{7}$ Septième	4 Octave*	$2\frac{2}{3}$ Quinte*
1 Piccolo	2 Doublette*	$2\frac{2}{7}$ Septième*
16 Tuba magna*	II-V Fourniture*	2 Doublette*
8 Trompette*	II-V Cymbale harmonique*	II-V Grand cornet*
4 Clairon*	16 Basson*	16 Bombarde*
	8 Basson*	8 Trompette*
	4 Clairon*	4 Clairon*

IV. POSITIF	V. RECIT	PÉDALE
16 Bourdon	16 Quintaton	32 Principal-basse
16 Montre	8 Flûte traversière*	16 Contrebasse
8 Flûte harmonique	8 Quintaton	16 Sousbasse
8 Bourdon	8 Viole de gambe	$10\frac{2}{3}$ Grosse quinte
8 Salicional	8 Voix céleste	8 Flûte
8 Unda maris	4 Flûte octaviante*	8 Violoncelle
4 Prestant	4 Dulciana	$6\frac{2}{5}$ Grosse tierce
4 Flûte douce*	$2\frac{2}{3}$ Quinte*	$5\frac{1}{3}$ Quinte*
2 Doublette*	2 Octavin*	$4\frac{4}{7}$ Septième*
1 Piccolo*	II-V Cornet harmonique*	4 Flûte
III-VI Plein jeu harmonique*	16 Bombarde*	32 Contre-bombarde
16 Clarinette basse*	8 Trompette*	16 Bombarde*
8 Cromorne*	8 Basson-hautbois	16 Basson*
4 Clarinette aiguë*	8 Clarinette	8 Trompette*
	8 Voix humaine	8 Basson*
	4 Clairon*	

PÉDALES DE COMBINAISON

Tirasses		Octaves Graves					Jeux de Combinaison						Copula du Grand-Choeur					

Effets d'orage · Grand-Choeur (Moteur général) · Grand-Orgue · Anches Pédale · Grand-Choeur · Grand-Orgue · Bombarde · Positif · Récit · Grand-Choeur · Grand-Orgue · Bombarde · Positif · Récit · Grand pédale collective · Grand-Choeur · Grand-Orgue · Bombarde · Positif · Récit · Trémolo · Grand pédale d'expression

SOURCE

François Sabatier, *Les aventures du grand orgue de Notre-Dame-De-Paris au XIXe siècle, II/1859-1963* (Paris: L'Orgue, 1975) 56–62.

X. ÉGLISE DE SAINT-PIERRE-DE-DREUX

Cavaillé-Coll Organ
Inaugurated by Saint-Saëns:
14 August 1868

Compass: Manuals, 54 notes: „C–"'F
Pedal, 30 notes: „C–'F

I. GRAND ORGUE		II. RÉCIT EXPRESSIF		PÉDALE	
16	Bourdon	8	Flûte traversière	16	Soubasse
8	Montre	8	Gambe	8	Grosse flûte ouverte
8	Flûte harmonique	8	Voix céleste	16	Bombarde
8	Salicional	4	Flûte octaviante	8	Trompette
4	Prestant	2	Octavin		
4	Octave	8	Trompette		
II-V	Plein jeu	8	Cor anglais/Hautbois		
8/16	Basson	8	Voix humaine		
8	Trompette				
4	Clairon				

SOURCE

Didier Decrette, *Histoire du Grand-Orgue de l'Église Saint-Pierre-de-Dreux* (Vernouillet: Les Vignes de la Brosse, 1977).

XI. ÉGLISE DE LA TRINITÉ

Cavaillé-Coll Organ
Inaugurated: 16 March 1869

Compass: Manuals, 54 notes: „C–"'G
Pedal, 30 notes: „C–'F

I. GRAND-ORGUE

16	Montre
16	Bourdon
8	Montre
8	Bourdon
8	Flûte harmonique
8	Gambe
4	Prestant
4	Flûte douce*
$2\frac{2}{3}$	Quinte*
V	Plein jeu*
V	Cornet*
16	Bombarde*
8	Trompette*
4	Clairon*

II. POSITIF

16	Quintaton
8	Principal
8	Flûte harmonique
8	Salicional
8	Unda maris
4	Prestant
4	Flûte douce
2	Doublette*
1	Piccolo*
V	Cornet*
16	Basson*
8	Trompette*
8	Clarinette

III. RÉCIT

8	Flûte traversière
8	Bourdon
8	Gambe
8	Voix céleste
4	Flûte octaviante*
2	Octavin*
8	Trompette*
8	Hautbois
8	Voix humaine
4	Clairon*

PÉDALE

32	Bourdon
16	Contrebasse
16	Sous-basse
8	Flûte
8	Basse
8	Violoncelle
4	Octave
16	Bombarde*
8	Trompette*
4	Clairon*
	Tacet
	Sonnette

PÉDALES DE COMBINAISON

	Tirasses				Anches				Accouplements au Grand-Orgue			
Appel des jeux Pédale	Grand-Orgue	Positif	Récit	Octaves Graves G.O.	Pédale	Grand-Orgue	Positif	Récit	Expression du Récit	G.O. sur machine	Positif	Récit	Récit sur Positif	Trémolo du Récit

SOURCE

Marcel Dupré, *Disposition des jeux aux consoles des orgues jouées par Marcel Dupré,* Bibliothèque Nationale, Rés. Vma. ms. 923 (Vol. I).

XII. CIRQUE D'HIVER SALLE DES CONCERTS PASDELOUP

I. GRAND-ORGUE	II. RÉCIT	PÉDALE (17 notes)
16 Bourdon	8 Gambe	à tirasse
8 Montre	8 Voix céleste	
8 Flûte	4 Flûte	
4 Prestant	Plein jeu	
	8 Trompette	
	8 Basson-hautbois	
	5 Pédales de Combinaison	

This was probably a second-hand organ bought by Cavaillé-Coll and installed in the Cirque d'Hiver. In 1880 it was bought by the Church of Saint-Denis-du-Saint-Sacrement and installed as their orgue-de-choeur.

XIII. ÉGLISE DE SAINT-VICTOR
Verdun (Meuse)

H. Jacquet, Père et fils, Bar-le-Duc.
This organ is "said to have been inaugurated by Saint-Saëns."

GRAND-ORGUE	RÉCIT	PÉDALE
16 Bourdon	8 Flûte harmonique	16 Flûte
8 Montre	8 Gambe	8 Flûte
8 Principal	8 Voix céleste	
8 Bourdon	4 Fugara	
8 Salicional	8 Basson-hautbois	
4 Prestant		
V Cornet		
8/16 Basson		
8 Quintaton		
8 Voix humaine		
8 Trompette		
4 Clairon		

PÉDALES DE COMBINAISON

Tirasse Grand-Orgue
Tirasse Récit
Copula
Anches Grand-Orgue
Expression
Trémolo

Transposition

SOURCE

Gustave Helbig, *Monographie des Orgues de France* Bibliothèque Nationale, Rés. Vmc. ms. 13 (Vol. 1) 728.

XIV. CHAMBER ORGAN OF GEORGE ASHDOWN AUDSLEY
Devon Nook, Duke's Avenue London, W., Chiswick

Organ built under Mr. Audsley's direction between 1865 and 1872.

Audsley adopted Italian nomenclature throughout in order to keep the specification uniform. Common designations for all stops appear to the right.

MANUAL I

8	Principale Grande	8	Open Diapason (unexpressive)

Swell No. 1

8	Flauto Tedesca	8	Clarabella
4	Flauto Traverso	4	Orchestral Flute
2	Piccolo	2	Piccolo
8	Oboe	8	Oboe

Swell No. 2

8	Flauto Primo	8	Doppel Flute
8	Flauto Secondo	8	Lieblich Gedeckt
8	Viola d'Amore	8	Viole (frein harmonique)
4	Ottava	4	Octave
V	Ripieno di Cinque	V	Dulciana Mixture
8	Tromba	8	Trumpet
8	Clarinetto	8	Clarinet
8	Voce Umana	8	Vox humana
	Tremolant[1]		Tremulant

APPENDIX E

MANUAL II (Enclosed in Swell No. 1)

8 Principale Dolce	8 Dulciana
8 Corno di Caccia	8 Keraulophone
4 Flauto d'Amore	4 Rohrflute

PEDAL

16 Principale	16 Open Wood
16 Contra-Basso	16 Bourdon
16 Contra-Saxophone	16 Saxophone (free reed)

COUPLERS

II - I 16' 8' 4'
I - Pedal
II - Pedal

[1]The tremolant effects every manual stop in the instrument but those enclosed in Swell No. 1 in a more delicate manner than those enclosed in Swell No. 2.

SOURCES

George Ashdown Audsley, *The Organ of the Twentieth Century* (New York: Dodd, Mead and Company, 1919) 334–36.

_____. "The Small Two-Manual Organ," *The Organ* (January 1925) 138-49.

XV. LA CHAPELLE DU CHÂTEAU DE VERSAILLES

Cavaillé-Coll Organ   Compass: Manuals, 54 notes: „C–"'F
Inaugurated: 21 February 1873   Pedal, 30 notes: „C –'F

GRAND-ORGUE	RÉCIT	PÉDALE
16 Bourdon	8 Violoncelle	16 Soubasse
8 Montre	8 Voix céleste	8 Flûte
8 Bourdon	8 Flûte douce	4 Flûte
8 Flûte harmonique	4 Dulciana (conique)	16 Basson
8 Salicional	V Plein jeu	8 Trompette
4 Prestant	16 Bombarde	
4 Flûte douce	8 Trompette	
2 Doublette	8 Cromorne	
	8 Voix humaine	
	4 Clairon	

PÉDALES DE COMBINAISON

Orage   Tirasse Grand-Orgue   Tirasse Récit   Octaves Graves G.O.   Anches Pédale   Copula G.O. sur machine   Récit au Grand-Orgue   Trémolo   Expression Récit

SOURCE

"L'Orgue de la Chapelle du Château de Versailles," *L'Orgue et les Organistes*, No. 5 (15 August 1924) 3–6.

XVI. ALBERT HALL
(Sheffield, England)

Cavaillé-Coll Organ   Compass: Manuals, 61 notes, „C–""C
Played by Saint-Saëns in   Pedal, 30 notes: „C–'F
Cavaillé-Coll's atelier, May 7, 1873
Destroyed by fire 14 July 1937

I. GRAND-ORGUE	II. POSITIF EXPRESSIF	III. RÉCIT
16 Montre	16 Quintaton	16 Bourdon
16 Bourdon	8 Principal	8 Diapason
16 Gambe	8 Nachtnorn	8 Flûte traversière
8 Montre	8 Unda Maris (,C–""C)	8 Viole de gambe
8 Diapason	4 Prestant	8 Voix céleste (,C–""C)
8 Flûte harmonique	4 Flûte douce	4 Flûte octaviante
8 Viole de gambe	2⅔ Quinte	4 Viole d'amour
8 Bourdon	2 Doublette	2 Doublette
4 Prestant	1 Piccolo	II–IV Cornet
4 Octave flûte	8 Cromorne	16 Cor anglais
2⅔ Quinte	8 Basson-hautbois	8 Trompette
V Fournitue	8 Voix humaine	4 Clairon harmonique
IV Cymbale		
16 Bombarde		
8 Trompette		
4 Clairon		

Plate 51. Albert Hall, Sheffield, England, the organ

IV. SOLO EXPRESSIF	PÉDALE
16 Bourdon	32 Principal basse
8 Diapason	16 Contrebasse
8 Flûte harmonique	16 Soubasse
4 Flûte octaviante	10 $\frac{2}{3}$ Quinte
2 $\frac{2}{3}$ Quinte	8 Basse
2 Doublette	8 Violoncelle
1 $\frac{3}{5}$ Tierce	4 Corno dolce
16 Tuba magna en chamade	32 Contre-bombarde
8 Trompette en chamade	16 Bombarde
8 Clarinette	8 Trompette
8 Musette	4 Clairon
4 Clairon en chamade	

PÉDALES DE COMBINAISON

Tirasses: Grand-Orgue, Positif, Récit, Solo

Anches: Pédale, Grand-Orgue, Positif, Récit, Solo

Accouplements au Grand-Orgue: Octaves graves, Positif, Récit, Solo

Grand-Orgue sur machine

Récit au Positif

Expression: Positif, Récit, Solo, Tremblant Positif, Tremblant Récit

Orage

SOURCES

Albert Dupaigne, *Le Grand orgue de la nouvelle Salle de Concert de Sheffield en Angleterre construit par A. Cavaillé-Coll à Paris.* (Paris: Plon, 1874).

Reginald Whitworth, "The Cavaillé-Coll Organ in the Albert Hall, Sheffield," *The Organ* (January 1925) 177.

_____. "The Cavaillé-Coll in Albert Hall," *The American Organist* (December 1937) 415–17.

Plate 52. Le Palais du Trocadéro, the organ

XVII. LE PALAIS DU TROCADÉRO (LA SALLE DES FÊTES)

Cavaillé-Coll Organ   Compass: Manuals, 56 notes: „C–'''G
Inaugurated: 7 August 1878   Pedal, 30 notes: „C–'F
Played by Saint-Saëns 28 Sept. 1878

I. GRAND-ORGUE
16 Montre
16 Bourdon
8 Montre
8 Flûte harmonique
8 Bourdon
8 Violoncelle
4 Prestant
4 Flûte douce*
2 Doublette*
V Dessus de Cornet*
V Plein jeu
16 Bombarde*
8 Trompette*
4 Clairon*

II. POSITIF
16 Bourdon
8 Principal
8 Flûte harmonique
8 Salicional
8 Unda maris
4 Flûte octaviante
2⅔ Quinte*
2 Doublette*
III-VI Plein jeu harmonique*
16 Basson*
8 Trompette*
8 Cromorne*

III. RÉCIT
16 Quintaton
8 Flûte harmonique
8 Cor-de-nuit
8 Viole de gambe
8 Voix céleste
4 Flûte octaviante
2 Octavin*
V Cornet*
I-III Carillon
16 Basson*
8 Trompette*
8 Basson-hautbois
8 Voix humaine
4 Clairon harmonique*

IV. SOLO
16 Bourdon
8 Diapason
8 Flûte harmonique
8 Violoncelle
4 Flûte octaviante
2 Octavin
16 Tuba magna*
8 Trompette harmonique*
8 Clarinette*
4 Clairon harmonique*

PÉDALE
32 Principal basse
16 Contrebasse
16 Sous-basse
16 Grosse Flûte
16 Violon basse
8 Grosse Flûte
8 Basse
8 Bourdon
8 Violoncelle
32 Contre-bombarde*
16 Bombarde*
16 Basson*
8 Trompette*
8 Basson*
4 Clairon*
4 Baryton*

APPENDIX E

PÉDALES DE COMBINAISON

| Tirasses | Octaves Graves | Anches | Accouplements de Grand-Orgue |

Orage · Grand-Orgue · Positif · Récit · Anches Pédale · Grand-Orgue · Positif · Récit · Solo · Grand-Orgue · Positif · Récit · Solo · G.O. sur machine · Positif · Récit · Solo · Récit au Positif · Trémolo Positif · Trémolo Récit · Expression Positif · Expression Récit

SOURCES

Joseph Bonnet, *Diagram of Stopknobs on (Ancien) Trocadéro Console—Préparation courante.* Bibliothèque Nationale, Rés. Vmb. 31.

Marcel Dupré, *Disposition des jeux aux consoles des orgues jouées par Marcel Dupré.* Bibliothèque Nationale, Rés. Vms. ms. 923, (Vol. I) 34–35.

XVIII. SAINT JAMES'S HALL
Picadilly (London, England)

No. 1

Gray & Davison Organ,   Compass: Manuals, 58 notes: „C–'''A
Opus 10086   Pedal, 30 notes: „C–'F
Completed: March 1858
Played by Saint-Saëns: 2 July 1879

I. GREAT	II. SWELL	PEDAL
16 Sub Bourdon	8 Stop Diapason	16 Open Diapason
8 Open Diapason	8 Flute Harmonique	8 Octave
8 Flute a Pavillon	8 Clarabella	4 Fifteenth
8 Salicional (,C–'''A)	8 Gamba or 8 Keraulophon	16 Bombarde
8 Bourdon (Bass)	8 Voix Celestes	
8 Clarionet Flute (Treble)	4 Principal	Manual to Pedal
8 Flute Harmonique	4 Flute Octaviante	Coupler
4 Octave	4 Fifteenth	
4 Gems Horn (sic)	II Mixture	
4 Flute	8 Solo Trompette Harmonique	
4 Flute Harmonique	8 Oboe	
3 Twelfth	8 Vox Humana	
2 Fifteenth		
2 Flageolet		
III Furniture		
II Mixture		
16 Contra Fagotto	3 Composition Pedals	
8 Trombone		
4 Clarion		

WIND PRESSURE:

Bass: 3"
'C –'''A: 3 1/2"
Reed Basses: 3 1/2"
Reed Trebles: 4"
Pedal: 4"

This specification is preserved by The English Organ Archive in Gray & Davison's Shop-Book 6, No. 10086 (serial numbers began at 10 001 in 1851.) The account is in Gray & Davison ledger, Vol. 6, page 223. The £722 cost of the organ broke down as follows: organ: £540, case: £130, decoration of pipe fronts: £50, stool: £2. The Shop-Book describes the organ as Manual and Pedal; although the stoplist for the Swell is written in pencil, it is doubtful if it were ever installed.

Gray & Davison provided a blower at ten shillings for each rehearsal and concert.

When this organ was removed in 1882, 13 ranks were reinstalled in Odiham Parish.

269

SOURCE

Dr. Michael Sayer, Honorary Archivest, English Organ Archive, Shrewsbury, England.

XVIII. SAINT JAMES'S HALL
Picadilly (London, England)
No. 2

Bryceson Brothers & Ellis Organ, 1882   Compass: Manuals, 58 notes: „C–'"A
Played at the premiere of Saint-Saën's   Pedal, 30 notes: „C–'F
Symphony No. 3 in C Minor, Op. 78, 9 May 1886.
(The composer conducted).
Played by Saint-Saëns: 21 June 1898.

I. GREAT (Enclosed)	II. SWELL (Enclosed)	PEDAL
16 Double Open Diapason	8 Open Diapason	16 Open Diapason
8 Open Diapason	8 Viola	16 Violone
8 Hohl Flute	8 Salicional	16 Bourdon
4 Principal	4 Harmonic Flute	8 Violoncello
4 Concert Flute	2 Flageolet	16 Trombone
2 Piccolo	8 Horn	
III Full Mixture	8 Oboe	
	Tremulant	

COUPLERS (Over Swell Keys)
Great to Pedal
Swell to Pedal
Swell to Great
Swell Octaves

The organ was mechanical action. The case was drab colored and decorated in dark brown, blue, red and gold. The mouths of the case pipes were gilded.

In 1905, when Saint James's Hall was closed, the organ was bought for £200 and presented to High Wycombe Town Hall.

SOURCE

The Rev. Bernard B. Edmonds, Suffolk, England.

E. & J. Abbey Organ
Inaugurated: 3 December 1890

Compass: Manuals, 56 notes; „C–"'G
Pedal 30 notes: „C–'F

I. GRAND-ORGUE	II. POSITIF	III. RÉCIT
16 Montre	8 Flûte harmonique	8 Diapason
16 Bourdon	8 Salicional	8 Flûte traversière
8 Montre	8 Cor de nuit	8 Viole de gambe
8 Flûte	8 Unda maris	8 Voix céleste
8 Bourdon	4 Dulciana	4 Flûte octaviante
8 Violoncelle	2⅔ Nazard	2⅔ Quinte
4 Prestant	2 Flageolet*	2 Octavin*
2 Doublette*	1⅗ Tierce*	IV–V Plein jeu*
V Cornet*	8 Trompette*	8 Trompette harmonique*
16 Basson*	8 Clarinette*	8 Hautbois-basson*
8 Trompette*		8 Voix humaine
4 Clairon*		4 Clairon harmonique*

PÉDALE

16 Contrebasse
16 Soubasse
8 Flûte
8 Bourdon
16 Bombarde
8 Trompette

PÉDALES DE COMBINAISON

Tirasses

Accouplements au
Grand-Orgue

Jeux de
combinaison

Efets d'orage
Grand-Orgue
Positif
Récit

Appel du Grand-Orgue

Positif
Récit
Octaves graves

Expression Récit

Grand-Orgue
Positif
Récit
Pédale

Forte général

Trémolo Récit

SOURCE

Le Monde Musical, advertisement for Abbey Organs, Special numéro, 1890 (?) Note: The article by W. L. Sumner, "The Organs of the Church of St. Séverin, Paris," *Musical Opinion* (April 1972) 367–69, contains many errors. The above is the original stoplist.

XX. SALLE PLEYEL

E. & J. Abbey Organ
Inaugurated: 19 November 1904

GRAND-ORGUE	RÉCIT	PÉDALE
8 Montre	8 Cor de nuit	16 Soubasse
8 Flûte harmonique	8 Viole de gambe	$10\frac{2}{3}$ Quinte
8 Violoncelle	8 Voix céleste	8 Basse
4 Prestant	8 Basson	

Salle Playel was completely renovated in 1927. A new organ was inaugurated by Marcel Dupré on 5 March 1930.

The Pleyel firm bought the Mutin-Cavaillé-Coll company and in October 1931 announced that they had entered the organbuilding business. Their first instrument, installed in one of the studios of the Pleyel building, was inaugurated by Dupré in October 1931. The traditional specificaiton of this organ, and the coincidence of eleven ranks, supports the assumption that this is the Abbey organ from the former Salle Pleyel.

As installed by Pleyel this organ had a three manual console. The first clavier, "Clavier d'accouplement," permitted the second (Grand-Orgue) and third (Récit) manuals to be coupled to it at 16′ 8′ and 4′ pitches. The Grand-Orgue and Récit coupled to the Pédale at 8′ and 4′.

XXI. AEOLIAN HALL
(135 New Bond Street, London, W. England)

Hutchings-Votey Organ
Built for The Aeolian Company   Compass: Manuals, 61 notes: „C–""C
Opus 922, 1903   Pedal, 30 notes: „C–'F

MANUAL I		MANUAL II	
Principale Doppio	16 Open Diapason	Bardone	16 Bourdon
Principale Maggiore	8 Open Diapason	Principale	8 Open Diapason
Principale Minore	8 Open Diapason	Violoncello	8 Violin Diapason
Flauto Primo	8 Gross Flute	Flauto Lontano	8 Rohr Flute
Flauto Traverso	8 Concert Flute	Quintatoni	8 Quintadena
Viola Pomposa	8 Gamba	Violino Primo	8 Salicional
Corno di Caccia	8 Gemshorn	Voce Angelica	8 Vox Celeste[2]
Violetta Marina	8 Dulciana	Viola D'amore	8 Aeoline
Ottava	4 Octave	Flauto Minore	4 Hohl Flute
Flauto Ottava	4 Flute Harmonique	Violetta	4 Violina
Flauto Piccolo	2 Piccolo	Flageoletto	2 Flageolet
Fagottone	16 Contra Fagotto	Seraphieno	V Cornet (String Mixture)
Trombetta	8 Trumpet	Baritono	8 Cornopean
Corno di Bassetto	8 Clarinet[1]	Oboe di Caccia	8 Orchestral Oboe
Saxophone	8 Saxophone	Voce Umana	8 Vox Humana
Tremolo	Tremolo	Companetta	Cathedral Chimes[3]
		Tremolo	Tremolo

AEOLIAN ECHO		PEDALE	
Contra Basse	16 Bourdon	Basso Profundo	16 Open Diapason
Principale	8 Open Diapason	Contra Basso	16 Bourdon
Pastorita	8 Rohr Flute	Basso Dolcina	16 Bourdon (from II)
Viola Pomposa	8 Gamba	Viola Pomposa	16 Violone
Violino Primo	8 Viol d'Orchestre	Violoncello	8 Cello
Viola d'amore	8 Aeoline	Flauto Grande	8 Flute
Voce Angelica	8 Unda Maris[2]	Trombono	16 Trombone
Flauto Minore	4 Chimney Flute		
Oboe di Caccia	8 Oboe		
Voce Umana	8 Vox Humana		
Tremolo	Tremolo		

Plate 53. Aeolian Hall, London

274

SPECIFICATIONS OF IMPORTANT ORGANS

DRAWKNOBS		COUPLERS	COMBINATION PISTONS
			(EACH MANUAL)
Right:	Manual I (Ebony)	II-I	
	Echo (Rosewood)	I - I 4'	Piano
Left:	Manual II (Ebony)	II - Pedale	Mezzo
	Pedale (Tulip)	I - Pedale	Mezzo Forte
		Echo - I	Forte
			Off

There is a balanced Swell Pedal for each manual division and Echo and a Balanced Crescendo Pedal.

[1]Free Reed Clarinet
[2]Celestes are each 49 notes: ,C–""C
[3]Chimes are 20 notes: ,A–"E
A Harp stop was ordered for this organ 30 October 1909.

The Aeolian Company subscribed to George Ashdown Audsley's premise that if Italian were the universal musical language it ought to be adopted for organ nomenclature. Consequently, many of their early organ's stops were lettered in Italian. However, to avoid confusion among its employees the company was careful in its contracts to "translate" each stop into standard organ terminology. We have, therefore, in the interest of clarity, rendered the Aeolian specification into its equivalent as a traditional organ stoplist.

SOURCES

Suggestive [sic] Specification, Aeolian Hall Organ, No. 922, Boston, 18 July 1901. Accepted by John W. Heins, Manager, Pipe-Organ Department.

Specification for an Aeolian Pipe-Organ prepared for The Orchestrelle Co., No. 932, 17 February 1903.

XXII. SALLE AEOLIAN
(32 Avenue de l'Opéra Paris)

Aeolian Organ Opus 1004
Inaugurated by Easthope Martin
December 1906
Contract dated 5 March 1906

Compass: Manuals, 61 notes: „C–""C
Pedal, 30 notes: „C–'F

MANUALE I		MANUALE II	
8 Principale Grande	Open Diapason	16 Bardone	Bourdon
8 Flauto Primo	Gross Flute	8 Flauto Lontano	Rohrflute
8 Viola Pomposa	Gamba	8 Violino Grande	Viole d'orchestre
8 Viola	Gemshorn	8 Violino Primo	Salicional
8 Viola d'Amore	Dolce	8 Violino Sordino	Aeoline
4 Principale Ottava	Octave	8 Voce Angelica	Vox Celeste
4 Flauto Ottava	Harmonic Flute	4 Violino Ottava	Violina
8 Tromba	Trumpet	V Serafieno	String mixture
8 Clarinetto	Clarinet	8 Baritono	Cornopean
Tremolo	Harp	8 Oboe di Caccia	Oboe
Arpa Grande	Harp	Tremolo	
		Campanetta	Chimes (20) in Echo box

ECHO (on Swell)		PEDALE	
8 Pastorita	Stopped Diapason	16 Violone	
8 Quintatoni	Quintadena	16 Contra Basso	Bourdon
8 Violino Distante	Aeoline	16 Basso Minore	Bourdon (Swell)
8 Onde Mare	Vox Celeste	8 Flauto Grande	Flute
4 Violetta	Violina	16 Sordono	Contra Fagotto
8 Voce Umana	Vox Humana		
Tremolo			

COUPLERS
II - I 8' 4"
II 16' 4' Unison Off
I 16' 4' Unison Off
Echo - I
II - Pedale
I - Pedale

COMBINATION PISTONS
(Five on each manual)

Piano
Mezzo
Mezzo forte
Forte
Release

SOURCE

Specification for an Aeolian Pipe-Organ prepared for Salle Aeolian, No. 1004, 5 March 1906.

XXIII. SALLE GAVEAU

Mutin Organ
Pedal, 30 notes: „C–'F

Compass: Manuals, 56 notes: „C–'''G

I. GRAND ORGUE

16	Bourdon
8	Montre
8	Flûte harmonique
8	Gambe
8	Bourdon
4	Prestant
2	Doublette
III	Fourniture
16	Basson
8	Trompette
4	Clairon

III. RÉCIT EXPRESSIF

8	Diapason
8	Flûte traversière
8	Gambe
8	Voix céleste
4	Flûte octaviante
2	Octavin
IV	Plein jeu
8	Trompette harmonique
8	Basson-hautbois
4	Soprano
	Recit 16'
	Récit Unisson
	Récit 4'

II. POSITIF EXPRESSIF

8	Principal
8	Salicional
8	Cor de nuit
4	Flûte douce
2	Flageolet
III	Carillon
8	Cromorne

PÉDALE

16	Contrebasse
16	Soubasse
8	Basse ouverte
8	Violoncelle
8	Bourdon
4	Flûte
16	Tuba magna

PÉDALES DE COMBINAISON

Tirasse Grand-Orgue
Tirasse Positif
Tirasse Récit
Appeles jeux de combinaison du Grand-Orgue
Récit au Grand-Orgue
Récit sur Positif
Positif sur Grand-Orgue
Octave grave du Grand-Orgue
Octaves aiguës du Grand-Orgue

Combinaisons ajustables: I, II, III, IV
Combinaisons fixes: I, f; II, ff à la Pédale

This was the first organ in Paris with adjustable combinations. However, it was so poorly placed, by the carelessness of an imprudent architect, that it could hardly be heard in the hall.

SOURCE

Jean Huré, *L'Esthètique de l'Orgue*, 130–31.

XXIV. CARNEGIE HALL
(New York City)

Frank Roosevelt Organ
Opus 468, 1891

Compass: Manuals, 61 notes: „C–""C
Pedal, 30 notes: „C–'F

GREAT	SWELL	PEDAL
16 Diapason	16 Bourdon Bass and Treble	16 Open Diapason
8 Open Diapason	8 Open Diapason	16 Bourdon
8 Gemshorn	8 Spitz Flöte	$10\frac{2}{3}$ Quint
8 Viola di Gamba	8 Salicional	8 Violoncello
8 Doppel Flöte	8 Stopped Diapason	16 Trombone
4 Octave	4 Octave	
4 Hohl Flöte	4 Flute Harmonique	
$2\frac{2}{3}$ Octave Quint	2 Flageolet	
2 Super Octave	III–V Dolce Cornet	
IV Mixture	8 Cornopean	
8 Trumpet	8 Oboe	
	Tremulant	

The entire organ, except for the Open Diapasons of the Great, is enclosed.

SOURCE

Rollin Smith, "The Organs of Carnegie Hall," *The American Organist* (July 1991) 46–49.

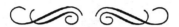

The Recordings of Camille Saint-Saëns

Saint-Saëns's recording career began at the age of 68 on Sunday after-noon, 26 June 1904 when, at the Paris studios of the Gramophone & Typewriter, Ltd., he recorded nine single-sided phonograph records: five sides of his own works for piano solo and four sides accompanying the celebrated contralto, Meyrianne Heglon. Curiously, on the latter four discs, his name does not appear on the label as accompanist. These were first listed in the G. & T. catalog supplement of November 1904.

He did not play for the phonograph again until 1919 when he recorded six sides for His Master's Voice—again in Paris. This session included four sides of solo selections and two sides as accompanist to the violinist, Gabriel Willaume.

Saint-Saëns also made rolls for the reproducing piano: eight for Welte-Mignon in 1905, three in Paris in 1907 for Hupfeld's DEA[1] — later issued by their licensee, Ampico (American Piano Company), and four for Aeolian Duo-Art recorded in New York City in June 1915.

Included with these recordings are five Aeolian Metrostyle 65-note piano rolls. These were not played by Saint-Saëns but, as was

---

[1]Saint-Saëns was disappointed with the DEA rolls. When they were played back for him and he was requested to sign them, he objected, saying, "I never played as badly as that!" (Arthur Dandelot, *Petits Mémoires Musicaux*, Paris: Editions Dandelot, 1930, p. 47).

Plate 54. Saint-Saëns recording Aeolian Duo-Art piano rolls, New York, 1915

Metrostyle's method for certain rolls in their Artist Series, "Interpretation was indicated by the composer." The dates are those of the monthly catalog in which the roll first appeared.

Solo Recordings by Saint-Saëns

AFRICA – IMPROMPTU CADENZA
G & T 3464F 035506   Recorded 26 June 1904

ALLEGRO APPASSIONATA, Op. 70
Metrostyle 100188   Catalog, February 1911

CONCERTO NO. 2 IN G MINOR, Op. 22, ALLEGRO SCHERZANDO
G & T 3467F 035509   Recorded 26 June 1904
Metrostyle 100021   Catalog, November 1910

GAVOTTE IN F, Op. 90, No. 3
Welte-Mignon C 802   Recorded 1905

PREMIÈRE MAZURKA, Op. 21
HMV 03286 v 2-035502   Recorded 1919

MAZURKA Op. 66, No. 3
Aeolian Duo-Art 5674-6   Catalog, September 1915

RHAPSODIE D'AUVERGNE, Op. 73
G & T 3474F 035510   Recorded 26 June 1904
Welte-Mignon C 800   Recorded 1905

SAMSON ET DALILA, ACT I: FINALE
Welte-Mignon C 797   Recorded 1905
Ampico 54686 H   Recorded 1907

SAMSON ET DALILA, IMPROVISATION
Aeolian Duo-Art 5696-6   Catalog, November 1915

SOUVENIR D'ISMAILIA, Op. 100
Metrostyle 100398   Catalog, November 1911

SUITE ALGERIÈNNE, Op. 60
  3. *Rêverie du soir (à Blidah)*
    Welte-Mignon X 801   Recorded 1905
    HMV 03284 v 035520   Recorded 1919
  4. *Marche militaire française*
    HMV 03285 v 035521   Recorded 1919

VALSE CANARIOTE, Op. 88
Metrostyle 100128   Catalog, December 1910

VALSE LANGOUREUSE, Op. 120
    Ampico 37234 H   Recorded 1907
    Metrostyle 100248   Catalog, April 1911

VALSE MIGNONNE, Op. 104
    G & T 3465F 035507   Recorded 26 June 1904
    Welte-Mignon C 803   Recorded 1905
    Aeolian Duo-Art 5673-6   Catalog, July 1915
    HMV 03287 v 2-035502   Recorded 1919

VALSE NONCHALANTE, Op. 110
    G & T 3466F 035508   Recorded 26 June 1904
    Welte-Mignon X 796   Recorded 1905
    Ampico 57234H   Recorded 1907
    Aeolian Duo-Art 5831-4   Catalog, November 1916

SCHUMANN: FAREWELL (ABSCHIED) FROM *FOREST SCENES*
    Welte-Mignon Y 806   Recorded 1905

CHOPIN: NOCTURNE IN F, Op. 15, No. 2
    Welte-Mignon C 807   Recorded 1905

Piano Accompaniment By Saint-Saëns

Meyrianne Heglon, Contralto

ASCANIO: AIR
    G & T 3469F 33470   Recorded 26 June 1904

RÊVERIE
    G & T 3470F 33471   "

SAMSON ET DALILA: "PRINTEMPS QUI COMMENCE"
    G & T 3471F 33472   "

LA SOLITAIRE (MÉLODIES PERSANES, Op. 26, No. 3)
    G & T 3473F 33473

Gabriel Willaume, violin

PRELUDE TO LE DÉLUGE
    HMV 03280 v 037920   Recorded 1919

ÉLEGIE, Op. 143
    HMV 03281 v 037921   "

Saint-Saëns's Testimonials for Harmoniums and Pianos

Estey Reed Organ

I have played the Estey organs and have been charmed by the quality of their sounds, which so closely resemble those of the pipe organ, and by the resources which they offer the performer.[1]

Mason & Hamlin Cabinet Organ, 1867

We, the undersigned, take pleasure in testifying that we regard the Mason & Hamlin Cabinet Organs as instruments in which all desirable improvements are to be found. The Automatic Swell expecially appears to us a remarkable success, and far superior in its capacity for varying the power of tone to anything which has hitherto been made. We recommend then, most especially these Cabinet Organs, for their excellent qualities; first, for the rendering of all sacred music, and also an an indispensable auxilliary of the pianoforte in the drawing room.[2]

> Édouard Batiste
> Auguste Durand
> Edmond Hocmelle
> C. Saint-Saëns

[1]This endorsement was probably secured during the Paris Exposition of 1867. It first appeared in the *Illustrated Catalogue of Cottage Organs Manufactured by J. Estey & Co., Brattleboro, Vermont* (New York: Biglow & Co., 1876) 22. It appeared in France in *MUSICA* from June 1908 to August 1909.

[2]*Mason & Hamlin Cabinet Organs*, Illustrated Catalogue (March 1880) 27.

The "Automatic Swell . . . is connected with the bellows . . . and is operated by in the

Orgue-Mustel

It is with the greatest pleasure that I take the opportunity to say how much I think of the Orgue-Mustel, unique in the world, and of the Célesta which has enriched the orchestra with a new and ever so valuable element.

I have played this marvellous instrument many times and it cannot help but be admired.[3]

Mustel Concertal, 1904

The Concertal has charmed and interested me to the highest degree. Thanks to this marvellous invention, everyone can interpret the most diverse things, not only the simplest, but those, like symphonic works, which requre every artistic resource. The most varied compositions benefit from the power and delicacy of its refined and amazing sound. The Concertal compliments the Orgue-Mustel and makes it available to everyone. It popularizes this ravishing instrument which, unique in the world, has retained my admiration for so many years.[4]

Welte-Mignon

Knowest thou the land, the land of the wonder? The wonder is the "Welte-Mignon," a modest name for a most wonderful thing. What a pity this invention was contrived long ago, for we could now hear Beethoven, Mozart, and Chopin himself, play.[5]

---

ordinary process of blowing. . . . To increase in loudness, blow faster; to diminish, blow more slowly, or stop blowing until the desired softness is attained."
[3]*Le Monde Musical* (15 January 1904) 24.
[4]*Le Guide du Concert: Numéro Saint-Saëns* (1914/1922) iv.
    This is the complete endorsement which appeared in Mustel publicity. The above citation contained only the second sentence.
[5]*Library of Welte-Mignon Music Records* (New York: De Lux Reproducing Roll Corporation, 1927) 191.

Knabe Piano, 1906

New York, 16 November 1906

Gentlemen:

You wish to know what I think of your pianos? I simply have the highest opinion possible of them. The ease and the evenness of the action, the limpidity and charm of the tone, above all, that rare quality possessed to sustain tone and sing like a human voice, as well as the varieties of the tone color met with, all combine in making the most magnificent and delightful instrument which it is my good fortune to play upon.

Very devotedly yours,
C. Saint-Saëns[6]

---

[6]*Eminent Musicians (New York: Wm. Knabe & Co., 1924).*

Thematic Catalog of Works for Harmonium and Organ

Solo Works

Original works for harmonium
Original works for organ
Transcriptions for organ

Chamber Music

Original works for harmonium/organ and instruments
Arrangements for harmonium and instruments

Organ and Orchestra

ORIGINAL WORKS FOR HARMONIUM

TROIS MORCEAUX POUR HARMONIUM, Op. 1

I. Méditation

II. Barcarolle

III. Prière

Composed:	1852
Published:	c. October, 1858
Publisher:	E. Girod
Plate No.:	E. G. 4109
Dedications:	I à Mr. Eugène Devivier
	II à Mademoiselle Berthe de Tinan*
	III à Madame Eugène Devivier

Other versions	Organ solo by Henri Busser (Alphonse Leduc, 1935; Plate No. A. L. 19026).
	Organ solo (I and II only) by Marilyn Mason (Boston: R. D. Row, 1954; Plate Nos. 2023-6 and 2024-6).

*As Berthe Pochet de Tinan, she later held a musical salon at her home in Paris and at her summer house in La Havre. There, during the summer of 1874, Gabriel Fauré played piano duets with André Messager and Saint-Saëns on several occasions.

The only authoritative version of Saint-Saëns's organ works is published by Durand; now in public domain, the music is available in an inexpensive reprint from Kalmus.

A six-volume edition of Saint-Saëns's organ works was published in Germany in 1991 by J. Butz. This is an unreliable and poorly documented series which, in addition to the original organ and harmonium works, includes manuscripts from the Bibliothèque Nationale never intended by the composer for publication, and simplified arrangements of other works originally published in harmonium collections presented here as original harmonium works! Some pieces have been provided with titles, and in many instances editorial markings and the original registrations have been changed or omitted. The sixth volume is an incomplete collection of organ transcriptions by others of various pieces by Saint-Saëns which were originally published by Durand.

ORIGINAL WORKS FOR ORGAN

FANTAISIE [E-flat]

Composed: 12 and 13 May 1857
Published: 1857
Publisher: Costallat (Richault et Cie., 1878)
Plate No.:   2745 (13152 R)
Dedication: Dediée à son ami Georges Schmitt (Richault edi-
                 tion only) (Manuscript: à mon ami M. G.
                 Schmitt)
Manuscript: No. 650 Bibliothèque Nationale
Performance: Played by the composer 3 December 1857 at the in-
                 auguration of the Cavaillé-Coll rebuild of the
                 organ of the Church of Saint-Merry, Paris.

TROIS RHAPSODIES SUR DES CANTIQUES BRETONS, Op. 7

I.

II.

III.

Composed:	I. Daurmeny, August 1866
	II. Daurmeny, Agust, 1866
	III. August, 1866
Published:	1866
Publisher:	1. Maeyens-Couvreur
	2. Pr. Pegiel, 1872
	Plate Nos.: J.B. 116 (1)
	J.B. 117 (2)
	J.B. 118 (3)
	3. Durand, 1880
	Plate No.: 2639
Dedication:	à Gabriel Fauré
Manuscript:	No. 655 Bibliothèque Nationale
Performances:	Played by the composer at the Trocadéro, 28 September 1878 and on his tour of Switzerland between 23 September and 3 October, 1896.
Themes:	I. Cantique des missionnaires, "Breudeur, ni'gler hok'emmo Deux ann tu all d'armor"
	II. Noël Breton, "Paraissez, monarque aimable"
Other versions:	Piano, 4 hands by Saint-Saëns (Maeyens-Couvreur, No. 1, 1866; No. II and III, 1867) Durand Plate No. 2640
	Harmonium by Saint-Saëns (Durand Plate No. 2641)
	Orchestra: Rhapsodie bretonne, Op. 7bis pour orchestre (sur les motifs de la 1e et de la 3e rapsodies de l'op. 7) by Saint-Saëns, November 1891. (Durand, 1892)
	Manuscript: No. 547 Bibliothèque Nationale

BÉNÉDICTION NUPTIALE, Op. 9

Composed:	1859
Published:	1868
Publisher:	Maeyens-Couvreur (Durand, 1880)
Plate No.:	D. S. & Cie. 2638
Dedication:	à Madame la Marquise de Mornay, née de Villers
Performance:	Played by the composer for the inauguration of the new organ of La Trinité, Paris, 16 March 1869 and on his tour of Switzerland between 23 September and 3 October 1896.
Transcriptions:	Piano à 4 mains par l'Auteur (Maeyens-Couvreur, 1868, Durand, 1880)
	Piano à 2 mains par l'Auteur (Durand, 1903) (Plate No. D. et F. 6287)

ÉLÉVATION OU COMMUNION, Op. 13

Composed:	c. 1856
Published:	September, 1865
Publisher:	Canaux et Maeyens-Couvreur. (In *La Chapelle au Couvent,* Publication spéciale de Musique Religieuse pour Voix de Femmes, edited by J. Lecocq and L. D. Besozzi.)
Plate No.:	J. B. 24
Dedication:	à Monsieur A. Chauvet
Manuscript:	1. No. 914 Bibliothèque Nationale *Cinq pièces inédits pour orgue ou harmonium.* This is 914d —*Morceaux pour harmonium, inédit.* No. III Andantino, "Communion ou 'O Salutaris'"
	2. No. 654 Bibliothèque Nationale *Elévation ou Communion pour Orgue* Dedication: à M. Alexis Chauvet.

Second Publication	
Published:	1880
Publisher:	Durand & Schoenwerk
	1. Grand Orgue Plate No.: D. S. & Cie. 2642 (1)
	2. Harmonium Plate No.: D. S. & Cie. 2642 (2)
Transcription:	Piano solo by Saint-Saëns (Choudens, 1886)

TROIS PRÉLUDES ET FUGUES, Op. 99

I.

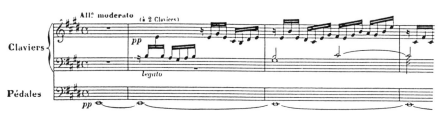

II.

III.

Composed:	Summer, 1894
Published:	1894
Publisher:	Durand
Plate No.:	D. & F. 4888
Dedications:	I à Charles-Marie Widor
	II à Alexandre Guilmant
	III à Eugène Gigout
Manuscript:	*Fugue in E.* No. 915 (4) Bibliothèque Nationale "Composed in the summer of 1894." After completing the fugue the composer continued with the *Prélude in B Major.* He first worked out the canon of the middle of the *Prélude* and then went on to the *Fugue.*
Performances:	Nos. I and III were played by the composer on his tour of Switzerland between 23 September and 3 October 1896.
Transcriptions:	2 pianos, 4 hands by Charles Malherbe (Durand, 1896)
	II. *Prélude* by Leon Boëllmann (Durand, 1896, Plate No. D. & F. 5160)

FANTAISIE [in D-flat], Op. 101

Composed:	1895
Published:	1896
Publisher:	Durand
Plate No.:	D. & F. 5032
Dedication:	à sa Majesté la Reine Elisabeth de Roumanie
Manuscript:	Chateau-Musée de Dieppe
Performances:	Played by the composer on his tour of Switzerland between 23 September and 3 October 1896.
Transcription:	Piano, 2 hands by Georges Grécourt (Paris: Lucien de Lacour, 1932)

MARCHE RELIGIEUSE, Op. 107

Composed:	November, 1897
Published:	1898
Publisher:	Durand
Plate No.:	D. & F. 5402
Dedication:	à Marie Christine, Reine Régente d'Espagne
Manuscript:	No. 653 Bibliothèque Nationale "Réçu à Paris 9 fevrier 1898."
Performances:	Played by the composer for Queen Christine in the Church of San Francisco, Madrid, November 1897. Played by the composer 6 November 1913, Paris, Salle Gaveau.
Transcriptions:	Piano, 4 hands by Gaston Choisnel (Durand, 1909) Orchestra by Roger Branga (Durand, 1929)

TROIS PRÉLUDES ET FUGUES, Op. 109

I

II

III

Composed:	Las Palmas, 1898
Published:	1898
Publisher:	Durand
Plate No.:	D. & F. 5421
Dedications:	I à Gabriel Fauré

299

	II à Albert Périlhou
	III à Henri Dallier
Manuscript:	No. 652 Bibliothèque Nationale
Correspondence:	Letter from Gabriel Fauré to Saint-Saëns, 14 July 1898:

Upon my return from London I found the superb *Préludes et Fugues* for organ which I will never be able to play properly and I had the great joy of seeing my name at the head of one of them. I thank you a thousand times for this pleasant and flattering surprise.

(Letter No. 18 [1.a. Gabriel Fauré] Bibliothèque Nationale, reproduced in Saint-Saëns et Fauré *Correspondence*, p. 60.

Transcription: 2 pianos by Gaston Choisnel (Durand, 1905)

FANTAISIE POUR ORGUE-AEOLIAN

Composed:	London, July 1906
Published:	1988 (Reconstructed by Rollin Smith, who translated the perforations of the player organ roll into musical notation.)
Publisher:	Rob. Forberg, Musikverlag
Manuscript:	No. 648 Bibliothèque Nationale. This incomplete first draft bears the heading: "Morceau écrit pour l'orgue AEolian."

The final 38-page autograph manuscript, signed and dated, was offered for sale in January 1989 by Hans Schneider, Musikantiquariat, Tutzing über München. Price: DM 16,000 ($8,677.00).

SEPT IMPROVISATIONS, Op. 150

I

II Feria Pentecostes

III

IV

V Pro Martyribus

VI Pro Defunctis

VII

Composed:	9 December 1916 to 12 February 1917
Published:	1919 (sic)
Publisher:	Durand
Plate No.:	D. & F. 9507
Dedication:	à Eugène Gigout
Manuscript:	No. 645 Bibliothèque Nationale
Performances:	Played by the composer:
	25 March 1917, Marseille, Théâtre des Nations (premiere)
	28 March 1917, Nice
	1 April 1917, Lyon
Transcription:	Piano, 4 hands by Lucien Gorban (Durand, 1918 [sic])

FANTAISIE [in C Major], Op. 157

Composed:	1919
Published:	1919
Publisher:	Durand
Plate No.:	D. & F. 9787
Dedication:	à sa majesté le Roi Manoel
Manuscript:	No. 647 Bibliothèque Nationale

TRANSCRIPTIONS FOR ORGAN

O SALUTARIS
extrait de la *Messe*, Op. 4

Composed:	1856
Transcribed:	1904
Published:	1904
Publisher:	A. Durand & Fils.
Plate No.:	D. & F. 6376
Dedication:	à Monsieur Gaston Choisnel
Performances:	Played by the composer for the first time at a benefit concert for the Association of Artists and Musicians at Salle Pleyel, 19 November 1904. He played it again at his "farewell recital" at Salle Gaveau, 6 November 1913.

LA PRÉDICATION AUX OISEAUX (ST. FRANÇOIS D'ASSISE)
Deux Légendes, No. 1 par Franz Liszt

Composed:	1863
Publisher:	Rózsavölgyi & Co., Budapest
Dedication:	à Madame la Baronne Cosima de Bülow (née Liszt)
Transcribed:	by Camille Saint-Saëns
Published:	1899
Publisher:	Rózsavölgyi & Co., Leipzig
	Heugel, Paris: 1923
Plate No.:	H. 28433
Performance:	Played by Saint-Saëns at his recital at the Trocadéro on 28 September 1878.
Correspondence:	Letter from Franz Liszt to Saint-Saëns, Weimar, 14 May 1882

(Saint-Saëns Archives, Chateau-Musée de Dieppe):
I am still quite struck with wonder at your *Prédication aux oiseaux.* You use your organ as an orchestra in an incredible way, as only a great composer and a great performer like yourself could. The most proficient organists in all countries have only to take off their hats to you.

Chamber Music

SIX DUOS POUR HARMONIUM ET PIANO, Op. 8

I. Fantasia et Fuga

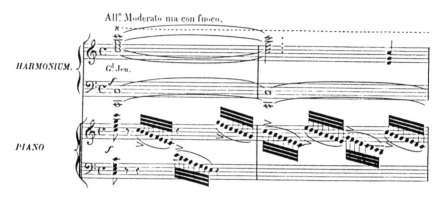

II. Cavatina

III. Choral

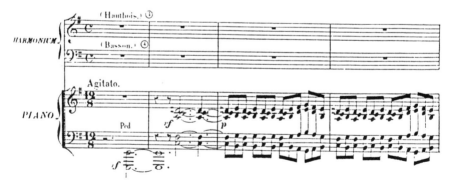

IV. Capriccio

V. Scherzo

VI. Finale

Composed:	April and May, 1858
Published:	c. October, 1858
Publisher:	E. Girod
Plate Nos.:	Girod: E. G. 4110
	Joubert: E. 2380 F (1)
	E. 2381 F (2)
	E. 2382 F (3)
	E. 2383 F (4)
	E. 2384 F (5)
	E. 2385 F (6)
Dedication:	à Lefébure-Wély
Manuscript:	Fantaisie et Fugue (sic) 6 pages, Harmonium part only: No. 915 Bibliothèque Nationale (collection Charles Malherbe)
Other version:	DUOS POUR DEUX PIANOS, Op. 8bis
	1. Fantaisie et Fugue
	2. Choral
	3. Scherzo
	4. Final
Arranged:	By Saint-Saëns in 1898
Published:	1898
Publisher:	E. Girod
Dedication:	à M. Gustave Lyon, inventeur du piano-double Pleyel.

SÉRÉNADE, Op. 15
pour piano, orgue, violon et alto ou violoncelle

Composed:	20 May 1865
Published:	1865
Publisher:	Choudens
Dedication:	à Princesse Mathilde Bonaparte Demidoff
Manuscript:	No. 893 Bibliothèque Nationale
Performances:	Premiered January 1866 at a soirée given by the Prince of Hohenzollern. Saint-Saëns (organ) and Julien Sauzay (piano). Performed again at Lubouc's by the Société des Concerts des Concerts Saint-Cécile, conducted by Weckerlin, 17 February 1866 and again Salle Pleyel, 2 April 1866 before an audience which included Berlioz, Gounod and Liszt.
	Played by the composer (organ) and Walter Damrosch (piano) at Carnegie Hall, New York City, 15 Novemver 1906.
Transcriptions:	Piano by Saint-Saëns (Choudens, 1886)
	Piano by Leon Boëllmann (Manuscript No. 17899 Bibliothèque Nationale)
	Piano, 4 hands by Leon Boëllmann (Manuscript No. 17900 Bibliothèque Nationale)
	Harmonium et piano by Albert Renaud (Choudens, Plate No.: A. C. 12,146)
Other version:	Song, Sérénade, Op. 15 to words by L. Mangeot
	ROMANCE, Op. 27

ROMANCE, Op. 27
pour violon, harmonium et piano

Composed:	1866
Published:	1868
Publisher:	Durand c. 1875
Plate No.:	D. S. & Cie. 2040
Dedication:	à Gustave Doré
Transcriptions:	Violin and piano by Gaston Choisnel (Durand, 1906, Plate No.: D. & F. 6743)
	Violin and orchestra by Saint-Saëns in 1921
Manuscript:	No. 667 Bibliothèque Nationale

QUATOUR
sur un fragment [Trio] de *l'Oratorio de Noël* pour violon, violoncelle, orgue-harmonium et piano

Composed:	1858
Published:	c. 1880
Publisher:	Durand
Dedication:	none
Plate No.:	D. & F. 3048

BARCAROLLE, Op. 108
pour violon, violoncelle, harmonium et piano

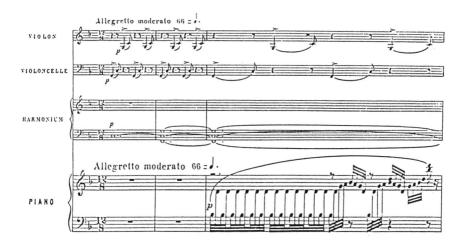

Composed:	7 March 1898
Published:	11 May 1898
Publisher:	Durand
Plate No.:	D. & F. 5403
Dedication:	Antonio Jeanbernat
Manuscript:	No. 738 Bibliothèque Nationale
Performances:	Premiered by La Trompette, 18 May 1898 Diémer (piano), Saint-Saëns (harmonium), Rémy (violin) and Jules Delsart (cello).
	Played in Barcelona, Spain at a concert given in Saint-Saëns's honor but which he did not attend. Performers included: Crickboom (violin), Pablo Casals (cello), Callado (piano) and Jeanbernat (harmonium).
Transcriptions:	For violin, viola, cello and piano by Saint-Saëns in April, 1909. (Durand Plate No. D & F. 7341).

Manuscript: No. 739, Bibliothèque Nationale

311

PRIÈRE, Op. 158
pour violoncelle et orgue

Composed:	Fall, 1919
Published:	November, 1919
Publisher:	Durand
Plate No.:	D. & F.
Dedication:	à André Hekking
Manuscript:	No. 839 Bibliothèque Nationale
Other version:	Violin and piano, Op. 158bis
Arranged:	1920 by Saint-Saëns
Publisher:	Durand
Plate No.:	D. & F. 9900
Manuscript:	No. 714 Bibliothèque Nationale

Durand paid Saint-Saëns 600 francs on 23 September 1919 for the version for cello and organ, and 500 francs on 12 73 July 1920 for the version for violin and piano. (Contracts, Boîte II, Dossier 2.)

MARCHE RELIGIEUSE DE LOHENGRIN
précédée du CHANT D'ELSA
par Richard Wagner
pour violon, harmonium et piano

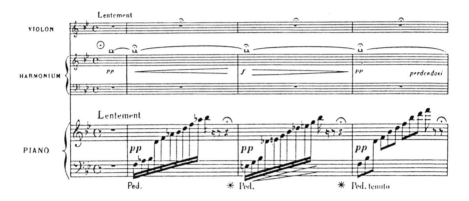

Composed:	Lohengrin was completed 1 January 1848
Dedication:	à Franz Liszt
Transcribed:	1868 by Camille Saint-Saëns
Published:	1869
Publisher:	Durand
Plate No.:	D. & F. 1023

Performances: Saint-Saëns included this transcription in his chamber
music concerts in Buenos Aires, Argentina, in June and July 1899.

Organ and Orchestra

TROISIÈME SYMPHONIE EN UT MINEUR, Op. 78

I

II

Composed:	August 1885–April 1886
Published:	1886
Publisher:	A. Durand et Fils
Plate No.:	D. S. 3700
Dedication:	à la mémoire de Franz Liszt
Manuscript:	Bibliothèque de l'Institut de France MS 2.500
Performances:	Premiered by the composer 19 May 1886, St. James's Hall, London; first performance in Paris on 9 January 1887, Jules Garcin conducting the Société des Concerts du Conservatoire; conducted by Saint-Saëns in London, 1895; conducted it a the Brussels Exposition 13 Oct. 1897; played the organ part at Salle Pleyel, 19 Nov. 1904; Academy of Saint Cecilia, Rome, 26 March 1906; Carnegie Hall, New York City, 15 Nov. 1906; Church of Saint-Martin, Vévey, 23 May 1913.
Correspondence:	The following letter acknowledging the dedication was written to Saint-Saëns by Franz Liszt twelve days before his death:

Very Dear Friend:

Pleased by the kindness of which you have given me much proof, I am whole-heartedly grateful to you. The success of your symphony in London gives me great pleasure, and it will continue to crescendo in Paris and elsewhere. For purposes of the dedication I ask that you use only my name – which I must now append to these few lines because of my poor eyesight.

> With devoted and cordial affection,
> Franz Liszt
> Weimar, 19 June 1886

(Chateau-Musée de Dieppe, quoted in Fallon, II, 375.)

Transcriptions:	Piano à quatre mains (by Léon Roques)
	Durand, 1886
	Plate No.: D. S. 3704
	Deux pianos à quatre mains (by Saint-Saëns)
	Manuscript dated Fin/Aout/
	MDCCCLXXXVII
	Durand et Cie., 1910
	Deux pianos – huit mains
	Durand et Cie., 1910

Piano solo (by Percy Goetschius)
Analytic Symphony Series, No. 28
Philadelphia: Oliver Ditson Co., 1931
Organ: Adagio only (by Émile Bernard)
Durand, 1897
Plate No.: D. & F. 5334

CYPRÈS ET LAURIERS, Op. 156

I. Cyprès

317

II. Lauriers

Composed:	End of February, 1919
Published:	1919
Publisher:	Durand
Plate No.:	D. & F. 9800
Dedication:	à Monsieur Raymond Poincaré, Président de la République Française
Performances:	Premiered at Ostende 18 April 1919
	Conducted by the composer at the Trocadéro on Sunday, 24 October 1920; Eugène Gigout, organist.
	26 October, Liège
	27 October, Brussels
	29 October, Rouen
Transcription:	2 pianos à 4 mains (Durand, 1919).

Variant Readings of the Trois Rhapsodies sur des cantiques Bretons

Saint-Saëns arranged his *Trois Rhapsodies Bretons* for piano four-hands, and harmonium; these versions, together with the organ solo version, were published concurrently by Durand. Interpretative directions vary from one version to another, and those who play the original for organ will be interested to see what additional suggestions the composer offered for performing the same work in a different medium. Each variant is compared by page, score and measure to the organ edition. Note that the Ⓖ in the harmonium score denotes the addition of 16′ and 4′ stops. A slash through the same circle, Ⓖ cancels the registration.

APPENDIX I

ORGAN			PIANO, FOUR HANDS	HARMONIUM
			RHAPSODIE I	
1	4	3	b. 6. sf over D-sharp	b. 6. sf over D-sharp
1	3	6	mf Expressive	mf
2	2	4	b. l. alto E tied to next measure	not tied
2	3	5	poco rit.	
2	3	6	a Tempo; 1.h. *Cantabile*	a Tempo
3	2	4		Ⓖ (Grand jeu, add 16′ 4′)
3	3	4		ff
5	3	1		f
5	4	3 to		
6	1	3	Dim.	sempre dim.
6	1	3	pp	pp
6	4	4	b. 6., 1.h.G-sharp tied to following meas.	
			RHAPSODIE II	
7	1	1		Ⓖ
7	1	2		Ⓖ
7	1	3		Ⓖ
7	2	3		Ⓖ
7	2	6		Ⓖ
7	4	7		a Tempo [off 16′]
8	3	4		cresc. to 8 4 3 *f*
9	3	2	b.4. Pedal A-sharp, B, C-sharp, B. The manuscript of the organ version reads this same variant. The pedal-board of the Madeleine went only to C.	b.4. Pedal: A-sharp, B, C-sharp, B.
10	1	1	Andantino	
10	1	2	Cantabile	
10	2	4	♩ ♫ m. 5: ♩ ♩	
12	1	1	cresc.	add 16′ poco. cresc.
12	1	5	mf	
12	2	2	dim.	
12	2	6	p	pp
12	3	2-3	——— *f*	
12	3	7	marcato	
12	3	9	cresc.	
12	4		♩ ♩♩ ♩ ♩♩ ♩ ♩	Ⓖ

13	1	1	marcatissimo	
13	3	1-2	◁————	

RHAPSODIE III

15	2	9	l.h. marcato	
15	3	1	b.2., r.h., F-sharp	b.2., r.h. F-sharp
15	4	11		off 16′
17	1	2		Ped. marcato
17	3	5	b.4. poco rit.	
20	1	12	Espressivo	
20	3	7	b.r., r.h. *dolce* >	
20	4	6	b.4., Pedal: ♩	
21	1	1	b.1., Pedal: ♫♩	
21	3	1	poco. rit.	
21	4	3	Pedal: ♫ ♪	Pedal: ⌐⌐ ♩

Bibliography

Adolophus, F. *Some Memories of Paris*. New York: Holt, 1895.

"Aeolian Hall in London." *The Music Trades* (26 March 1904) 19–22.

Aldrich, Richard. *Concert Life in New York*. New York: Putnam, 1941.

Audsley, George Ashdown. *The Organ of the Twentieth Century*. New York: Dodd, Mead and Co., 1919.

_____. "The Small Two-Manual Organ." *The Organ*, No. 15 (January 1925) 138–49.

Beale, S. Sophia. *The Churches of Paris*. London: Allen, 1893.

de Bertha, A. "Franz Liszt." *Bulletin français de la S.I.M.* (November 1907) 1160–84.

Bonnal, J. Ermend. "Saint-Saëns à Saint-Séverin." *Bulletin Trimestriel des Amis de l'Orgue*, No. 24 (December 1935) 6–8.

Bonnerot, Jean. *Camille Saint-Saëns*. Paris: Durand, 1923.

Bonnet, Joseph. *Diagram of Stopknobs on (Ancien) Trocadéro Console— Préparation courante*. Bibliothèque Nationale, Rés. Vmb. 31.

_____. "Preface." *Historical Organ Recitals*, Vol. V. New York: G. Schirmer, 1929.

Bourdon (Chanoine), A. *Notice sur le grand-orgue de Notre-Dame-de-Saint-Dizier, construit par M. Cavaillé-Coll*. Bar-le-Duc: Numa Rolin 1863. (A forty-seven-page promotional monograph written by the former maître-de-chapelle of Rouen Cathedral and the Superior of the Maîtrise Saint-Évode.)

Bowers, Q. David. *Encyclopedia of Automatic Musical Instruments*. Vestal, New York: Vestal Press, 1972.

Bridge, Frederick. *A Westminster Pilgrim*. London: Novello, 1918.

Briquet, Marie. *Correspondance et papiers de Saint-Saëns et inventaire des portraits et du mobilier conservés au Musée Saint-Saëns de Dieppe 1939–1950.* Bibliothèque Nationale Rés. Vmd. ms. 11. (Letters are copied completely or in resumé.)

Brook, Barry S. "The simplified plaine and easie code system for notating music, a proposal for international adoption." *Fontes Artis Musicae* (May–September 1965) 156–60.

Busser, Henri. *De Pelléas aux Indes Galantes.* Paris: Fayard, 1955.

Cain, Georges. *À Travers Paris.* Paris: Flammarion, 1909.

Campbell, Margaret. *The Great Violinists.* Garden City: Doubleday & Co., 1981.

de Castéra, Réne. "Les Variations de M. Saint-Saëns." *L'Occident* (March 1903) 527–30.

Cavaillé-Coll, Aristide. "De l'Orgue et son architecture." *Revue Générale de l'Architecture* (1872) 1–17.

Cellier, Alexandre. "Une Heure avec Camille Saint-Saëns." *L'Orgue*, No. 73 (October–December 1954) 122–24.

Christ, Yvan. *Églises de Paris.* Paris: Éditions des Deux Mondes, 1956.

Clunn, Harold P. *The Face of Paris.* London: Spring Books, n.d. (c. 1960).

Clutton, Cecil. "The Grand Orgue at St. Merry, Paris." *The Organ*, No. 112 (April 1949) 145ff.

_____. "Modern French Organbuilding." *The American Organist* (September 1939) 295–99.

Colin, Charles. "Réception du Grand Orgue de Saint-Sulpice." *La France musicale* (4 May 1862) 137–38.

Collin, Charles. "Memoires." *Bulletin de l'Association des Ancien Élèves de l'École Niedermeyer* (January–March 1922) 3.

Collin, Charles–René. "Souvenirs artistiques." *La Flûte Harmonique*, No. 31/32 (1984) 12–41.

Cortot, Alfred. "Saint-Saëns." in *La Musique Française de Piano.* 3 vols. Paris: Éditions Rieder, 1930, pp. 55–108.

Dandelot, Arthur. *Petits Mémoires Musicaux.* Paris: Éditions de "La Nouvelle Revue," 1936.

_____. *La Vie et l'Œuvre de Saint-Saëns.* Paris: Éditions Dandelot, 1930.

Decrette, Didier. *Histoire du Grand Orgue de l'Église Saint-Pierre-de-Dreux.* Vernouillet: Les Vignes de la Brosse, 1977.

Delhommeau, Abbé. *Orgues et Organistes de la Cathédrale de Luçon.* Luçon, 1966.

Dieterlen, Michel. *L'Harmonium, une aventure musicale et industrielle.* Doctoral thesis, Université de Reims, 1982.

_____. "L'Orgue expressif de la Maison d'Éducation de la Légion d'-Honneur de Saint-Denis." *La Flûte Harmonique,* No. 17 (1er trimestre 1981) 5–23.

Discours prononcés aux funérailles de C. Saint-Saëns. Le Samedi 24 décembre 1921 au cimetière Montparnasse. (Contains eulogies by Eugène Gigout, Carol-Bénard, C. Joubert, Edmond Haraucourt, Ch.- M. Widor and Léon Bérnard.)

Doré, Gustave. *Temps et contretemps.* Fribourg: Éditions de la libraire de l'Université, 1942.

Douglass, Fenner. *Cavaillé-Coll and the Musicians.* 2 vols. Raleigh: Sunbury Press, 1980.

Dufourcq, Norbert. "L'Enseignement de l'orgue au Conservatoire National avant la nomination de César Franck (1872)." *L'Orgue,* No. 144 (October–December 1972) 121–25.

_____. *Le grand orgue et les organistes de Saint-Merry de Paris.* Paris: Librairie Floury, 1947.

_____. "Les grandes formes de la musique d'orgue." *La Revue musicale,* No. 172 (February–March 1937) 83–95.

_____. "Les grandes orgues historiques de Saint-Merry." *Bulletin Trimestriel des Amis de l'Orgue,* No. 12 (December 1932) 7.

_____. *Les grandes orgues de Saint-Merry de Paris à travers l'histoire.* Paris: L'Association des Amis de l'Orgue, 1983.

_____. "Saint-Merry." *Les Monuments Historiques de la France* VIII/2–3 (April–September 1962) 165–71.

Dulcken, Ferdinand Quentin. *Liszt Organ Method.* Boston: Mason & Hamlin Organ & Piano Company, 1891.

Dupaigne, Albert. *Le Grand Orgue de la nouvelle Salle de Concert de Sheffield en Angleterre construit par A. Cavaillé-Coll à Paris.* Paris: Plon, 1874.

Duplessy, E. *Paris Religieux: Guide artistique, historique et pratique dans les églises, chapelles, pélerinages et oeuvres de Paris.* Paris: Roger et Chernoviz, 1900.

Dupré, Camille. "Quatre organistes (Chauvet, Saint-Saëns . . .)." *La Chronique musical* (16 February 1867).

Dupré, Marcel. *Disposition des jeux aux consoles des orgues jouées par Marcel Dupré.* Bibliothèque Nationale, Rés. Vma. ms. 923.

_____. *Marcel Dupré raconte. . . .* Paris: Bonnemann, 1972.

Durand, Jacques. *Quelques souvenirs d'un éditeur de musique.* Paris: A Durand & Cie., 1924.

Eschbach, Jesse, and Robert Bates. *César Franck: Fantaisie für die Orgel in Drei Versionen.* Bonn–Bad Godesberg: Forberg, 1980.

(Estey). *Illustrated Catalogue of Cottage Organs Manufactured by J. Estey & Co., Brattleboro, Vermont.* New York: Biglow & Co., 1876.

Fage, Adrien de la. *Quinze visites musicales à l'exposition universelle de 1855.* Paris: Chez Tardif, 1856.

Fallon, Daniel M. "Saint-Saëns and the Concours de Composition Musicale in Bordeaux." *Journal of the American Musicological Society* xxxi (Summer 1978) 309–25.

_____. *The Symphonies and Symphonic Poems of Camille Saint-Saëns.* 2 vols. Ph.D. dissertation, Yale University, 1973.

Fauré, Gabriel. "Camille Saint-Saëns." *La Revue Musicale* (February 1922) 97–100.

Fétis, François-Joseph. *Rapport du jury: Fabrication des instruments de musique, Exposition de 1855.* Paris: Napoleon Chaix de Cie., 1857.

_____. "L'Orgue mondaine et la musique érotique à l'église." *Revue et Gazette musicale* (6 April 1856) 1–2.

Feuillet, Alfred. "Georges Schmitt." *Revue de musique sacrée ancienne et moderne* (15 October 1863) 352–55.

Foster, Myles Birket. *History of the Philharmonic Society.* London: 1912.

Galerne, Maurice. *L'École Niedermeyer.* Paris: Éditions Margueritat, 1928.

Garay, Martin. *L'Église Saint-Merry de Paris.* Paris: Association pour la Culture par les Loisirs et le Tourisme, c. 1982.

Gastoué, Amédée. "A Great French Organist, Alexandre Boëly, and His Works." *The Musical Quarterly* XXX/3 (July 1944) 336–44.

Gavoty, Bernard. *Louis Vierne*. Paris: Albin Michel, 1943.

Gérard, Yves. *Saint-Saëns and the Problems of Nineteenth-Century French Music Seen through the Saint-Saëns Archives*. Unpublished monograph, Paris (December, 1969).

Grace, Harvey. *Modern French Organ Music*. An address given on 14 May 1918.

_____. "Saint-Saëns's New Organ Works." *The Musical Times* LVIII/896 (October 1917) 448–50. Review of the just-published *Sept Improvisations*.

Gros, Adrien. "Des morceaux chantés pendant la célébration du service divin." *Revue de musique sacrée ancienne et moderne* (15 Septembre 1862) 376.

Guide du Concert. Special number devoted to Saint-Saëns. Paris: 1914. Enlarged and reissued in 1922.

Guilmant, Alexandre. "Organ Music and Organplaying." *The Forum* (March 1898) 83–89.

Hamel, Pierre-Marie. *Rapport sur les travaux de grand orgue de l'église de la Madeleine à Paris*. Paris: Maulde et Renou, 1846.

Harding, James. *Saint-Saëns and His Circle*. London: Chapman & Hall, 1965.

Harkins, Elizabeth Remsberg. *The Chamber Music of Camille Saint-Saëns*. Ph.D. dissertation, New York University, 1976.

Head, Sir Francis. *A Faggot of French Sticks; or, Paris in 1851*. New York: Putnam, 1852.

Helbig, Gustave. *Monographie des Orgues de France*. Bibliothèque Nationale Rés. Vmc. ms. 13 (1–2); Rés. Vmc. ms. 14 (1–2).

_____. *La Grande Pitié des Orgues de France*. Bibliothèque Nationale Rés. Vmc. ms. 15 (1–4).

Henderson, Arthur M. "Church and Organ Music; Memories of Some Distinguished French Organists: Fauré." *The Musical Times* (September 1937) 817–19.

_____. "Visits to Saint-Saëns Recalled; Memories of a Famous Organist." *The Diapason* (February 1951) 24.

Hervey, Arthur. *Masters of French Music*. London: Osgood, McIlvaine & Co., 1894.

Hillairet, Jacques. *Le Colline de Chaillot*. Paris: Editions de Minuit, 1977.

Horowitz, Joseph. *Conversations with Arrau*. New York: Knopf, 1982.

Houle, Michael. *Cyclic Techniques in the Symphonies of Saint-Saëns, d'Indy, Franck and Chausson and the Extension and Development of These Techniques in Other French Symphonies through the Turn of the Century*. Master's thesis, University of California at Los Angeles, 1968.

Hughes, Allen. "Saint-Saëns's Organ Music: A Case of Unjust Neglect." *The New York Times* (Sunday, 7 February 1982) Section 2.

Huré, Jean. "Eugène Gigout." *L'Orgue et les Organistes* (15 December 1925) 5–6.

_____. "Franz Liszt." *L'Orgue et les Organistes* (15 January 1925) 27–30.

_____. "Inauguration d'un orgue à la Salle Pleyel." *Le Monde Musical* (30 November 1904) 314, 319.

_____. "Saint-Saëns: Organiste honoraire de Saint-Séverin." *Le Guide du Concert* (Numéro spécial Saint-Saëns, 1914/1922) 9–10.

Huybens, Gilbert. *Aristide Cavaillé-Coll: Liste des travaux exécutés*. Orgelbau-Fachverlag Rensch: ISO Information, 1985.

Jouve, (Abbé). "Inauguration de l'orgue de la paroisse Saint-Thomas-d'Aquin." *Revue de musique sacrée ancienne et moderne (15 June 1862) 260–61*.

Kelterborn, Louis. "A Few Reminiscences of Camille Saint-Saëns." *The Musician* (May 1906) 250.

Klein, Grégor. *Le Grand Orgue de Saint-Sulpice*. Paris: La Flûte Harmonique, 1981.

Klein, Herman. "Saint-Saëns as I Knew Him." *The Musical Times* (February 1922) 90–93.

Kobbé, Gustave. *The Aeolian Pipe-Organ and Its Music*. New York: The Aeolian Company, 1919.

Kriéger, Antoine. *La Madeleine*. Paris: Desclée de Brower, 1937.

Lamazou, (Abbé) Pierre-Henri. *Étude sur l'orgue monumental de Saint-Sulpice et de la facture d'orgue moderne*. Paris: Repos, 1863.

_____. *Grand Orgue de l'église métropolitaine Notre-Dame-de-Paris, reconstruit par A. Cavaillé-Coll*. Paris: Plon, 1868.

_____. "Lefébure-Wély." *L'Illustration musicale* (February 1863).

_____. "Les Organistes Français." *Revue et Gazette musicale* (4 May 1856) 140–41.

Laurens, L. C. "Des Fonctions du grand orgue pendant les offices." *Revue de musique sacrée ancienne et moderne* (15 August 1864) 290–96.

Lauth, F. "Une Anecdote sur A. Périlhou (1895)." *Bulletin Trimestriel des Amis de l'Orgue*, No. 29 (March 1937) 17–18.

Lefébure-Wély, Louis-James-Alfred. *Méthode Théorique et Pratique pour le Poïkilorgue*, Op. 9. Paris: Canaux et Nicou-Choron, 1839.

Levien, John. *Impressions of W. T. Best.* London: Novello, 1942.

Lioncourt, Guy de. "Les Idées de M. Camille Saint-Saëns." *Les Tablettes de la Schola Cantorum, Bulletin mensuel* (July 1919).

Liszt, Franz. *Letters of Franz Liszt.* Edited by La Mara. Translated by Constance Bache. New York: Greenwood Press, 1969.

Lostalot, A. D. "Inauguration du Grand Orgue de Notre-Dame-de-Paris." *L'Illustration* (21 March 1868).

Locard, Paul. *Les Maîtres contemporains de l'orgue.* Paris: Librairie Fischbacher, 1901. The chapter, "Saint-Saëns, organiste" appeared in *Le Monde Musical* (31 October 1901) 306–7.

Lonergan, Walter F. *Historic Churches of Paris.* London: Downey, 1896.

Long, Marguerite. *At the Piano with Fauré.* New York: Taplinger Music Company, 1981. Originally published as *Au piano avec Gabriel Fauré.* Paris: R. Juilliard, 1963.

Mason, Daniel Gregory. "Great Modern Composers, No. 9: Camille Saint-Saëns, A Modern Classicist." *The New Music Review* (May 1915) 196–99.

Mason & Hamlin Cabinet Organs, Illustrated Catalog. Boston: March 1880.

Ménil, F. de. "L'École de Musique Niedermeyer." *MUSICA* (July 1903) 149,

Mignan, Édouard. *Les Grandes Orgues de la Madeleine et ses Organistes.* Paris: Alsatia, 1958.

Le Monde Musical (31 October 1901). Special issue devoted to Saint-Saëns.

Morel, Fritz. "Camille Saint-Saëns, organiste." *Musik und Gottesdienst* No. 5 (1971) 132–33; No. 6 (1972) 127–39. Translated into French by Marie-Odile Servajean in *L'Orgue*, No. 160/161 (October–December 1977) 103–16.

Moulis, Adelin. "Un grand musicien ariégeois méconnu: Albert Périlhou." *L'Orgue*, No. 159 (July–September 1977) 89–96.

MUSICA, No. 57 (June 1907). Special issue devoted to Saint-Saëns.

Nietzel, Otto. *Camille Saint-Saëns*. Berlin: Harmonie, 1899.

Niedermeyer, Louis. "Un Nouveau Pédalier de M. Wolff." *La Maîtrise* (December 1857) 139–40.

Un Organiste. "Un Cours d'Improvisation par Marcel Dupré." *L'Orgue et les Organistes* (15 October 1925) 7–9. This unsigned review of Dupré's book was probably written by Jean Huré, editor of the journal. He quotes several reminiscences of Saint-Saëns which are to be found in his *Ésthetique de l'Orgue* (p. 172) and in *Guide du Concert* (pp. 9–10).

"Organs and Organplaying." *The Orchestra* (3 May 1872) 73–75.

"L'Orgue de la Madeleine." *L'Illustration, Journal Universal.* (7 November 1846) 147–48.

"L'Orgue de la Chapelle du Château de Versailles." *L'Orgue et les Organistes*, No. 5 (15 August 1924) 3–6.

d'Ortique, Joseph. "Inauguration des orgues de Saint-Merry à Paris." *La Maîtrise* (15 December 1857) 141–43.

Ory, Pascal. *Les Expositions Universelles de Paris*. Paris: Editions Ramsay, 1982.

Payne, Donald I. *The Major Chamber Works of Saint-Saëns*. Ph.D. dissertation, University of Rochester, 1965.

Perkins, John F., and Alan Kelly. "The Gramophone & Typewriter, Ltd. Records of Camille Saint-Saëns." *Recorded Sound*, The Journal of the British Institute of Recorded Sound, No. 79 (January 1981) 25–27.

Petit, (Chanoine). "Les Grandes Orgues de l'Eglise Notre-Dame-de-Saint-Dizier." *L'Orgue*, No. 68/71 (1953/1954) 1–15.

Philipp, Isadore. "Saint-Saëns: pianiste et organiste." *MUSICA* (June 1907) 70. Percursory article on Saint-Saëns as a pianist. The last paragraph refers to his incomparable virtuosity and his prodigious knowledge of registration effects and his charming improvisations. Philipp regards the *Rhapsodies Bretonnes* as his masterpiece.

_____. "Souvenirs de Saint-Saëns." *Revue Internationale de Musique* (April 1939) 907.

Pierre, Constant. *Le Conservatoire Nationale de Musique et de Déclamation.* Paris: Imprimerie Nationale, 1900.

Pincherle, Marc. *Musiciens peints par eux-mêmes*. Lettres de compositeurs écrites en français (1771–1910). Paris Cornuau, 1939.

Pollei, Paul Cannon. *Virtuoso Style in the Piano Concertos of Camille Saint-Saëns*. Ph.D. dissertation, Florida State University, 1975.

Pontecoulant, Ad. de. *La Musique à l'Exposition de 1867*. Paris: Bureau de l'art musical, LXV.

Poulenc, Francis. *Emmanuel Chabrier*. Paris: La Palantine, 1961.

Ratner, Sabina Teller. *The Piano Works of Camille Saint-Saëns*. Ph.D. dissertation, University of Michigan, 1972.

Raugel, Félix. *Les Grandes Orgues des Églises de Paris*. Paris: Librairie Fischbacher, 1927.

_____. "The Organ of Saint-Merry and Saint-Nicolas-des-Champs." *The Organ* (April 1923) 230–36.

Regnault, Henri. *Correspondance de Henri Regnault*, recueille et annotée par Arthur Duparc. Paris: Charpentier & Cie., 1884.

Report of the Department of Music to the President of the Pan-Pacific International Exposition, 1915. Manuscript in the San Francisco Archives, San Francisco (California) Public Library.

Richardson, Joanna. *Princess Mathilde*. London: Weidenfeld & Nicholson, 1969.

Roger, Louis. "Inauguration du Grand Orgue de Saint-Sulpice." *Revue de musique sacrée ancienne et moderne* (15 May 1862) 230–34.

Sabatie, Paul. Letter, La Chapelle Saint-Remy (Sarthe), 20 October 1955. Quoted in Seth Bingham's "Glimpses Over the French Horizon, Part 3." *The American Organist* (June 1959) 202–3.

Sabatier, François. *Les aventures du grand orgue de Notre-Dame-de-Paris aux XIXᵉ siècle*. 2 vols. Paris: L'Orgue, 1974/1975.

_____. "Remarques à propos d'un manuscrit inédit de Pierre Veerkamp." *L'Orgue*, No. 195 (July–September 1985) 1–11.

Sadoul, Georges. *Dictionary of Films*. Paris: Éditions du Seuil, 1965. Translated by Peter Morris. Berkeley and Los Angeles: University of California Press, 1972.

Saint-Saëns, Camille. "Conseils pour l'étude du piano." *Le Monde Musical* (15 February 1899) 53.

_____. *École Buissonnière — Notes et Souvenirs*. Paris: Lafitte, 1913. Twenty-three of the 36 chapters were translated by Edwin Rich and published as *Musical Memories* by Small, Maynard & Co., Boston, 1919.

_____. "Music in the Church." *The Musical Quarterly* II/1 (January 1916) 1–8.

_____. *On the Execution of Music, and Principally of Ancient Music.* Translated by Henry P. Bowie. San Francisco: The Blair-Murdock Co., 1915.

_____. *Outspoken Essays on Music.* Translated by Fred Rothwell. Boston: Small, Maynard & Co., 1922.

_____. *Portraits et Souvenirs.* Paris: Société d'édition artistique, 1899.

_____. "Preface." *Recueil de Noëls,* Op. 15. Fourteen Preludes or Pieces for Organ Composed by A. P. F. Boëly on the Cantiques of N. Denizot. Paris: Costallat, 1902.

_____. "Thoroughness in Music Study." *The Etude* (December 1913) 853–54. An interview obtained especially for *The Etude* by G. Mark Wilson with the Greatest Living French Composer.

Saint-Saëns, Camille, and Gabriel Fauré. *Correspondance: soixante ans d'amitié.* Edited by Jean-Michel Nectoux. Paris: Heugel, 1973.

Scherperel, Loretta Jane Fox. *A Study of the Solo Organ Works of Camille Saint-Saëns.* DMA Performance document. University of Rochester, 1978.

Schmitt, Georges, and Charles Simon. *Nouveau Manuel complet de l'organiste.* Paris: Encyclopédie Roret, 1855. New edition, 1905.

Schoenstein, Louis J. *Memoirs of a San Francisco Organ Builder.* San Francisco: Cue Publications, 1977.

Servières, Georges. *Saint-Saëns.* Paris: Alcan, 1923.

Smith, Rollin. "A Pair of Rockefeller Organs." *The Tracker* (Summer 1976) 13–14.

_____. "Alexandre Guilmant: Commemorating the 150th Anniversary of His Birth." *The American Organist* (March 1987) 50–58.

_____. "Camille Saint-Saëns." *MUSIC* (November 1971) 24–26.

_____. "Franz Liszt and the Organ." *The American Organist* (July 1986) 67–73.

_____. "The Organs of Carnegie Hall." *The American Organist* (July 1991) 46–49.

_____. *Toward an Authentic Interpretation of the Organ Works of César Franck.* New York: Pendragon Press, 1983.

Spark, William. *Musical Memories*. London: Sonnenschein, 1888.

Stiven, Frederic B. *I n the Organ Lofts of Paris*. Boston: Stratford, 1923.

Stokan, David Stephen. *A Stylistic and Performance Analysis of Variations for Piano by Saint-Saëns, Fauré and Dukas*. D.Mus. dissertation, Indiana University, 1979.

Todd, Frank Morton. *The Story of the Exposition*. New York: Putnam, 1921.

Tournemire, Charles. *Petite Méthode d'Orgue*. Paris: Éditions Max Eschig, 1949.

_____. *Précis d'éxécution, de registration et d'improvisation à l'orgue*. Paris: Éditions Max Eschig, 1936.

Vallas, Léon. *La Véritable Histoire de César Franck*. Paris: Flammarion, 1950. Translated by Hubert Foss as *César Franck*. New York: Oxford University Press, 1951.

_____. *Vincent d'Indy*. 2 vols. Paris: Michel, 1950.

Valois, J. de. "Paris, les grandes orgues de Saint-Merry." *L'Orgue*, No. 50 (January–March 1949) 25.

Van Wye, Benjamin. "Ritual Use of the Organ in France." *Journal of the American Musicological Society* (Summer 1980) 287–325.

Viardot, Paul. "Saint-Saëns Gai." *Le Guide du Concert* (Numéro Saint-Saëns 1914/1922) 13–14.

Viardot, Pauline. "La Jeunesse de Saint-Saëns." *MUSICA* (June 1907) 83–84.

Vierne, Louis. *Journal*. Paris: Les Amis de l'Orgue, 1970.

_____. *Mes Souvenirs*. Paris: Les Amis de l'Orgue, 1970. Originally these memoirs were published serially in the *Bulletin Trimestriel des Amis de l'-Orgue* from September 1934 to September 1937.

_____. "La Musique religieuse de Saint-Saëns." *Le Guide du Concert* (Numéro Saint-Saëns 1914/1922) 37–39.

Viollet-le-duc, Eugène-Emmanuel. "Les Églises de Paris." *Paris Guide*. Paris: Librairie Internationale, 1867.

Vuillermoz, Émile. *Saint-Saëns*. Les Laboratoires G. Beytout, 1935.

Wedgewood, James. *Some Continental Organs and Their Makers*. London: Wm. Reeves, 1910.

(Welte). *Library of Welte-Mignon Music Records.* New York: De Lux Reproducing Roll Corporation, 1927.

Widor, Charles-Marie. *Notice sur la vie et les oeuvres de M. Camille Saint-Saëns.* Lu dans la séance publique annuelle du samedi 2 decembre 1922. Paris: Firmin-Didot, 1922.

Index

Numbers in bold type indicate pages that contain illustrations.